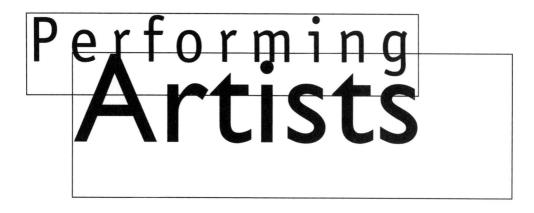

Performing Artists

Performing Artists

Volume 3 ★ N–Z

Molly Severson

U·X·L

An imprint of Gale Research Inc.,
an International Thomson Publishing Company

I(T)P

NEW YORK • LONDON • BONN • BOSTON • DETROIT • MADRID
MELBOURNE • MEXICO CITY • PARIS • SINGAPORE • TOKYO
TORONTO • WASHINGTON • ALBANY NY • BELMONT CA • CINCINNATI OH

Performing Artists: From Alvin Ailey to Julia Roberts

Molly Severson, *Editor*

Staff

Carol DeKane Nagel, *U·X·L Developmental Editor*
Thomas L. Romig, *U·X·L Publisher*

Mary Kelley, *Production Associate*
Evi Seoud, *Assistant Production Manager*
Mary Beth Trimper, *Production Director*

Cynthia Baldwin, *Art Director*

H. Diane Cooper, *Permissions Associate (Pictures)*
Margaret A. Chamberlain, *Permissions Supervisor (Pictures)*

Marty Somberg/Somberg Design, Ann Arbor, MI *Cover Design*
The Graphix Group, Fenton, MI *Typesetting*

∞™ This book is printed on acid-free paper that meets the minimum requirements of American National Standard for Information Sciences—Permanence Paper for Printed Library Materials, ANSI Z39.48-1984.

ISBN 0-8103-9868-0 (Set)
ISBN 0-8103-9869-9 (Volume 1)
ISBN 0-8103-9870-2 (Volume 2)
ISBN 0-8103-9871-0 (Volume 3)

Printed in the United States of America

I(T)P™ U•X•L is an imprint of Gale Research Inc.,
an International Thomson Publishing Company.
ITP logo is a trademark under license.

Contents

Performing Artists by Field of Endeavor xi

Reader's Guide xvii

Biographical Listings

Volume 1: A-F

Abdul, Paula 1
Ailey, Alvin 4
Allen, Debbie 10
Allen, Tim 15
Alonso, Alicia 22
Alonso, Maria Conchita 30
Astaire, Fred 35
Baez, Joan 40
Baryshnikov, Mikhail 47

Beatles 53

Bergen, Candice 61

Blades, Rubén 67

Brooks, Garth 71

Brown, Bobby 77

Cage, Nicolas 81

Candy, John 87

Carey, Mariah 93

Carrey, Jim 97

Carvey, Dana 101

Cher 106

Clapton, Eric 113

Connery, Sean 120

Cosby, Bill 126

Costner, Kevin 131

Cruise, Tom 138

Crystal, Billy 146

Culken, Macauley 152

d'Amboise, Jacques 156

Davis, Bette 162

Day-Lewis, Daniel 168

Depp, Johnny 172

Dogg, Snoop Doggy 178

Eastwood, Clint 182

Estefan, Gloria 190

Estevez, Emilio 195

Fishburne, Laurence 201

Fonda, Bridget 208

Foster, Jodie 212

Fox, Michael J. 220

Freeman, Morgan 226

Photo Credits 233

Index 235

Volume 2: G-M

García, Andy 249

Garland, Judy 252

Glover, Danny 258

Goldberg, Whoopi 264

Grant, Amy 271

Grant, Cary 275

Greene, Graham 280

Guy, Jasmine 284

Hall, Arsenio 289

Hammer 295

Hanks, Tom 299

Harris, Neal Patrick 306

Hepburn, Katharine 309

Hines, Gregory 314

Hoffman, Dustin 319

Hopkins, Anthony 323

Houston, Whitney 330

Huston, Anjelica 335

Ice-T 341

Jackson, Janet 347

Jackson, Michael 350

Joffrey, Robert 355

Julia, Raul 360

Keaton, Michael 363

Kelly, Gene 369

lang, k. d. 374

Lee, Brandon 380

Lee, Spike 384

Letterman, David 393

Los Lobos 399

Ma, Yo-Yo 404

Madonna 407

Mark, Marky 413

Marley, Bob 417

Martin, Steve 425

McFerrin, Bobby 432

Midler, Bette 435

Midori 442

Mitchell, Arthur 446

Moreno, Rita 451

Morita, Noriyuki "Pat" 458

Myers, Mike 464

Photo Credits 471

Index 473

Volume 3: N-Z

Nirvana 487

Norman, Jessye 492

N.W.A. 498

O'Connor, Sinead 502

Olivier, Laurence 507

Olmos, Edward James 512

Parton, Dolly 519

Pavarotti, Luciano 523

Pearl Jam 526

Perez, Rosie 533

Pfeiffer, Michelle 537

Poitier, Sidney 544

Presley, Elvis 552

Price, Leontyne 556

Public Enemy 561

Queen Latifah 567

Redford, Robert 571

The Red Hot Chili Peppers 580

Roberts, Julia 585

The Rolling Stones 592

Rose, Axl 599

Roseanne 606

Schwarzenegger, Arnold 610

Seinfeld, Jerry 615

Sinbad 620

Smith, Will 624

Snipes, Wesley 628

Stallone, Sylvester 635

Stewart, Patrick 641

SWV 645

Tallchief, Maria 648

10,000 Maniacs 653

Townsend, Robert 656

Washington, Denzel 662

Weaver, Sigourney 668

Williams, Robin 675

Williams, Vanessa 681

Winfrey, Oprah 687

Photo Credits 695

Index 697

Performing Artists by Field of Endeavor

Comedy:

Allen, Tim 15

Candy, John 87

Carrey, Jim 97

Carvey, Dana 101

Cosby, Bill 126

Crystal, Billy 146

Goldberg, Whoopi 264

Martin, Steve 425

Morita, Noriyuki "Pat" 458

Myers, Mike 464

Roseanne 606

Seinfeld, Jerry 615

Sinbad 620

Williams, Robin 675

Dance:

Abdul, Paula 1

Ailey, Alvin 4

Allen, Debbie 10

Alonso, Alicia 22

Astaire, Fred 35

Baryshnikov, Mikhail 47

d'Amboise, Jacques 156

Garland, Judy 252

Guy, Jasmine 284

Hines, Gregory 314

Joffrey, Robert 355

Kelly, Gene 369

Mitchell, Arthur 446

Moreno, Rita 451

Perez, Rosie 533

Tallchief, Maria 648

Film and Television:

Allen, Debbie 10

Allen, Tim 15

Alonso, Maria Conchita 30

Astaire, Fred 35

Baryshnikov, Mikhail 47

Bergen, Candice 61

Blades, Rubén 67

Cage, Nicolas 81

Candy, John 87

Carrey, Jim 97

Carvey, Dana 101

Cher 106

Connery, Sean 120

Cosby, Bill 126

Costner, Kevin 131

Cruise, Tom 138

Crystal, Billy 146

Culken, Macauley 152

Davis, Bette 162

Day-Lewis, Daniel 168

Depp, Johnny 172

Eastwood, Clint 182

Estevez, Emilio 195

Fishburne, Laurence 201

Fonda, Bridget 208

Foster, Jodie 212

Fox, Michael J. 220

Freeman, Morgan 226

García, Andy 249

Garland, Judy 252

Glover, Danny 258

Goldberg, Whoopi 264

Grant, Cary 275

Greene, Graham 280

Guy, Jasmine 284

Hall, Arsenio 289

Hanks, Tom 299

Harris, Neal Patrick 306

Hepburn, Katharine 309

Hines, Gregory 314

Hoffman, Dustin 319

Hopkins, Anthony 323

Houston, Whitney 330

Huston, Anjelica 335

Ice-T 341

Jackson, Janet 347

Julia, Raul 360

Keaton, Michael 363

Kelly, Gene 369

Lee, Brandon 380

Lee, Spike 384

Letterman, David 393

Madonna 407

Martin, Steve 425

Midler, Bette 435

Moreno, Rita 451

Morita, Noriyuki "Pat" 458

Myers, Mike 464

Olivier, Laurence 507

Olmos, Edward James 512

Parton, Dolly 519

Perez, Rosie 533

Pfeiffer, Michelle 537

Poitier, Sidney 544

Presley, Elvis 552

Queen Latifah 567

Redford, Robert 571

Roberts, Julia 585

Roseanne 606

Schwarzenegger, Arnold 610

Seinfeld, Jerry 615

Sinbad 620

Smith, Will 624

Snipes, Wesley 628

Stallone, Sylvester 635

Stewart, Patrick 641

Townsend, Robert 656

Washington, Denzel 662

Weaver, Sigourney 668

Williams, Robin 675

Williams, Vanessa 681

Winfrey, Oprah 687

Music:

Abdul, Paula 1

Allen, Debbie 10

Alonso, Maria Conchita 30

Astaire, Fred 35

Baez, Joan 40

Beatles 53

Blades, Rubén 67

Brooks, Garth 71

Brown, Bobby 77

Carey, Mariah 93

Cher 106

Clapton, Eric 113

Dogg, Snoop Doggy 178

Estefan, Gloria 190

Garland, Judy 252

Grant, Amy 271

Guy, Jasmine 284

Hammer 295

Houston, Whitney 330

Ice-T 341

Jackson, Janet 347

Jackson, Michael 350

Kelly, Gene 369

lang, k. d. 374

Los Lobos 399

Ma, Yo-Yo 404

Madonna 407

Mark, Marky 413

Marley, Bob 417

McFerrin, Bobby 432

Midler, Bette 435

Midori 442

Moreno, Rita 451

Nirvana 487

Norman, Jessye 492

N.W.A. 498

O'Connor, Sinead 502

Parton, Dolly 519

Pavarotti, Luciano 523

Pearl Jam 526

Presley, Elvis 552

Price, Leontyne 556

Public Enemy 561

Queen Latifah 567

The Red Hot Chili Peppers 580

The Rolling Stones 592

Rose, Axl 599

Smith, Will 624

SWV 645

10,000 Maniacs 653

Williams, Vanessa 681

Reader's Guide

Performing Artists: From Alvin Ailey to Julia Roberts features biographies of 120 popular singers, actors, dancers, comedians, musicians, and television personalities who have made an impact on the performing arts. Selected and written especially with students in mind, the entries focus on the early lives and motivations of the performers as well as highlights (and lowlights) of their careers.

Arranged alphabetically over three volumes, the biographies open with the birth dates and places of the individuals and, where necessary, with death dates and places. Each entry features a portrait of the biographee, a three- to nine-page essay on the performer's life and career, and a list of sources for further reading. Additionally, sidebars containing interesting details about the performers are sprinkled throughout the text, as are 25 movie stills and other action shots. A cumulative index providing easy access to the people and works mentioned in *Performing Artists* concludes each volume.

Comments and Suggestions

We welcome your comments on this work as well as your suggestions for individuals to be featured in future editions of *Performing Artists: From Alvin Ailey to Julia Roberts*. Please write: Editor, *Performing Artists*, U·X·L, 835 Penobscot Bldg., Detroit, Michigan 48226-4094; call toll-free: 1-800-877-4253; or fax 1-313-961-6348.

Nirvana

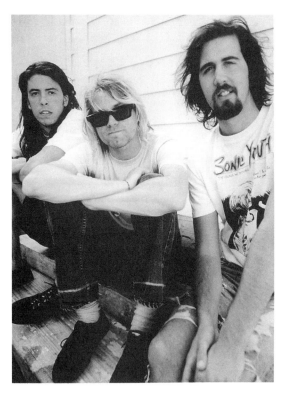

ROCK BAND

The group Nirvana, already famous for helping to create the sound of "grunge" rock, became infamous with the news of lead vocalist Kurt Cobain's suicide in April 1994. Only 27 years old, Cobain's tragic death threw the music world into a state of shock and denial. His many fans mourned his passing and questioned why one so young and so talented would choose to end his life. When a reporter for *People* spoke to a 20-year-old fan keeping a vigil outside of the house where Cobain shot himself, the fan echoed the thoughts of many: "I came here looking for answers. But I don't think there really are any. I was hoping it was a dream. Ever since I heard the news, I wanted to wake up."

"Kurt spoke to us in our hearts. That's where the music will always be. Forever."—Krist Novoselic

In the beginning

Nirvana began as three Seattle musicians who played what has become known as "grunge" rock. Decidedly punkish in their musical style—albeit at a slower pace than was the hallmark of punk rock—strident in their lyrics, and unapologetic of their outspoken offstage personalities, the group nonetheless went from the "underground" status of their initial release, *Bleach,* to mega-stardom with their first major-label effort, *Nevermind,* within the space of a few years. The latter, featuring Kurt Cobain on guitar and vocals, Chris Novoselic on bass, and David Grohl on drums, jumped to the Number One spot on the *Billboard* rock chart and was cited in many music critics' Top Ten lists just months after its release.

Cobain and Novoselic grew up near Seattle, in Aberdeen, Washington, a secluded logging town 70 miles southwest of Seattle known largely for its overcast climate. Cobain's youth was often chaotic—he lived in a trailer park with his cocktail waitress mother after the breakup of his parents' marriage. Before his parents split up, Cobain's mother recounted in *Rolling Stone,* he "got up every day with such joy that there was another day to be had. When we'd go downtown to the stores, he would sing to people." After the divorce, though, Cobain's personality underwent a transformation. "I think he was ashamed," his mother continued, "and he became very inward—he just held everything."

Until the age of nine, Cobain listened mostly to the Beatles. Then his father introduced him to heavier fare—Led Zeppelin, Kiss, and Black Sabbath. He started playing drums and hanging around with an Aberdeen group called the Melvins. Melvins leader Buzz Osborne took Cobain to a Black Flag concert, where he got his first taste of hard-core punk. Cobain was awed; he began to experiment with the guitar and tried to form a band. "I learned one Cars song and AC/DC's 'Back in Black,'" he told *Elle.* "And after that I just started writing my own. I didn't feel it was important to learn other songs because I knew I wanted to start a band." After repeatedly failing to get a group together, Osborne suggested that Cobain hook up with Chris Novoselic, a tall, shy Aberdeen kid two years older than Cobain.

Cobain and Novoselic bound by punk

According to Nirvana's record company press biography, Cobain and Novoselic had met at the Grays Harbor Institute of Northwest Crafts, where they were apparently "gluing seashells and driftwood on burlap" and making mobiles of macaroni. Like Cobain, Novoselic had moved around a lot as a kid—they felt they were both misfits in a way. They further shared an appreciation for the hard-core music that was generally shunned by their heavy metal-loving peers. A tape of the San Francisco punk band Flipper cemented their commitment to the genre. "It made me realize there was something more cerebral to listen to," Novoselic told *Elle*. Exhibiting total rebellion against what they saw as the red-necked, macho establishment of their hometown, they spray-painted phrases antireligious and sexual on cars and bank buildings. For one offense Cobain was arrested and fined.

Cobain's mother kicked him out of the house after he quit high school. Homeless, he slept on friends' couches and even briefly found lodging under a bridge. By 1987, however, he and Novoselic were beginning to gain a reputation as Nirvana and were a hit at parties at Evergreen State College in Olympia.

With the help of Melvins drummer Dale Crover, the trio began to record, finishing ten songs in one afternoon taping session. The resulting demo was submitted to Sub Pop, Seattle's then-underground label, the directors of which signed them to a record contract right away. In 1988, after changing drummers, the band recorded *Bleach* in six days for $606.17. The album moved slowly at first, but eventually sold 35,000 copies between its debut and the release of the band's second effort, which caused a surge of *Bleach* sales.

Caught in bidding war

After *Bleach,* Nirvana began looking for yet another drummer, this time settling, in the fall of 1990, on Dave Grohl of the Washington, D.C., band Scream. This lineup returned to the studio to find that the Nirvana sound had improved significantly. When Sub Pop sought a distributor for the upcoming second album, a bidding war ensued among record labels interested in buying Nirvana out of their Sub Pop contract. The group eventually signed to DGC, home of giants Guns 'N' Roses and Cher, for $287,000. Rumors persisted, however, that the label had shelled out up to $750,000 to obtain the trio. Cobain commented in *Spin* that those reports were "journalism through hearsay," adding that "the numbers kept getting bigger so that a lot of people believed that we were signed for a million dollars."

The group had mixed feelings about signing to a major label; they feared they would be labeled "sellouts" for trading their underground status for the promise of big money. But the opportunity to get their music heard by a larger audience—and thus spread their message to the mainstream—mitigated these concerns. Nirvana released *Nevermind* in the spring of 1991; the record took three weeks to record and earned the trio $135,000. Producer Butch Vig instinctively felt that the unintelligible, but mesmerizing, cut "Smells like Teen Spirit" would be a hit, even before it was completed in the studio. "It was awesome sounding," he told *Rolling Stone.* "I was pacing around the room, trying not to jump up and down in ecstasy."

Nevermind *a Sensation*

Vig's prophecy came true: The *Nevermind* single "Smells Like Teen Spirit" soared to Number One after only a few months of airplay. The accompanying video, featuring a somewhat sinister high school pep rally—Cobain has said the song is about teenage apathy—complete with tattooed cheerleaders, a bald custodian, writhing fans, and pointedly unkempt band members, received heavy rotation on MTV. "Smells" earned perhaps the ultimate tribute when it was lampooned by rock parodist "Weird Al" Yankovic, whose own video was entitled "Smells Like Nirvana." And yet the most distinguishing aspect of *Nevermind* may have been that, as *New York Times* contributor Karen Schoemer pointed out, "Nirvana didn't cater to the mainstream; it played the game on its own terms.... What's unusual about [the album] is that it caters to neither a mainstream audience nor the indie rock fans who supported the group's debut album." Calling the release "one of the best alternative rock albums produced by an American band in recent years," Schoemer continued, "*Nevermind* is accessible but not tame. It translates the energy and abandon of college rock in clear, certain terms."

In 1993 Nirvana released *In Utero,* the band's long-awaited follow-up to *Nevermind.* The album received a great critical response and sales soared. Fans who feared that Nirvana's music would either become mainstream or lacking the passion of *Nevermind* were reassured. According to Gary Susman in *People,* "The dramatic hallmarks of *Nevermind* remain intact [in *In Utero*]: the sudden dynamic shifts, Cobain's unerring sense of songcraft and his inventive bursts of guitar fire, and bassist Krist Novoselic and drummer Dave Grohl's heart-stopping rhythms." (Novoselic reclaimed the original spelling of his name—Krist—to emphasize his Croation roots; the band as a whole was very sensitive to the political upheaval affecting the Croation and other peoples of the former Yugoslavia during the early 1990s.)

Cobain's *suicide*

Yet fame and fortune seemed to intensify the anguish that Cobain felt. As listeners of his songs knew, Cobain struggled with his unhappiness, pain and anger. Toward the end of his life rumors abounded—his band was breaking up, he was once again taking heroin. And indeed it appeared that Cobain had slipped back into his old drug habits. In March 1994 Cobain almost died of an overdose of prescription drugs and alcohol while in Rome, Italy. His wife, alternative-rock star Courtney Love, was so concerned that she and some friends intervened by trying to scare Cobain into dealing with his addiction. The intervention failed, however, when Cobain ran away from the California treatment center where he'd been admitted. Police believe that on April 5, Cobain locked himself in a room above his garage and shot himself in the head. He left a suicide note for Love and his 19-month-old daughter, Frances Bean. The note suggested that his chronic stomach pain was becoming unbearable and that the passion was gone from his life. According to *People* his final written words were: "It's not fun for me anymore. I can't live this life."

In the fall of 1994, with the professional fate of Novoselic and Grohl still uncertain, DGC released a recording of Nirvana's MTV "Unplugged" concert. One of the highlights of Nirvana's career, the show (and album) features such standouts as the single "About the Girl," an inspired "Come as You Are," and a howling rendition of Leadbelly's "Where Did You Sleep Last Night?" "The music is terrific, but the album is ultimately sad," wrote Gary Graff in his *Detroit Free Press* review. "Nirvana … proves so adept at handling the 'Unplugged' [acoustic] setting that it's just a reminder of the talent and potential that was lost earlier this year."

A planned compilation of other material was postponed when the surviving members of the band found working on it too emotionally taxing. Despite this tragic end, Nirvana will be remembered as the band that broke alternative rock through to the mainstream, thus paving the way for a generation of musicians whose work may never have been heard but for the innovations of Nirvana.

Sources

Elle, April 1992.

Detroit Free Press, October 30, 1994.

Guitar Player, February 1992.

Newsweek, January 27, 1992.

New York Times, January 8, 1992; January 13, 1992; January 26, 1992.

People, December 23, 1991; October 11, 1993; April 25, 1994.

Pulse!, March 1992.

Rolling Stone, November 28, 1991; February 20, 1992.

Spin, January 1992.

Time, September 20, 1993; April 18, 1994.

Additional information for this profile was obtained from a David Geffen Company press biography, 1991.

Jessye Norman

Born September 15, 1945
Augusta, Georgia

"If a performer is truly committed, then the audience will be the first to know and will respond accordingly. Of course, love is the thing that propels us all. It's what carries us along—that's the fuel!"

OPERA SINGER

American soprano Jessye Norman is hailed as one of the world's greatest opera and concert singers and performers. Since the early 1970s she has starred at leading opera houses, concert halls, and music festivals throughout Europe, North America, and three other continents. She has also enjoyed a prolific recording career with over 40 albums and several Grammy awards to her credit and is even recognized as the inspiration for the title character in the 1982 French film *Diva*, directed by Jean-Jacques Beineix.

Norman's voice has been resoundingly praised for its mastery of expression, technical control, and sheer power, while her diverse song repertoire spans standard and obscure operas to German lieder (classical songs), avant-garde works, and even popular ballads. As a performer, she is known for her magnetic and dramatic personality, and, with her imposing physical presence, cuts an impressive figure before audiences. According to Curt Sanburn in *Life*,

Norman onstage creates the perception of one who "veritably looms behind her lyrics."

Born into a musical family in Augusta, Georgia, at the close of World War II, she was encouraged in her youth to be a singer. Norman's mother, an amateur pianist, saw that all the children in the family took piano lessons, while her father, a successful insurance broker, sang frequently in the family's Baptist church. As a young girl Norman loved singing and performed wherever she had the opportunity—at church, school, Girl Scout meetings, even a supermarket opening; yet she never formally studied voice until college. "I was completely sure I would be a psychiatrist," she recalled in an interview with Charles Michener for *Vanity Fair*.

Norman fell in love with opera the first time she heard a Metropolitan Opera radio broadcast." I was nine and I didn't know *what* was going on, but I just loved it, she told Michener. "After that I listened religiously." Soon after, Norman mastered her first aria, "My Heart at Thy Sweet Voice," from French composer Camille Saint-Saens's *Samson and Delilah*. At 16 she traveled to Philadelphia with her school choral director for the Marian Anderson Scholarship competition and, while most of the participants were much older and more experienced and thus she failed to win, she received positive comments from the judges. On her return trip to Georgia she visited the music department at Howard University in Washington, D.C., and sang for Carolyn Grant, who would later become her vocal coach. After hearing Norman's voice, Grant recommended the budding soprano for a full-tuition four-year scholarship to the university when she came of college age.

Norman graduated from Howard with honors in 1967 and during her university career won many fans who heard her sing in the university choral group and local church choirs. She went on to complete a summer of postgraduate study at the Peabody Conservatory in Baltimore, Maryland, before obtaining her master's degree at the University of Michigan in Ann Arbor. While at Michigan, Norman worked with two renowned teachers of voice, French baritone Pierre Bernac—a famous teacher of the art song—and Elizabeth Mannion. To finance her graduate school studies Norman auditioned for and received grants from various musical foundations and in 1968 received a scholarship from the Institute of International Education that allowed her to enter Bavarian Radio's International Music Competition in Munich, Germany. When Norman was on a U.S. State Department musical tour of the Caribbean and Latin America that year she received word that she had won the prestigious European contest. Subsequently, she received offers to perform and work in Europe and moved overseas in 1969, following the path of many American singers who began their careers in the celebrated concert and opera halls of Europe.

Gained international acclaim early in career

Norman enjoyed rapid success in Europe. In December 1969 she signed a three-year contract with the venerable Deutsche Opera in West Berlin and was a sensation in her debut—at the age of 23—as Elisabeth in German composer Richard Wagner's *Tannhauser*. Norman thereafter received other primary roles with the opera company, in addition to numerous offers to sing concerts and operas throughout Europe. In 1970 she made her Italian debut in Florence in George Frideric Handel's *Deborah* and the following year her busy opera schedule included performances in Wolfgang Amadeus Mozart's *Idomeneo* in Rome, Giacomo Meyerbeer's *L'Africaine* in Florence, and Mozart's *Marriage of Figaro* at the Berlin Festival. Later in 1971 Norman auditioned for and won the opportunity to sing the role of the Countess in a Philips recording of *Figaro* with the BBC Orchestra under the direction of Colin Davis. The recording was a finalist for the prestigious Montreux International Record Award competition and brought Norman much exposure to listeners in Europe and the United States.

In 1972 Norman performed in a Berlin production of Giuseppe Verdi's *Aida,* a role in which she debuted later that year at the famed Italian opera stage La Scala, in Milan. Also in 1972 she sang in a concert version of *Aida* at the Hollywood Bowl in California, followed by a performance at Wolf Trap in Washington, D.C., with the National Symphony Orchestra, and an acclaimed Wagner recital at the prestigious Tanglewood Music Festival in Massachusetts.

Norman's triumphs of 1972 continued when she returned to Europe in the fall and debuted at the Royal Opera House in Covent Garden, England, as Cassandra in Hector Berlioz's *Les Troyens*. She also made her debut at the prestigious Edinburgh Music Festival that year. As a result of these victories, much acclaim and excitement awaited her first-ever New York City recital the following year when she appeared as part of the Great Performers series at Alice Tully Hall in Lincoln Center. Norman's performance, which included songs by European masters Wagner, Strauss, Brahms, and Satae, was hailed by Donald Henahan in the *New York Times* as one of "extraordinary intelligence, taste and emotional depth."

Took temporary leave of opera

In the mid-1970s, wanting to more fully develop her vocal range, Norman made the decision to stop performing operas temporarily to concentrate on concert performances. She told John Gruen in the *New York Times* of her desire to master a broad repertoire. "As for my voice, it cannot be categorized—and I like it that way, because I sing things that would be considered in the dramatic, mezzo or spinto range. I like so many different kinds of music that I've never allowed myself the limitations of one particular range."

The decision to take a half-decade leave from opera prompted criticism in concert circles. "I was considered difficult to deal with because I said 'No' so much," she noted in *Vanity Fair*. "But my voice was changing and it needed time to develop. It takes years to get that understanding of how your voice works, years before you're able to divorce yourself from that horrible word we call technique and are able to release your soul."

Over the years Norman's technical expertise has been among her most critically praised attributes. In a review of one of her recitals at New York City's Carnegie Hall, *New York Times* contributor Allen Hughes wrote that Norman "has one of the most opulent voices before the public today, and, as discriminating listeners are aware, her performances are backed by extraordinary preparation, both musical and otherwise." Another Carnegie Hall appearance prompted these words from Bernard Holland in the *New York Times*: "If one added up all the things that Jessye Norman does well as a singer, the total would assuredly exceed that of any other soprano before the public. At Miss Norman's recital ... tones were produced, colors manipulated, words projected and interpretive points made—all with fanatic finesse."

Norman returned to the operatic stage in 1980 in a performance of Strauss's *Ariadne auf Naxos* in Hamburg, Germany, and in 1983 made her debut with New York City's Metropolitan Opera company in its gala centennial season opener of *Les Troyens*. Norman shone among the star-studded cast, as Henahan wrote in his review. "Miss Norman ... is a soprano of magnificent presence who commanded the stage at every moment," he declared. "As the distraught Cassandra she sang grippingly and projects well, even when placed well back in the cavernous sets."

Although Norman has had great success performing in full-scale opera productions, her formidable physical stature has somewhat limited the availability of stage roles to her and she has increasingly directed her opera singing to condensed concert versions. One of the standards in her repertoire is "Liebestod" ("Love of Death"), the finale from Wagner's *Tristan und Isolde,* in which a despondent and soon-to-expire Isolde sings to her dead beloved, Tristan. Henahan reviewed Norman's performance of

Norman has earned numerous awards and honors, including first prize in vocal competition from the National Society of Arts and Letters in 1965; Grammy awards in 1980, 1982, and 1985; and *Musical America*'s Outstanding Musician of the Year Award in 1982. She was named a commander in France's Order of Arts and Letters in 1984, and she holds honorary degrees from Howard, Yale, Harvard, and Brandeis universities, the University of Michigan, and the Juilliard School of Music.

"Liebestod" at the 1989 New York Philharmonic season opener: "Although she has never sung the complete role on any stage, she has handled this fearsome 10-minute challenge with increasing vocal authority and dramatic insight.... Hers is a grandly robust voice, used with great intelligence and expression."

Inspired lavish ovations

Norman's performances have sparked seemingly endless ovations from audiences throughout the world—a reported 47 minutes in Tokyo in 1985 and 55 minutes in Salzburg the next year. Another pinnacle of her career came in 1987 with the Boston Symphony Orchestra at Tanglewood; her program of Strauss songs, which featured the final scene from Strauss's opera *Salome*, prompted both critical acclaim and more than ten minutes of applause from the audience. Michael Kimmelman wrote in the *New York Times* on the power of that particular performance: "Ms. Norman's voice seems to draw from a vast ocean of sound.... No matter how much volume Sieji Ozawa requested from his orchestra during the fiery scene from 'Salome,' it seemed little match for her voice. Yet, as always, what made the soprano's performance particularly remarkable was the effortlessness with which she could hover over long, soft notes.... And there is also the quality of sound she produces: even the loudest passages are cushioned by a velvety, seductive timbre."

Over the years Norman has not been afraid to expand her talent into less familiar areas. In 1988 she sang a concert performance of Francis-Jean-Marcel Poulenc's one-act opera *La Voix humaine* ("The Human Voice"), based on Jean Cocteau's 1930 play of the same name, in which a spurned actress feverishly pleads to keep her lover on the other end of a phone conversation. Although Henahan noted in the *New York Times* that Norman's "characteristic ... style puts great emphasis on tragic dignity," and that the role perhaps called for less restraint, he nonetheless admired her as among those artists "driven to branch out into unlikely roles and whole idioms that stretch their talents interestingly, if sometimes to the breaking point."

Other of Norman's diverse projects have included her 1984 album *With a Song in My Heart,* which contains numbers from films and musical comedies, and a 1990 performance of American spirituals with soprano Kathleen Battle at Carnegie Hall. Norman told William Livingstone in *Stereo Review* that one of her objectives as a performer is "to communicate, to be understood in many ways and on many levels." In 1989 she was invited to sing the French national anthem—"La Marseillaise"—in Paris during the celebration of the bicentennial of the French Revolution. Norman, who sings nearly flawless French (in addition to German and Italian), was particularly honored by the opportunity. "It makes you feel really good that people at home think you are worth their interest, but it's incredible to be so warmly received in a foreign country," she told Livingstone. "I love watching the faces of the people who are listening as I sing these songs and know that they understand."

In the *New York Times* interview with Gruen, Norman described the reverence with which she approaches her work. "To galvanize myself into a performance, I must be left totally alone. I must have solitude in order to concentrate—which I consider a form of prayer. I work very much from the text. The words must be understood, felt and communicated.... If you look carefully at the words and absorb them, you're halfway home already. The rest is honesty—honesty of feeling, honesty of involvement."

Sources

Chicago Tribune, July 7, 1992.

Ebony, March 1988; July 1991.

Greenfield, Edward, Robert Layton, and Ivan March, *The New Penguin Guide to Compact Discs and Cassettes,* Penguin, 1988.

The International Encyclopedia of Music and Musicians, 10th edition, edited by Oscar Thompson, Dodd, 1975.

Life, March 1985.

Los Angeles Times, February 2, 1986; April 27, 1992.

Musical America, January 1991; July 1991; September/October 1991; November/December 1991.

Music and Musicians, August 1979.

Newsweek, December 6, 1982.

New York, April 1, 1991; April 29, 1991; May 20, 1991.

New Yorker, April 1, 1991; May 20, 1991.

New York Times, January 21, 1973; January 23, 1973; December 15, 1982; September 18, 1983; September 27, 1983; November 24, 1983; January 26, 1986; August 25, 1987; February 20, 1988; March 6, 1989; September 22, 1989; March 19, 1990; February 11, 1992.

Opera News, June 1973; February 18, 1984; February 16, 1991; July 1991.

Stereo Review, October 1989; February 1991; July 1991; August 1991; September 1991.

Vanity Fair, February 1989.

Washington Post, August 7, 1972.

N.W.A

"We like to be real ... wake up and smell the coffee."

RAP GROUP

The pioneering rappers in N.W.A. saw themselves as reporters, and the stories they covered are not pretty. Having grown up amidst drug deals and gang violence in the Compton section of Los Angeles, the members of N.W.A. rapped about urban America's ugliest realities and offered no apologies for the brutality and cynicism of their lyrics. *Orlando Sentinel* correspondent Robert Hilburn wrote: "Pushing the imagery much further than anyone before, N.W.A. features sirens and gunshots as back-drops to its ... tales of drug dealing and police confrontations....The defiant N.W.A. refuses to pass judgment or offer itself as a role model. The group's name echoes its bold, incendiary nature: Niggers With Attitude."

N.W.A. formed in Los Angeles in the late 1980s, when an admitted former drug dealer decided to invest his earnings in a record company. The leader of the group, Eazy-E, founded Ruthless Records "with money gained illegally on the streets," according to *Rolling Stone*. He then recruited some of his friends to form a rap act, most notably Ice Cube, who wrote many of the raps on the group's debut album. Other N.W.A. members included producers Dr. Dre and Yella and mixer M. C. Ren.

In 1989 N.W.A. released their debut album, *Straight Outta Compton,* a vivid evocation of the bitter and dangerous world from which the group's members emerged. The work was decidedly controversial—one song derided police, making claims of brutality. *Richmond Times-Dispatch* contributor Mark Holmberg described the album as "a preacher-provoking, mother-maddening, reality-stinks" diatribe that "wallows in gangs, doping, drive-by shootings, brutal sexism, cop slamming and racism." However, a reviewer for *Newsweek* acknowledged that *Straight Outta Compton* "introduced some of the most grotesquely exciting music ever made."

A *Newsweek* reviewer added, "Hinting at gang roots, and selling themselves on those hints, they project a gangster mystique that pays no attention [to] where criminality begins and marketing lets off." Defending the group's stance, Ice Cube told *Rolling Stone:* "Peace is a fictional word to me.... Violence is reality.... You're supposed to picture life as a bowl of cherries, but it's not. So we don't do nothin' fake."

Work fueled controversy

Because of its controversial lyrics, little air time was granted to *Straight Outta Compton*—even by rap radio stations—and MTV refused to show the group's debut video, claiming it "glorified violence." Despite this lack of mainstream exposure the album sold a million copies, making stars of its five Compton natives. Criticism rained down on the group—the F.B.I. officially condemned one of N.W.A's songs for encouraging violence against law-enforcement officers—and the group members were allegedly harassed by police officers during a concert at Detroit's Joe Louis Arena. Ice Cube told the *Richmond Times-Dispatch* that the group's negative image among authority figures didn't bother N.W.A. "We don't want the key to any cities," he announced. "We like to be real ... wake up and smell the coffee, this is the way it is."

Their defiant attitude firmly established, N.W.A.'s members became premier performers of "gangster" rap, an arm of rap music that chronicles often violent and squalid urban conditions. As M. C. Ren explained in *Rolling Stone,* "We don't go around telling people, 'Don't do drugs,' or preaching safe sex, cause everybody's gonna do what they want regardless."

Violence and profanity condemned

The group's subject matter and its lyrics, rife with four-letter words and

After he left the group, Ice Cube was also the target of N.W.A.'s insults, with one song, "B.A."—for traitor Benedict Arnold—pointedly addressing him.

sexual suggestion, aroused heated controversy among critics. Some reviewers felt that N.W.A. glamorized gang violence. In the *Washington Post*, David Mills wrote: "The hard-core street rappers defend their violent lyrics as a reflection of 'reality.' But for all the gunshots they mix into their music, rappers rarely try to dramatize that reality—a young man flat on the ground, a knot of lead in his chest, pleading as death slowly takes him in. It's easier for them to imagine themselves pulling the trigger." On the other hand, *Wichita Eagle-Beacon* correspondent Bud Norman noted that while N.W.A.'s members refused to condemn the violence they describe, "they don't make it sound like much fun.... They described it with the same nonjudgmental resignation that a Kansan might use about a tornado."

Ice Cube answered the charges against N.W.A.'s lyrics. "We're not trying to make a buck off of violence," he told the *Richmond Times-Dispatch*. "We're not on the good side or the bad side of anything. We're in the middle, like a reporter would do. We tell [listeners] what's going on. If you want to go bad, you got to deal with the consequences." He added: "If you don't like it, if you don't understand it, don't buy the records. Don't come to the concert."

Second album topped charts

After *Straight Outta Compton* Ice Cube left the group to pursue a solo career—allegedly, according to *Rolling Stone,* because of a financial dispute. Because Ice Cube had written many lyrics, the group's 1991 album, *Efil4zaggin,* marked a new direction for N.W.A. Nonetheless, the new release occupied the number one spot on the charts without a hit single or play on radio stations and MTV. Once again, the group caused controversy. The title of the album, read backwards, is Niggaz4life. Although the group's members referred to themselves with this word, many found it offensive. In addition, N.W.A.'s references to women—most often insulting—caused an uproar. As Alan Light in *Rolling Stone* remarked, "the second half of the album ... stands as a graphic, violent suite of misogyny [women-hating] unparalleled in rap."

The unbridled success of *Efil4zaggin* among both black and white listeners startled and dismayed critics. The group earned substantial media attention as "experts" tried to explain N.W.A.'s appeal. Some suggested that the bad attitude and raunchy lyrics of what a reviewer for *Time* called a "rap mural of ghetto life, spray-painted with blood" uniquely appealed to listeners. Helping to launch sales of the album was a new group of customers—white middle-class teenagers—who latched on to the hard-core sound of N.W.A. As M. C. Ren explained, "White kids have been seeing so many negative images of blacks in the media for most of their lives. Now they have a chance to see something real. White kids got hip."

Efil4zaggin would be the group's last record together; all would go on to solo careers. Ice Cube continued to sell well as a solo artist and was acclaimed for his role in John Singleton's film *Boyz N the Hood*. Eazy-E maintained Ruthless Records and released solo albums, though critical praise for his work was minimal. He nonetheless managed to stay in the public eye through his ongoing feud with Dr. Dre, who went on to tremendous success as a solo artist, much sought-after producer, and recruiter of talent like Snoop Doggy Dogg. Though N.W. A.'s output was limited, its influence has been extremely widespread, establishing the place of the now-pervasive gansta rap in mainstream popular culture.

Sources

Houston Post, June 18, 1989.

Newsweek, March 19, 1990; July 1, 1991.

Orlando Sentinel, October 26, 1990.

Richmond Times-Dispatch, June 30, 1989.

Rolling Stone, June 29, 1989; August 8, 1991.

Time, July 1, 1991.

Washington Post, September 2, 1990; March 19, 1991.

Wichita Eagle-Beacon, August 3, 1989.

Sinead O'Connor

Born December 8, 1966
Dublin, Ireland

"I don't want to be perceived as a pop star; that leaves you very little room to develop. I want to be perceived as a human being."

SINGER AND SONGWRITER

With her clean-shaven head and shapeless clothes, Sinead O'Connor's appearance is as distinctive and startling as her music. She weaves pop, jazz, and Celtic sounds together as she sings about such assorted topics as religion, history, and personal relationships. Despite the critical and popular acclaim her work has received, she seems to garner more attention from her outspoken and often sensational public protests.

O'Connor was the third of four children born into a middle-class Dublin family. Her parents separated when she was nine years old, and she was left to live with her mother, who was abusive. O'Connor ran wild in the streets of Dublin. She was arrested several times for shoplifting and expelled from a series of Catholic schools before landing in reform school at the age of 14. "I have never—and I probably will never—experienced such panic and terror and agony over anything," she stated in *Rolling Stone*. In this "very Dickensian" place, troublemakers were punished by being forced to sleep on the floor of a hospice for the dying that was also housed in the building. "You're there in the pitch black," she recalled. "There were rats everywhere, and ... old women moaning and vomiting," she recalled in *People*.

Ironically, O'Connor's first musical break came out of this nightmarish predicament. She had begun strumming a guitar and making up songs for emotional release; a teacher overheard and asked O'Connor to sing at her wedding. The bride's brother then asked her to cut a song with his band, In Tua Nua. O'Connor was released shortly thereafter and sent to a boarding school in Waterford where she promptly landed in trouble again—this time for singing in pubs when she was still underage. She ran away to Dublin, where she joined a band and supported herself by being a street performer, waitressing, and delivering telegrams in a French-maid costume.

Begins recording career

Nigel Grainge heard O'Connor sing in 1985 and immediately asked the young performer-songwriter to come to London and record a demo tape for his company, Ensign Records. When he listened to the completed product, it was "shivers-down-the-spine-time," he told Janet Lambert in *Rolling Stone*. While waiting to begin work on her album, O'Connor met U2's guitarist, the Edge, and began working with him on the soundtrack for the 1986 film *The Captive*. Their collaboration led to her being tagged a "U2 protégée," but in fact, O'Connor does not care for the group's music, which she finds "too bombastic." Simplicity, she insists, is her ideal.

When the time came to record her album in the fall of 1986, O'Connor found her plain style at odds with her producer's fondness for lush string arrangements behind lilting Celtic melodies. "I just wanted to keep it as simple as possible, with none of this mucking about with violins," explained O'Connor in *People*. Friction between artist and producer resulted in an album so horrible that Ensign scrapped it and let O'Connor return to the studio to produce herself. The result was her debut album, *The Lion and the Cobra*, whose title refers to a psalm about overcoming adversity. Critics had high praise for the finished product, immediately ranking O'Connor with two other boundary-stretching female vocalists, Laurie Anderson and Kate Bush. Within seconds, wrote Richard J. Grula in *Interview*, O'Connor's voice moves from "an ethereal whisper hanging over your shoulder" to "a torrid scream raging outside your window."

Album receives critical praise

"[*The Lion and the Cobra*] covers an unusually wide range of ground," Lambert commented in *Rolling Stone*. "There's light, Pretenders-style pop on the first single, 'Mandinka,' syncopated dance funk on 'I Want Your (Hands on Me)' and symphonic strings on the six-and-a-half-minute 'Tray.' O'Connor twists conventional song structure and stretches pop singing while maintaining her melodic sense: on 'Just Call Me Joe' her voice is a lullaby croon; on 'Never Get Old' it soars above the jazzy piano chords into ecstatic, wordless cries. There's a faint Irish aura throughout, whether in the spoken Gaelic that dramatically opens 'Never Get Old,' in the occasional snatches of folk airs or in the effective use of drone. But what really holds *Lion* together is the strong individuality of O'Connor's voice." The album went on to sell over 500,000 copies.

Her follow-up release, the 1991 *I Do Not Want What I Haven't Got,* was an even greater success. Writing in *Rolling Stone,* Mikal Gilmore praised the album: "It opens with a prayer for strength and wisdom and closes with another, offering a brave, fearful thanks for equanimity. Yet it is what comes through those prayers—a journey through rage and heartbreak to grace—that ultimately makes this record so memorable and so powerful. In any event the memory of a hard loss burns at the heart of this album. Somebody, it seems—apparently a mentor as much as a lover—has shattered the singer's trust, and the fallout from that ordeal spills into nearly every song." The video for the number-one single from the album, the Prince-penned "Nothing Compares 2 U," was named MTV's video of the year. In addition, O'Connor was nominated for four Grammy awards—winning in the best alternative album category. Citing her objection to the commercial nature of the Grammys, O'Connor refused this award.

Controversy surrounds O'Connor

O'Connor attracted massive media attention in May 1990 by refusing to appear on the television show *Saturday Night Live* when the comedian Andrew Dice Clay was scheduled to host. As a woman sensitive to feminist issues, O'Connor felt it would be hypocritical to appear on the same stage as a man whose monologues contain degrading and abusive comments about women. In September of the same year O'Connor refused to play at the Garden State Arts Center in New Jersey if "The Star Spangled Banner" was played prior to her performance. While the Center complied with her request, they vowed never to invite her to perform there again. The incident incited public outrage and a number of radio stations refused to air her songs.

O'Connor's most outrageous act, however, occurred on the October 3, 1992, broadcast of *Saturday Night Live*. After finishing an a cappella protest song she tore up a picture of Pope John Paul II. Public reaction was swift and overwhelmingly negative. As explanation for her act, O'Connor claimed that the Catholic Church's opposition to divorce, abortion, and birth control is essentially anti-woman. The fallout from this and her other controversial acts affected her popularity and record sales. In fact, at Bob Dylan's Thirtieth Anniversary concert at Madison Square Garden in 1993 she was met with loud boos and jeers. As the band began to play the song she was scheduled to sing, she cut them off and sang the Bob Marley song "War," which was the same song she had sung before ripping up the photograph of the pope.

O'Connor's next album, *Am I Not Your Girl?*, was released in late 1992. In a departure from her earlier work, O'Connor offered a collection of soft pop standards. The critical reaction was mixed. Parke Puterbaugh of *Stereo Review* wrote, "[*Am I Not Your Girl?*] is not the place you'll go to hear torch songs and show tunes identified with the likes of Peggy Lee ('Why Don't You Do It Right?'), Sarah Vaughn ('Black Coffee') and Billie Holiday ('Gloomy Sunday').... [But] her haunting version of Loretta Lynn's 'Success Has Made a Failure of Me' works as illuminating autobiography and her cool, gauzy vocals put across Rodgers and Hart's 'Bewitched, Bothered, and Bewildered' with surprising panache."

Though several sources reported that O'Connor had announced her retirement after the commercial failure of *Am I Not Your Girl?*, she proved that her need to make music was still strong with the 1994 release of *Universal Mother*. Some critics praised the effort and seemed to be welcoming O'Connor back into the pop mainstream, but the album, which debuted at Number 36 on the *Billboard* 200 album chart, displayed a rapid decline in sales in the first weeks after its release. Still, few observers of the music scene were ready to count O'Connor out altogether. Rather, it seemed that America, anyway, may simply have needed more time to recover from O'Connor's assault on its values.

O'Connor lives in London, England, with her son Jake. Although no longer married, she remains close friends with former husband John Reynolds. In an article she wrote for *Ms.* magazine, O'Connor explained: "I felt I should get married in order to make myself happy and that this in turn would make John and my son Jake happy. We've decided that we didn't like living together as man and wife and we'd rather be friends." In this same article O'Connor put greater value on her person than on her career. "My songs are not the most important thing in my life—they're just a written account of it. I don't want to be perceived as a pop star; that leaves you very little room to develop. I want to be perceived as a human being."

Sources

High Fidelity, March 1988.

Humanist, January/February 1993.

Interview, March 1988; December 1992.

Ms., May/June 1992.

New York, March 8, 1993.

New York Times, September 11, 1994.

People, May 16, 1988.

Rolling Stone, April 21, 1988; January 26, 1989; March 22, 1990; October 29, 1992.

Stereo Review, January 1993.

Time, November 9, 1992; June 21, 1993.

Washingtonian, December 1988.

Laurence Olivier

Born May 22, 1907, Dorking, Surrey, England
Died July 11, 1989, West Sussex, England

ACTOR AND DIRECTOR

As king among actors of the modern era and the first lord of the British theater, Laurence Olivier mesmerized audiences for years with his versatility, boldness, and charisma. His range was remarkable, for he played with equal skill and believability romantic heroes and eccentrics. His talent also extended to the realms of directing and producing, and his contribution to theater and film remains a testament to his genius. Actor Anthony Hopkins told *People* magazine, "He was the greatest actor of the twentieth century."

Olivier was born on May 22, 1907, in Dorking, in Surrey, England, about 20 miles southwest of London. His father was an Anglican clergyman and the relationship between the two was strained. Clear in his dislike for his son, Olivier's father remained distant throughout his life. The youngest of three children, Olivier remembered in his autobiography, *Confessions of an Actor,* "I have always thought that

"I am fortunate in that, however unexciting or even distasteful a role may seem to me at first, with the first glimmer of invention or imagination I become lost in the magical wonder of being in its grip; one is barely conscious of the process by which one pours oneself into it and it into itself."

the initial trouble between me and my father was that he couldn't see the slightest purpose in my existence. There, in splendid relief, was his beautiful daughter, his eldest child, and three years younger was his son and heir and the only one he needed, thank you very much." His father was economical in the extreme, carving paper-thin slices of meat for his family and forcing Olivier to bathe in the same water used first by the father and then by the first-born son. The cool indifference and sometimes raging temper of his father alienated Olivier and kept him always on guard. Recalling his childhood, Olivier once stated, "I was frightened. More than anything else, I was terrified."

Fortunately for Olivier, his mother provided great warmth and love for her youngest child. Some of his sweetest childhood memories are centered on his mother. When he was three they moved to London, where his bedroom overlooked a park. His mother taught him the names of the trees and flowers there, and from her he learned his lifelong love of gardening.

As a young man Olivier was impressed by the pageantry and drama he witnessed during his father's church services. He used to reenact the service and imitate his father as part of his play. He also used to set up a wooden chest by his nursery curtains and perform parts from plays he had seen at his brother's school, usually with his mother as an audience. From the ages of five through nine Olivier managed to be regularly, if reluctantly, spanked by his mother for his repeated acts of lying. "It was a compulsion in me to invent a story and feel it so convincingly that it was believed at first without doubt of suspicion," Olivier recalled. This habit continued until he realized that it truly pained his mother to have to punish her youngest son.

School launches acting career

In 1916 Olivier attended his older brother's school, All Saints, after a vocal audition. Fourteen boys attended the school, whose choir was renowned and whose dramatic society began the training that would launch Olivier into the acting profession. Here he played in such Shakespearean works as *Twelfth Night* and *The Taming of the Shrew*. Although his acting was applauded, Olivier's academic performance was only average. He was physically awkward and often lonely. "I was a muddled kind of boy, a weakling," Olivier recalled. "As a child I was a shrimp, as a youth I was a weed—a miserably thin creature whose arms hung like wires from my shoulders." Where he won his classmates approval was with his mimicry. He often impersonated the school's staff, as well as film stars, for the amusement of his fellow students.

In 1920, when Olivier was only 12, his mother died from a brain tumor. In later years he often remarked, "I don't think I ever got over it." When she died Olivier lost his greatest ally and the major provider of love in his young life. He persevered, however, and remembering "I learnt that great suffering could in some mysterious way sometimes implant in its victim an unexpected strength. I have managed to cling to that belief throughout my life, and in any really appalling circumstances it has given me a small, narrow shelf that could afford me a moment's rest."

In 1921, when it was time to enter higher classes, Olivier was admitted to St. Edward's School. Most of the students there were the sons of clergymen whose reduced tuition allowed them a good education at a reasonable price. He continued his acting while there and during the winter break of 1923-24, Olivier first realized that acting would become his career. According to Olivier, he was at home taking his bath in used water and feeling sad because he had seen his brother sail off to India to be a rubber planter. With his father in the room, Olivier asked when he might be expected to follow his brother to India. As Olivier often told it, his father answered: "Don't be such a fool; you're not going to India, you're going on the stage."

So in June 1924 Olivier was admitted on full scholarship to the Central School of Speech and Drama. With only the meager allowance given by his father, Olivier often was hungry. He struggled and worked to secure parts that would provide income. His reputation began to grow and soon the roles he was seeking came his way. In 1930 Olivier was offered a film role, and because he needed the money he accepted. It was after the New York run of Noel Coward's *Private Lives* that Hollywood first courted Olivier. With the advent of talking pictures, the need for stage actors grew and Hollywood went to Broadway to find performers who were trained in speech and elocution.

Makes movies in Hollywood

Hollywood offered Olivier stardom when he first arrived, casting him in the romantic lead of Heathcliff in *Wuthering Heights* and MGM planned an appearance opposite Greta Garbo in *Queen Christina*. This might have tipped him inescapably toward a movie career, but Garbo rejected him in favor of old lover and slipping star John Gilbert. Thereafter, Olivier rejected star roles in favor of character parts. He took a delight in mime, accent, and character make-up. Such parts as Darcy in *Pride and Prejudice*, Maxim de Winter in *Rebecca*, Nelson in *That Hamilton Woman*, and Hurstwood, the hotel manager ruined by love in *Carrie*, are performances by a skilled actor, not the appearances of a star.

Among Olivier's greatest achievements are the three Shakespearean plays he produced and directed for the screen—*Henry V, Hamlet,* and *Richard III.* Also starring in these films, Olivier used only half the original text but conveyed the essence of Shakespeare by using strong visual images. *Henry V* was Olivier's first film as director, and it was made at government request to bolster the morale of an England struggling to survive World War II. To do so, Olivier concentrated on portraying the brave soldiers who emerge victorious in battle through improvised solutions. The project was even dedicated to the men of the Royal Air Force who fought in the Battle of Britain. Olivier excelled as a director by creatively using such film techniques as swiftcuts and dissolves to effectively bring a Shakespearean play from the stage to the screen. *Hamlet* and *Richard III* were also well received, and all three gave Olivier the chance to enjoy working in the medium of film as much as he had always enjoyed working in live theater.

His films of the 1950s and 1960s mostly recreated his stage hits *The Entertainer, Othello, The Three Sisters,* and *The Dance of Death.* One exception is *The Prince and the Showgirl* which he directed and starred in opposite Marilyn Monroe, and which was largely unsuccessful. He also appeared in some cameos chosen from the range of international film and television productions that could always use an imposing figure and an impressive voice.

Despite declining health in the 1970s and 1980s, Olivier continued to work. Among his roles were a complaining Moriarty in *The Seven-Per-Cent Solution,* Nazi hunter Ezra Lieberman in *The Boys From Brazil,* and the former Nazi of *Marathon Man.* All these characters are effective creations by a man who enjoyed playing diverse and challenging parts.

Married three times

Olivier was married three times to actresses with whom he worked. His first wife was Jill Esmond, who he married in 1930. Their marriage was later acknowledged by Olivier to be little more than a sham. Olivier once claimed that Jill "could not and did not try to deceive herself into believing that she was in the slightest degree in love with me, and she knew that I was fully aware of it." In 1935 Olivier met Vivian Leigh, and within a few years the two were involved in an affair. In 1940 he obtained a divorce and married Leigh. Their relationship began to dissolve in the 1950s as Leigh's behavior became increasingly volatile and self-destructive. Divorcing Leigh in 1960, Olivier married Joan Plowright in 1961. The two remained married until Olivier's death in 1989.

Olivier remarked in his autobiography that unlike stage work, "films and television do not usually tax one's energies beyond their normal capacities." Yet it is evident that Olivier gave to most of them the benefit of a superb technique. It was to the live theater, however, that Olivier pledged his greatest love and support. Of it he once said, "I believe in the theater; I believe in it as the first glamorizer of thought. It restores dramatic dynamics and their relationship to lifesize.... I believe in anything that will keep our domains, not wider still and wider, but higher still and higher in the expectance and hope of quality and probity."

Sources

Current Biography, H. W. Wilson, 1979, 1989.

Fairweather, Virginia, *Cry God for Larry: An Intimate Portrait of Sir Laurence Olivier,* Calder & Boyars, 1969.

Newsweek, July 24, 1989.

New York Times, July 12, 1989; October 21, 1989.

Olivier, Laurence, *Confessions of an Actor,* Viking Penguin, 1982.

People, July 24, 1989.

Edward James Olmos

Born February 24, 1947
Boyle Heights, California

"Face to face over tea and croissants, Olmos is quietly compelling. Pockmarked cheeks, ridged forehead, a jumble of lower teeth, his is a face to wonder over, to respect."—David Mills

ACTOR

Edward James Olmos was recognized by his fellow actors as an intense, disciplined performer long before he became known to the general public for his portrayal of Lieutenant Martin Castillo on the television series *Miami Vice*. Today he has several prestigious awards and nominations as proof of his acting talent. Yet Olmos maintains that the citations he has received for his public service work mean more to him than any number of Emmys or Oscar nominations. Each year he makes approximately 150 public-speaking engagements, encouraging disadvantaged people of all types to pursue an education and gain control of their own destinies.

Education is important

Olmos's passion for education is a legacy from his parents. His father left Mexico City at the age of 21 with nothing more than a sixth-grade education, but after settling in Los Angeles, he returned to school and eventually earned a high school degree. The actor's mother left school after the eighth grade, but she too completed her education after her children were grown, and the importance of school was always strongly emphasized in her household. The Olmoses divorced when Edward was eight years old. It was a traumatic time for the child, who responded by becoming obsessively involved with baseball. He described the sport to *New York*'s Pete Hamill as "the one thing I enjoyed doing, that would make me stop thinking about my own problems. I was lucky. It could have been drugs. It could have been drinking. But it was baseball." Practicing every day, he developed a tremendous sense of self-discipline that stayed with him into his adult life. In the 1991 film *Talent for the Game*, Olmos played a major-league catcher and scout. He told a reporter for *Parade*, "Doing this film was like going down the road not taken."

Pedro Olmos was certain that his son would become a professional ball player, but at the age of 13 the boy suddenly announced his intention to become a singer and dancer instead. By the time he graduated from high school, he was making a living doing just that, fronting a band called Pacific Ocean. The group was regularly booked at the Sunset Strip's top clubs. "I sang terrible," Olmos admitted to Hamill, "but I could scream real good and I could dance. So I'd dance for five minutes, then come back and sing a couple more screams, then dance again." During the day he attended college, studying with characteristic intensity. He even brought his textbooks to Pacific Ocean's gigs and delved into them during breaks. At first he majored in psychology and criminology, but eventually he gravitated toward dance and theater in the hopes of improving his singing. Before long, however, he fell in love with acting and decided to make it his profession.

By the time he was 25 years old, Olmos was married and the father of two. He supported his family by running an antique-furniture delivery business, while working in experimental theater by night and hustling for bit parts on television. Frequently he was cast as a sullen bartender or two-bit crook on shows such as *Kojak* or *Hawaii Five-O*, where, he told *Time* reporter Elaine Dutka, "I was the only person Jack Lord [star of *Hawaii Five-O*] shot in the back, ever.... That's how bad I was."

Won breakthrough role in Zoot Suit

In 1978 Olmos won the role that would transform his life. It was a part in Luis Valdez's *Zoot Suit*, a musical drama based on a 1942 case in which a group of Hispanic youths were wrongly convicted of murder. Olmos played "El Pachuco," the narrator and conscience of the story. Strutting and posing in an embodiment of angry machismo, he delivered a performance of "extraordinary, electric power," wrote Hamill. "He seemed to pour everything he knew into the role.... And he stylized the character into a figure of equal menace and sympathy." *Zoot Suit* electrified Los Angeles. According to *Playboy* contributor Marcia Seligson, it "awakened the city ... to its Hispanic population, to its racial tensions and to the Chicano community's fight for identity." Scheduled for a ten-day run at the Mark Taper Theater, *Zoot Suit* actually ran for a year and a half before moving on to Broadway. Its success was not repeated in New York—the play closed after just seven weeks—but Olmos's brilliance was acknowledged all the same when he was nominated for a Tony Award.

The days of fighting for one-line parts in TV cop shows were over. Olmos was now offered featured parts in major films. Wary of becoming locked into stereotypical Hispanic roles, he selected his projects carefully. He put his unique stamp on the films *Wolfen* and *Blade Runner,* playing a tormented man-dog in the former and a brilliant multiethnic in the latter. Next came a film that was deeply meaningful to the actor: A PBS "American Playhouse" presentation entitled *The Ballad of Gregorio Cortez.* It was the tale of a Mexican folk hero who had traditionally been portrayed as a fierce bandit. When Olmos and director Robert Young researched the story, however, they discovered that Cortez was actually an impoverished rancher and dedicated family man, who had become the subject of the largest manhunt in Texas history on the basis of a misinterpreted word. Together, they transformed the outlaw legend into what Pat Aufderheide called in *Mother Jones* "a tragic misunderstanding across linguistic and cultural barriers."

Some Hispanics protested this interpretation at first, fearing that the film would demean their hero, but after its release, *The Ballad of Gregorio Cortez* was recognized as a "breakthrough film for Hispanics, with its evocation of an individual's ordinary humanity denied by discrimination, stereotyping, and ignorance." Olmos spoke Spanish exclusively in the picture, which carried no subtitles. "I wanted to put non-Spanish speaking viewers in the same predicament as the law-abiding citizens of that community," the actor explained to Dutka. "I wanted the audience to be in the shoes of Gregorio Cortez."

Promotes Cortez *himself*

No major studio chose to distribute *The Ballad of Gregorio Cortez* after its PBS broadcast, and it seemed likely to fade into obscurity. Olmos refused to let that happen. He rented a Hollywood theater and showed the film every Saturday morning for free, waiting for word of mouth to broadcast its merits. Then he began traveling extensively to promote Cortez on the film-society circuit. His dedication to this project was such that he turned down more than $500,000 worth of standard acting work at this time in order to continue his promotional efforts. He has explained that although the parts he was offered in *Red Dawn, Scarface,* and *Firestarter* would have been lucrative, they held no meaning for him. He also turned down a part in television's *Hill Street Blues* because it would have required him to sign an exclusive five-year contract prohibiting him from working on any other projects. His principles were straining the family's finances, however; at one point, friends held a fund-raiser to help defray the cost of his travel expenses.

In 1984 television producer Michael Mann offered Olmos the role of Lieutenant Martin Castillo on a new program called *Miami Vice.* Although the actor badly needed the money, he turned down the offer because, like the *Hill Street Blues* part, it involved an exclusive contract. Mann continued to call, each time increasing his financial offer to Olmos, but the actor, who was developing some new projects with *Gregorio Cortez* director Robert Young, continued to refuse. Finally, after five offers, Mann agreed to Olmos's demand for a non-exclusive contract, the first one granted in the history of television. The next morning, Olmos was in Miami, ready to begin creating the character of Martin Castillo.

A dark, puzzling figure, Castillo soon came to represent the moral center of *Miami Vice* and was considered by many critics to be the most interesting and complex character in the series. "He's mysterious because you don't know very much about his life," Olmos described his creation to Seligson in *Playboy.* "Actually, he's a fairly normal guy who has been beaten back by life. In one early episode, it was revealed that he had lost his family and all his friends, he was betrayed by his own country, by the CIA. So what he learned about life made him very bitter." Olmos went on to say that the Castillo character is very strict with himself and very disciplined, and "I would like to think of myself and my own values that way. He embodies concepts that I think are essential to getting to the highest level of understanding oneself—discipline, determination, perseverance and patience."

Enthusiastic as he was about his own character, however, Olmos never hesitated to point out the shortcomings of *Miami Vice,* even while it was still on the air. Aufderheide quoted him as calling the program "highly stylized" and "uneven in content"; to Seligson, he commented: "The show definitely has a tendency to perpetuate stereotypes and also is chau-

Olmos on the set with high school teacher Jaime Escalante, whom Olmos portrayed in *Stand and Deliver*, 1988.

vinistic to women. I have gotten into intense discussions with the producers about that and I've had some big blowouts with them over it.... Women are just used as decor.... It's a male-oriented show."

Nominated for Oscar for Stand and Deliver

He voiced no such ambiguities about his next film project, *Stand and Deliver.* He told Seligson, "It's one of the most uplifting films I've ever seen.... I tell you, if I never do another thing in my life but this, I will be forever grateful to have been given the opportunity to make it." *Stand and Deliver* is the true story of Jaime Escalante, a Bolivian-born math teacher who came to a gang-ridden East Los Angeles high school and inspired 18 of his students to take, and pass, the Educational Testing Service's advanced placement calculus test. Along the way, he also taught them to have pride in themselves and to take control of their own destinies.

To prepare for his role as Escalante, Olmos attended the teacher's classes, gained 40 pounds, and spent hundreds of hours studying tapes of the Bolivian's speech patterns and manner-isms. (He even asked to move in with Escalante, but the teacher's wife drew the line there.) The finished film grossed more than nine times its modest cost and won Olmos an Academy Award nomination. "The film is

Since the making of *American Me*, the "Mexican mafia" has reportedly threatened Olmos's life. Four people associated with the film have mysteriously died since its release.

really about the triumph of the human spirit," the actor told Seligson. "It's about something we've lost—the joy of learning, the joy of making our brains develop. It evokes the same feelings as *Rocky, Chariots of Fire, The Miracle Worker.* Response to the film has been monumental.... Never have I done anything that has gotten this response. People thank me; they talk about the value of education and how that's lacking in our political struc-ture.... There have been standing ovations at performances.... It was a God-sent project and I'm really happy that Jaime Escalante is alive and well today." Olmos has enlisted the help of several major corporations in a pro-ject to place a copy of *Stand and Deliver* with every school, library, prison, hospital, youth organization, or any other organization that could benefit from its uplifting message.

In 1992 Olmos directed, coproduced, and starred in *American Me.* Based loosely on fact, the movie centers on Chicano drug lord Santana (Olmos) and is set in a California State Prison. Against a series of flash-backs, Santana recalls how he became involved in gangs as a youth in L.A. and how he helped to establish a "Mexican mafia" from behind prison walls. In an interview with *USA Today,* Olmos revealed his opinion of the story: "The basic story, I thought was just extraordinary. How inside of the prisons organized crime was building, touching society on the daily level."

Olmos's most recent project was *Menendez: A Murder in Beverly Hills,* which aired in May 1994 on CBS. In it Olmos played Jose Menendez, the real-life father of Lyle and Erik Menendez, who was allegedly killed by his sons due to years of sexual and mental abuse. In his review for *People,* David Hildbrand praised Olmos's performance: "Edward James Olmos is outstanding as Jose Menendez, the driven, demanding father, who spits at both his sons at one time or another, 'You disgust me!'"

Olmos spends as much time being an activist as he does acting. He was recently involved in an effort to make peace between Los Angeles's warring gangs; he works with disabled and sexually abused children; he makes public-service announcements to speak out against drug abuse; and he speaks frequently to children in juvenile halls, inner-city schools, and on Indian reservations, spreading the word that it is possible to improve one's lot in life, even against heavy odds. He told Seligson that these speaking engagements are far more rewarding than acting, and serve as "an extraordinary source of energy.... After an hour of speaking with those kids, I walk away with a buzzing feeling inside. Because you're one person giving to more than three hundred people who are giving back to you.... If I do two or three schools in one day, I go home and I'm careening off the walls and just feel great about what I've done with my life that day. I'm in love with life; yeah, it's very rewarding. These are the most fulfilling moments that I've spent on this earth. That and just staying with my family are the two things that give me the most joy."

Sources

Mother Jones, April 1988.

Newsweek, March 14, 1988.

New York, September 29, 1986.

Parade, March 17, 1991.

People, May 23, 1994.

Playboy, June 1989.

Time, April 4, 1988; July 11, 1988.

USA Weekend, May 20-22, 1994.

Washington Post, March 21, 1992.

Dolly Parton

Born January 19, 1946
Sevier County, Tennessee

SINGER, SONGWRITER, AND ACTRESS

"I never doubted I'd make it."

Few country singers have had greater success in the pop market than Dolly Parton, the curvaceous blonde from Tennessee's Smoky Mountains. "As much as anyone," wrote Gene Busnar in *Superstars of Country Music*, "Dolly has extended the connections between folk traditions and contemporary styles." Much attention has been lavished on Parton's gaudy attire, cascading wigs, and outgoing, chatty personality, but beneath the surface glitter lurks a genuine musician determined to enjoy her life and art. As Margo Jefferson observed in *Ms.* magazine, Parton "is making no effort to hide or disguise her origins. She is indelibly country. The vibrato and light twang of her voice evoke the Anglo-Saxon ballads of the Southern mountains, and the jigs and reels of the early string bands. Her rhythmic fluidity suggests the affinity for black blues and church singing that always lies beneath the surface of so much country music. And she has been experimenting with assorted styles since her first recordings." Concerning Parton's association with the stereotypical "dumb blonde," those who know her characterize her as an astute businesswoman with unrelenting ambitions. Busnar stated, "Dolly makes it crystal clear that she is the brains behind all those ... wigs." The performer herself put it more succinctly in *Ms.:* "If people think I'm a dumb blonde because of the way I look, then they're dumber than they think I am. If people think I'm not very deep because of my wigs and outfits, then they're not very deep.... If I was trying to really impress men or be totally sexy, I would dress differently."

Parton's affinity for fancy hairstyles and jewel-studded dresses stems in large part from her impoverished upbringing in Sevier County, Tennessee. She was born near the Smoky Mountains in 1946, the fourth of 11 children of Robert Lee and Avie Lee Parton. According to Busnar, "The pain of growing up poor and hungry weighed heavily on the young girl and, like Cinderella in the fairy tale, Dolly dreamed that someone would magically turn her shack into a palace and her raggedy clothes into magnificent gowns." Parton's romantic visions of wealth soon gave birth to an iron determination to succeed. If she wanted to get rich and give her farmer parents an easier life, she realized she would have to make a name for herself. "I knew I'd be the first member of my family in generations to leave the mountains and actually go out in the world," she said in Busnar's account. "I never doubted I'd make it." Parton began writing songs and singing at the age of seven. She made her professional debut on a Knoxville radio show at ten and secured a guest appearance at the Grand Ole Opry at twelve. Parton told *Ms.,* "I got so much applause, it just confirmed what I believed. I thought: Well, this is for me. I am definitely destined to be a star. I'm going to make a lot of money. I'm going to buy Mama and Daddy a house. We're going to have clothes, cars...."

Starts singing career

First, however, Parton graduated from high school. Intuitively she felt that she would need an education to help her manage the fantastic career she had planned. Immediately after graduation, she packed a cardboard suitcase and moved to Nashville to begin her career. On her first night in town she met a handsome contractor, Carl Dean, in a Nashville laundromat. They married and pursued their separate interests—Parton a singing career, Dean a small business buying and selling farm equipment. Within a year, in 1967, Parton had landed a starring role on the popular *Porter Wagoner Show.* She began recording duets with Wagoner, who was already a country-music superstar, and both their careers were strengthened by the association. Busnar wrote, "With the addition of Dolly, Wagoner was able to successfully combine traditional folk elements with rock and pop influences to put on a show rivaled only by Johnny Cash and his troupe. However, Dolly was already looking not only beyond Porter Wagoner, but also beyond the confines of the entire Nashville scene."

In the mid-1970s several female artists began crossing over from country to pop. Parton, who had never sold more than 200,000 copies of an album decided to gamble on her marketability in the pop music business. It was a daring move for a performer so strongly identified with country—she not only ran the risk of alienating her country fans, she also ran the risk of being too eccentric a personality to attract pop listeners. She was fond of saying, "I'm not leavin' country, I'm just takin' it with me," as she fired her back-up band and signed on with a Los Angeles-based management company. For Parton, the move to Hollywood was a smart one. Her subsequent songs "Here You Come Again," "Islands in the Stream," and "Nine to Five" were million-sellers that appealed as much to her old fans as to her new ones. She also landed film work in the movies *Nine to Five*, *The Best Little Whorehouse in Texas*, *Rhinestone*, and *Steel Magnolias*. Only *Rhinestone* failed to show a hefty profit. By 1981 Parton was an international star. Women especially liked her earthy humor and—surprisingly—her figure-enhancing gowns. Jefferson noted, "Isn't it pleasant to be reminded that ruffles, pleats, drapes, sequins, curls, lashes, hoops, spangles, powders and paints can be simply toys—entertainment and sports for women quite apart from their value in the game [with men]?" Parton, Jefferson said, returned the joy to femininity.

Hospitalized for exhaustion

Like many performers, Parton finally succumbed to the stress of her profession. In 1982 she fainted during a performance and was hospitalized for exhaustion and a host of medical problems. According to Scot Haller in *People*, the crowds "were faced by a different Dolly: hoarse, overweight, unhealthy and unhappy." After a long recuperation at her home in Nashville, Parton began working again. In 1987 she was given a prime-time television variety show, *Dolly*, that failed in the ratings. The movie *Rhinestone* served as proof that she was not a guaranteed draw at the box office. Still, Parton has continued to enjoy a healthy career between her music and her pet project, a theme park called Dollywood that she built near her mountain home in Tennessee. Busnar analyzed Parton's musical talents: "In her typical fashion, Dolly often jokes about not being a particularly good singer. But, in fact, she is one of our best and most important contemporary female vocalists. Although she is often imitated, Dolly has an unmistakable quality in her voice that somehow combines elements of

Awards

Parton has won numerous awards, including Grammys for *Here You Come Again* in 1978 and, with Emmylou Harris and Linda Ronstadt, for *Trio* in 1988, and People's Choice awards in 1980 and 1988. She was nominated for an Academy Award for the song "Nine to Five" in 1981. The Academy of Country Music named Parton female vocalist of the year for 1980 and named *Trio* Album of the Year for 1987.

traditional American folk music, the strength and power of religious music, and her own unique brand of fun." Busnar added, most importantly, that Parton's "songwriting skills have helped her become an awesome force in the music business." Nothing more forcefully demonstrated this than the record-breaking success of pop star Whitney Houston's rendition of Parton's "I Will Always Love You." The theme to Houston's worldwide smash film *The Bodyguard* is actually Parton's farewell to early mentor Porter Wagoner, with whom her relationship was always stormy. Parton's original recording is a quiet, moving tribute of subtle power, but it was Houston's over-the-top performance that brought the song international renown, numerous awards, and substantial royalties for the songwriter.

Alanna Nash praises Parton for another aspect of her career in Ms., namely her astute (and independently made) career decisions and her preservation of family and marital ties. Dolly Parton has realized the American dream on her own terms, wrote Nash. "Throughout her ... career, Parton has followed the classic female paradigm of using the access that comes with personal achievement to create opportunities for those we love.... [She] has come to symbolize the Smoky Mountains heritage. For Parton, this heritage has not only meant preserving the old ways, but also making the most out of what you have, and then showing others how to do it too." Parton, who is said to be looking forward to performing until she turns 100, told People that the way she looks and dresses is the way she chooses to look and dress. "The personality is for real," she said. "I don't have to put on makeup to feel like Dolly. I am Dolly."

Sources

Busnar, Gene, *Superstars of Country Music,* J. Messner, 1984.

Life, March 1987.

Ms., June 1979; July 1986.

Nash, Alanna, *Dolly Parton,* ReedBooks, 1978.

New York Times Magazine, May 9, 1976.

People, August 2, 1982; July 9, 1984; May 5, 1986.

Rolling Stone, October 23, 1975; August 15, 1977.

Simon, George T., *The Best of the Music Makers,* Doubleday, 1971.

Luciano Pavarotti

Born October 12, 1935
Modena, Italy

OPERA SINGER

Luciano Pavarotti is considered by many to be the greatest male singer since Enrico Caruso, and in his prime—the mid-1970s—he was probably the century's best lyric tenor. He is known for his extraordinary vocal capacity, earning the nickname "King of the High Cs" for his execution of the string of high notes in Gaetano Donizetti's fiendishly difficult *La Fille du regiment.* His voice, at once capable of sweetness and immense volume, is considered the ideal medium for Italian opera's celebrated *bel canto* works, those works calling for purity of tone and articulation even in the upper register. Pavarotti has embraced such works gleefully, and with both his extraordinary voice and his endearing, puckish personality, he is largely perceived as the opera performer who best recalls previous greats such as Caruso and Jussi Bjoerling. As Hubert Saal noted in a 1976 *Newsweek* article, "More than any other tenor today, Luciano Pavarotti ... summons up the legendary golden age of singing."

"When my daughter was seven, she thought I was a thief, because she never saw me go to work. For her, singing is not work. Probably she is right!"

Born in Modena, Italy, in 1935, Pavarotti sang from early childhood. At home, he was often exposed to recordings by Caruso, Bjoerling, and Benaimino Gigli. Though an impressive singer, Pavarotti aspired in his youth to a career as a professional soccer player. His mother, however, urged him to pursue a more realistic career, and in the 1950s he trained as a teacher. He subsequently taught at an elementary school for two years, but with his father's encouragement he continued to train his voice. Pavarotti's efforts proved successful in 1961 when he won a music contest and secured the role of Rodolfo in Giacomo Puccini's *La Boheme* in nearby Regia Emilia. His success in Puccini's great opera led to further roles in such works as Donizetti's dramatic masterwork *Lucia di Lammermoor.*

Masters the bel canto *repertoire*

Throughout the early 1960s, Pavarotti continued to distinguish himself in the *bel canto* repertoire, enjoying particular success with celebrated soprano Joan Sutherland in Donizetti operas, including *L'Elisir d'amore* and the aforementioned *Lucia di Lammermoor*. In still another Donizetti work, *La Fille du regiment,* he awed audiences by soaring through the difficult string of high Cs that mark the opera's highlight. Word soon spread through the opera world of Pavarotti's extraordinary capacity for sustained vocal purity, and in 1967 he made his American debut as Rodolfo in a San Francisco Opera production of *La Boheme*. The following year he reprised the role at the Metropolitan Opera, whereupon he won great praise for his supremely beautiful singing. By the end of the decade Pavarotti was recognized as a supreme force in *bel canto* opera, distinguishing himself further with his performances on recordings of *La Fille du regiment* and Bellini's *Beatrice di Tenda.*

Aside from mastering the *bel canto* repertoire, Pavarotti also earned distinction with his performances in works by Giuseppe Verdi, who is often considered Italy's master opera composer. Among Pavarotti's greatest Verdi roles at this time was the duke in *Rigoletto,* in which capacity he inevitably astounded audiences with his rendition of the well-known "Donna e mobile." As his voice grew in richness and depth, Pavarotti broadened his own repertoire to include other Verdi operas, notably *Il Trovatore,* where his rousing interpretation of Manrico's call to war often inspired wild enthusiasm from opera lovers. Other roles Pavarotti assumed at this time included Cavaradossi in Puccini's *Tosca* and the Calaf—though on recording only—in Puccini's *Turandot*. "Nessun dorma," the tenor centerpiece of this work, has become a mainstay of Pavarotti's solo performances.

Strengthens status in opera world

In the 1980s, Pavarotti strengthened his status as one of the opera world's leading figures. Since his first appearance on the Metropolitan Opera's stage, Pavarotti has expanded his repertoire with considerable success, undertaking works ranging from Wolfgang Amadeus Mozart's *Idomeneo* to Verdi's *Aida,* while continuing to appear in those works—notably *La Boheme, Lucia di Lammermoor,* and *Rigoletto*— which helped establish him as one of the century's great tenors. Televised performances of Pavarotti in many of his greatest roles have enabled him to not only sustain his status but considerably broaden his appeal, reaching millions of viewers each time one of his opera performances, solo concerts or recitals is broadcast. He has also shown increasing flexibility as a recording artist. While he continues to appear on recordings of complete operas—with *Idomeneo* and Bellini's *Norma* among his most impressive records from the 1980s— he has also released collections of Italian folk songs and even an album of compositions by popular composer Henry Mancini.

In 1994 Pavarotti teamed with fellow singers José Carreras and Placido Domingo for a highly acclaimed series of performances and recordings. *3 Tenors in Concert 1994,* a live recording culled from the trio's landmark Dodgers Stadium concert, debuted in the Number Four position on the *Billboard* 200 pop album chart, vividly illustrating the mainstream penetration of classical singing, much of which is owed to Pavarotti's work of the 1970s and 1980s.

Pavarotti seems comfortable with his vast popularity. Although mobbed in public and worshipped in opera houses, he stays committed to serving his art. Unabashed in proclaiming his own pursuit of fame and acclaim—"I want to be famous everywhere," he told *Newsweek*'s Hubert Saal—he greatly reciprocates his fans' dedication and shows a marked appreciation for the attention he is accorded by music lovers everywhere. "I tell you," he confided to Saal, "the time spent signing autographs is never long enough."

Sources

Esquire, June 5, 1979.

Newsweek, March 15, 1976.

New York, May 18, 1981; January 27, 1986.

New Yorker, October 15, 1973; June 21, 1993.

Opera News, December 10, 1983; March 29, 1986.

Time, October 25, 1976.

Pearl Jam

Pearl Jam "are darling guys."
—*Lynn Woolsey*

ROCK GROUP

Pearl Jam is one of the hottest young acts in the rock world. Propelled by the gloomy vocals of singer Eddie Vedder, the muscular playing of guitarists Mike McCready and Stone Gossard, the groove of drummer Dave Abbruzzese, and the melodic but funky bass work of Jeff Ament, they have risen from Seattle's bubbling underground to the position of rock superstars. Pearl Jam made its debut in 1991 with the hard-rocking album *Ten*. Its sound recalled the heavy rock of the 1970s and was initially labeled "grunge" and lumped with the work of Nirvana and other Seattle bands. After *Ten*'s release, the band toured for 18 months and gained a reputation as an excellent live act. Its videos became MTV favorites, and teenagers all over the country identified with singer Vedder's manic stage presence, his obvious sincerity, and his songs about abuse and adolescent angst.

Ten *a huge success*

Ten would remain in the *Billboard* Top 200 for years and would become one of the most successful debuts in history, selling over eight million copies. This incredible success, however, led to media over-exposure, especially for Vedder—who appeared on *Newsweek*'s cover and was

described by the *Philadelphia Inquirer* and other sources as "the sex symbol of the grunge world." Because of this success some questioned Pearl Jam's artistic credentials. With the release of their second album, *Vs.*, in October 1993, Pearl Jam proved they were more than alternative pinup boys. A critical and popular success, *Vs.* displayed a band that had grown beyond the flannel-fringed heavy Seattle sound and embraced a more diverse and fully formed style. Pearl Jam's roots reach back to the mid-1980s underground scene of Seattle, Washington. In 1984 guitarist Stone Gossard and bassist Jeff Ament helped found the pioneering Seattle grunge rock group Green River. Green River recorded several albums on the indie (independent) label Sub Pop, including *Rehab Doll*, which *Guitar Player* called their best disc.

After Green River dissolved in 1988, Gossard, Ament, and drummer Jeff Turner joined with singer Andrew Wood to form Mother Love Bone. MLB was a more bluesy outfit than Green River; Ament told *Guitar Player* that it gave him and Gossard "the room to let our personalities shine." MLB's two records, 1989's *Shine* (on Stardog/Polydor) and 1990's *Apple* (Polydor) were both well received but Wood died of a heroin overdose on the eve of *Apple*'s release and MLB's potential was left unfulfilled.

With Wood's death, Gossard moved toward a hard-edged groove and produced a tape called "Stone Gossard Demos 91," which contained instrumental versions of several songs that would appear on *Ten*. He soon began jamming with Mike McCready, an explosive lead guitarist whose own band, Shadow, had also recently broken up. When McCready and Gossard brought in Ament, who had been playing around Seattle with a funky group called War Babies, the three sensed something special. "I knew we had a band," McCready told *Rolling Stone*, "when we started playing that song 'Dollar Short.'"

What the group did not have, however, was a vocalist. Hoping to spark some interest, Gossard passed "Stone Gossard Demos 91" to some friends, including Jack Irons, formerly of the Red Hot Chili Peppers. Irons, who was living in San Diego, gave it to another San Diego "scenester" named Eddie Vedder.

Vedder, an Evanston, Illinois, native, was working days at a petroleum company and building a career as a singer and songwriter by night. He listened to Gossard's tape and liked what he heard. A few mornings later, while surfing, he got a rush of words for the song "Dollar Short." When he got home, he recorded himself singing over three of the instrumentals and sent the tape, which he titled "Mamasan," north.

Vedder joins group

When Ament and Gossard heard Vedder's songs, one of which was "Alive," they knew they had something. Two weeks later Vedder went to Seattle and a week after that Pearl Jam was a functioning band. Initially named Mookie Blalock (for the New Jersey Nets guard, whose number, 10, also became the title of their debut), the band soon renamed itself Pearl Jam, allegedly taking the name from the homemade jam made by Vedder's great-grandmother Pearl.

In September 1991, less than a year after Vedder had first arrived in Seattle, Pearl Jam released their debut album, *Ten. Ten* became one of the most successful debut albums in rock, and Vedder's lyrics and tortured baritone were a big part of its appeal. "Vedder," *Spin* wrote, "is an extremely serious, extremely sincere young man, and most importantly, his sincerity translates. His fans make an emotional connection with him." According to *Guitar Player*, many looked to his emotion-driven music "for comfort, solidarity, and a sense of connectedness." Among *Ten*'s songs, *Rolling Stone* described "Once," "Even Flow," and "Deep" as conveying "a nearly overwhelming sense of empathy for the disenchanted"; "Why Go," and "Jeremy" as delving "into the battered psyche of the neglected child"; and "Black," "Porch," and "Alive" as imparting "an almost primal yearning." As *Rolling Stone* reviewer Kim Neely wrote, "The most intriguing aspect of the songs is that, despite their often sad subject matter, they are oddly celebratory." She added that "*Ten* is the sort of album that makes you want to stand on a mountain and yell."

But while *Ten* became wildly popular, critical assessment was mixed. The *Boston Phoenix* called *Ten* "magnificent," though Nirvana's Kurt Cobain told *Rolling Stone* it had been made by a "bunch of careerists." As for the hit "Alive," *Chicago Tribune* critic Greg Kot described it as "a shapeless mess of verses, anthemic chorus that comes out of nowhere, and 'Free Bird' guitar finale," referring to the Lynyrd Skynyrd song of the 1970s. For Kot and others *Ten* was the product of "a group of '70s metal heads repackaged as a '90s alternative band."

Gain praise for live performances

While critics had mixed opinions about *Ten,* they had no trouble agreeing that Pearl Jam was one of the very best live acts. *Spin* described them as "such an intense experience that even nonbelievers walk away with newfound respect for the raw emotional energy the group conjures." A reviewer from *Stereo Review* wrote, "When I heard Pearl Jam in a club last summer, I almost lost all sense of time and space—not just because they were loud, but because they played as if their lives depended on it."

Interestingly, Vedder, who was always the focal point of Pearl Jam live, began his performing career as a desperately shy young man. It was only to incite complacent crowds while performing away from the familiar Seattle audience that he transformed himself. With the help of Soundgarden's Chris Cornell, he began to act out the desperation of his songs. He climbed stage scaffolding, flung himself into the crowd, and conveyed with his body the suffering and emotion so characteristic of his voice.

Another transformation for the band came with the addition of Austin, Texas-bred funk drummer Dave Abbruzzese, who replaced Dave Krusen soon after the release of *Ten.* "Dave ... added a whole new dimension to the group, and we've gotten a hell of a lot better and tighter," lead guitarist Mike McCready told *Guitar Player.* The band toured for 18 months between 1992 and 1993. They played on MTV's *Unplugged,* opened the European leg of U2's Zooropa '93 tour, and appeared with rock legends Keith Richards and Neil Young. The *New York Times* described their performance at the 1992 Lollapalooza traveling music festival as "long suffering and elegiac." Reviewer Jon Pareles noted that while "Pearl Jam's artists were constantly leaping around," their music wasn't "festive." Of Vedder, Pareles said, "[His] voice has a despairing groan at its core, and he acts out the lyrics with an earnestness that can illuminate the song or, at times, make him look like Joe Cocker."

Success increases exposure

Ten's incredible success brought further opportunities and exposure. A&M re-released *Temple of The Dog,* a 1991 tribute to Mother Love Bone's Andrew Wood featuring Ament, Gossard, McCready, and Vedder, along with Soundgarden's Chris Cornell and Matt Cameron. Guitarist Gossard released a side project titled *Shame* with some friends, calling that group Brad. And the band as a whole contributed the songs "Breath" and "State of Love and Trust" to the *Singles* movie soundtrack and "Crazy Mary" to *Sweet Relief*—a benefit album for songwriter Victoria Williams, who contracted multiple sclerosis and couldn't afford health care insurance. (Vedder's father, whom Vedder was led to believe was only a family friend until after his death, was a victim of multiple sclerosis.)

Success also brought pressures and temptations. Abbruzzese told *Modern Drummer* that all the touring left him "with a sense of feeling scattered." "Throughout that first tour," he said, "I kept remembering all the times that as a fan I used to really like a band and want a piece of their time and how I used to feel when they snubbed me.... So I went out of my way not to take out my frustrations or emotions on the kids."

For his part, Vedder worked very hard to stay down-to-earth. He answered fan mail personally and at one point after the release of the band's second album, *Vs.,* he gave out his home phone number on a nationally broadcast radio program. Moreover, he retained his slacker life style, crashing on friends' couches and carrying many of his possessions around in a beat-up old suitcase. A writer at *Spin* commented, "The guy can obviously afford a car that works, but he [avoids showiness] like the plague he imagines it to be."

Vs. *is released*

In October 1993 the band released its eagerly awaited second album, *Vs.* It entered the charts at Number One and sold 350,000 copies in its first day of release. Unlike its predecessor, *Vs.* met with virtually unqualified critical endorsement. *Newsweek* hailed it as "an absolutely first rate rock-and-roll album: streamlined, propulsive and full of urgency"; the *Chicago*

Tribune described it as "hard rock that is as supple and subtle as it is crunching"; and *Rolling Stone* called it "the band's turf statement—a personal declaration of the importance of music over idolatry."

Recorded outside of San Francisco and produced by Brendan O'Brien, *Vs.* exposed an improved and more fully realized band. Where *Ten* had verged on heavy metal, *Vs.* grooved like the Red Hot Chili Peppers while displaying both Vedder's knack for melody and the guitar pyrotechnics of Mike McCready and Stone Gossard. The *Chicago Tribune* credited drummer Dave Abbruzzese for the improvement and wrote, "The album feels tighter and yet more limber—the songs swing." As a reviewer for *Modern Drummer* wrote, "Abbruzzese punches Pearl Jam into wider more dynamic expressions than the band achieved with its debut, while lending an infectious warmth that percolates from the bottom up."

Vs. also displayed a command of rock styles that went far beyond *Ten*'s Led Zeppelin-style riffs. The album contains thrashing punk rock and wah-wah chords that recall the 1970s R&B classic "Theme From Shaft." Two nearly acoustic tracks, "Daughter" and "Elderly Woman Behind the Counter in a Small Town," are among its most affecting. And, according to the *New York Times*, *Vs.* contains echoes of "R.E.M., the Police, the Allman Brothers, Jefferson Airplane, the Rolling Stones, and the Beatles," among others.

Vedder sings of pain

Lyrically, Vedder's dark tremulous voice returned "again and again to issues of abuse, power and rage" on *Vs.*, according to *Newsweek*. For instance, "Rearviewmirror" begins, "I took a drive today/Time to emancipate/I guess it was the beatings/Made me wise." But "instead of succumbing to despair," a *New York Times* reviewer wrote, "Vedder insists that the struggle to survive is heroic. And when the band's riffs kick in, it's not hard to believe him."

Writing in the *New York Daily News*, Jim Farber explored Vedder's use of "the abused child['s]" narrative voice. Farber pointed to "Daughter," a song in which "both mother and child disown each other," and "Leash," "where Vedder writes: 'I can't ... believe I came from you people.'" According to Farber, Vedder "constantly expresses a victim's sense of powerlessness," and as such, "plug[s] directly into [our society's] victim-abuse culture." Farber theorized that this explains "Pearl Jam's cultural resonance" and that ultimately, "Vedder represents the inner child as raging rock star bringing a virtual therapy session of pain to the public forum."

Whatever the roots of Vedder's lyrics, given its whopping sales and lyrical and musical growth, Pearl Jam definitely has a bright future ahead. As Abbruzzese told *Modern Drummer,* "There are so many avenues for us to explore, and we get tastes of that every time we jam. Maybe the greatest thing about this band is that the jamming aspect never takes a back seat. That's why I love the word "Jam" in the band's name. I can never see the music just stopping for us." (The jam would stop for Abbruzzese, however, in the fall of 1994 when he was abruptly fired by the band.)

In May 1994 Pearl Jam sent a memo to the Justice Department claiming that ticket broker Ticketmaster's "huge" share of the ticketing market allows it to inflate prices and engage in monopolistic practices. Because there is virtually no competition for Ticketmaster, Pearl Jam's members accused them of essentially ripping off their customers. Earlier that year the group had intended to mount a low-cost tour, asking promoters to keep service charges at no more than 10 percent of the ticket's value. Appearing before a congressional panel on June 30, the group testified that Ticketmaster told promoters to ignore their requests.

Late in 1994 Pearl Jam released a third disc, *Vitalogy.* Though the album doesn't feature any one instantly memorable song such as "Jeremy" or "Alive," with its further explorations of the band's familiar themes of pain and abuse, the album should satisfy the legions of Pearl Jam fans.

Sources

Boston Phoenix, October 15, 1993.

Chicago Tribune, March 30, 1992; October 17, 1993.

Daily News (New York), October 17, 1993.

Detroit Free Press, November 20, 1994.

Guitar Player, February 1992; January 1994.

Modern Drummer, December 1993.

Newsweek, October 25, 1993.

New York Times, August 11, 1992; October 24, 1993.

Philadelphia Inquirer, October 19, 1993.

Rolling Stone, October 31, 1991; February 4, 1993; October 28, 1993.

Spin, December 1993.

Stereo Review, January 1992.

Time, June 20, 1994.

Rosie Perez

Born c. 1968
Brooklyn, New York

ACTRESS, DANCER,
CHOREOGRAPHER

"Honey, I can give drama. I'm from Brooklyn!"

Rosie Perez, whose closest revelation of her age has been "under 25," claims to be having a hard time sleeping these days—her career is not moving fast enough for her. In just a few short years she went from being a science student to becoming one of the most sought-after pop music choreographers in the industry and a rising actress. "I'm very happy with the way things are going for me right now," she revealed in an interview with Frank Spotnitz for *Entertainment Weekly,* "but I still feel like they're going too slow. I want it all."

Rosa Mary Perez was born in Brooklyn, New York, daughter of Ismael Serrano and Lydia Perez. Raised in Brooklyn's mostly Puerto Rican Bushwick district, Perez is one of ten brothers and sisters who grew up watching their parents dance "salsa" on weekends and holidays. Her mother was a singer in Puerto Rico, and music always filled the house. In her *Entertainment Weekly* interview, Perez reminisced: "Growing up with nine brothers and sisters was an early lesson in assertiveness training. In a family like that, you have to compete for attention." Despite the poverty in her neighborhood, Perez and her family had fun. Describing her youth in a *Vogue* article, Perez said "I didn't know I had secondhand clothes; I just thought my mother had bad taste."

A good student who excelled in science, Perez moved to Los Angeles at the age of 18 to attend UCLA, where she studied marine biology as a biochemistry major. It was while dancing at a trendy Los Angeles Latin club that she was first invited to dance on the television show *Soul Train*. After doing a couple of shows, Perez quit, but while she was there she met Louis Silas, Jr., senior vice-president of black music at MCA records. Silas asked if she wanted to be in a recording group, and although Perez declined, she kept in touch with him.

Launches choreography career with Bobby Brown

One day Silas asked if she would choreograph for one of his artists who was coming out with his third solo album. Silas wanted him to have a younger appeal and asked Perez to find some dancers who could dance "hip-hop" with him. Perez at first refused because she had no experience, but after hearing the music decided to go ahead. The artist's name was Bobby Brown and the project was a success.

After seeing Brown on the television program *Soul Train*, a new Motown recording group (The Boys) asked Perez to choreograph their show. With the double successes of Bobby Brown and The Boys, offers poured in. She and her partners, Heart & Soul, found themselves busy creating the stage and/or video choreographies for many artists, including Diana Ross and urban acts Al B. Sure, LL Cool J, Heavy D & the Boyz, and for such record labels as Motown, PolyGram, and Capitol. The next step was the small screen, with Perez choreographing the Fox television program *In Living Color*. When a *GQ* contributor asked her to define her dancing style, Perez (who considers herself a better choreographer than a dancer) replied, "Clearness. Quickness. Difficult combinations. I'll never do a move on a four count—usually just a two and move on. That's what earns me respect with the club people." She then laughingly added: "Here's my dancer's arrogance. I haven't seen anybody who can articulate hip-hop like I do, in such a lean, crisp way and still be authentic. There are a lot who try and do it, and it comes off very corny. I still got the flavor."

Takes on acting in Do the Right Thing

In her press biography, Perez told how her movie career was launched. "While I was choreographing The Boys, I was dancing at the Funky Reggae Club in Los Angeles. Spike Lee was having his birthday party there and the band EU was performing. The band asked me to dance onstage; afterwards Spike introduced himself to me. His partner Monty Ross, gave me their phone number and asked me to call. I forgot all about it until I was leaving to go back to Brooklyn (the school semester had finished) and decided to call them. They were really excited and asked me if I would be in Los Angeles long. When I told them I was returning to Brooklyn in a couple of days, they started screaming and Spike said, 'This is fate.' I didn't know what he meant by that, because he never mentioned the possibility of a movie until a month later. When I told him I had to return for the new school semester in Los Angeles, he offered me the role of Tina in *Do the Right Thing.* Instead of finishing that semester, I decided to do the movie, and it changed my life."

In an interview with *Newsweek,* Perez described her movie debut experience as possibly the best and worst thing that happened to her. There was a nude scene involving an ice cube that, she has said, made her feel "raped" by the camera. When Hispanic groups criticized her for promoting a stereotype, Perez defended the film—"I was not portraying something that's not really out there"—but informed her agent she didn't want to play any "Tinas" in the future.

Perez's television work includes *21 Jump Street, Criminal Justice,* and *WIOU.* Perez was unhappy with her newscaster role on *WIOU,* however, because she felt stereotyped as the "newsroom tramp." A week after Perez asked to be written out, the show was canceled and she was offered a role in the film *White Men Can't Jump.*

Film career rapidly progresses

Perez's role as Woody Harrelson's feisty girlfriend in the basketball-themed film *White Men Can't Jump* was originally written for a caucasian woman who'd gone to an Ivy League school. But writer/director Ron Shelton was so impressed by the instant chemistry between Perez and Harrelson that, without making major changes to the script, the role was transformed from that of a Barnard graduate to a former Brooklyn disco queen.

In quick succession, Perez's acting credits went on to include the films *Night on Earth, Untamed Heart, Fearless,* and *It Could Happen to You.* Similar to her part in *White Men Can't Jump,* Perez's role in *Fearless* was originally written for a non-Hispanic woman. Such well-established stars as Winona Ryder and Jodie Foster were said to have wanted it. Undaunted, Perez fought for a chance to audition and the director was so impressed he rewrote the part to reflect Perez's accent and style. Though the film's life at the box office was short, critics were beside themselves with praise for Perez. She was nominated for an Academy Award for her work as a young mother traumatized by the death of her child in a plane crash. With a successful acting career well under way, Perez concluded in a *Preview* interview: "Minorities can play regular roles too. And being a minority you have a responsibility to help other minorities along the way."

Sources

Entertainment Weekly, April 3, 1992.

Essence, October 1993.

Hispanic, April 1993.

Newsweek, May 4, 1992.

Preview, April 1992.

Vibe, December 1993/January 1994.

Additional information on Perez was provided by Baker-Winokur-Ryder Public Relations.

Michelle Pfeiffer

Born in 1957
Santa Ana, California

ACTRESS

It takes only one glimpse of Michelle Pfeiffer to realize that she is no ordinary Hollywood beauty. Called "drop-dead gorgeous" by *Time* and chosen one of the ten most beautiful women in the world by *Harper's Bazaar,* the actress has left an indelible impression on the acting world and movie audiences alike since her career soared in the mid-1980s. And it's no wonder. Blonde, with huge almond-shaped blue eyes, the sultry Pfeiffer has been likened to such icons of the silver screen as Greta Garbo and Carole Lombard. But while her beauty cannot be questioned, Pfeiffer's more subtle and perhaps enduring appeal comes from what director Jonathan Demme termed her "strength of character" and "decency of spirit," in *Vanity Fair.* It has been these qualities that have allowed Pfeiffer, a blend of sweetness and steel, to explore a wide range of roles, maintain her integrity, and achieve a hard-won celebrity status in recent years.

"Every time I do a movie, I think this is the one where they're going to find me out, that I'm a total and utter fraud. And everytime I get to say to myself, 'Well, you got away with it again.'"

Grew up as "California girl"

Deemed a "rarefied version of a West Coast prom queen, sandblasted to a razor-cheeked fineness" by *Vanity Fair*, Pfeiffer grew up as a typical Southern California girl—surfing at Huntington Beach, hanging out at Life Guard Station 17, and attending boarding school in Colorado Springs. Having studied stenotyping and working as a cashier in a local supermarket, Pfeiffer won recognition—and an agent—when she was chosen Miss Orange County at age 19. The slow but steady ascent of her acting career began with a few theater classes and a TV debut, followed by the landing of minor roles in the feature films *Falling in Love Again, Hollywood Knights,* and *Charlie Chan and the Curse of the Dragon Queen.* What Pfeiffer anticipated was going to be her big break came in 1982 when she was offered the lead in the musical *Grease 2.*

Despite the massive promotional hype surrounding the movie, *Grease 2* proved unsuccessful and Pfeiffer's career remained stagnant. According to *Newsweek,* her keen portrayal of Stephanie, head punkette of the Pink Ladies gang, might have worked against her: "Pfeiffer's uncanny ability to make people believe she's the character she's playing boomeranged. As a bubble-gum popping high-school vixen, she gave a sly, delectably sluttish performance." While this stereotype of just another blonde beauty, as limited as the character she portrayed, put Pfeiffer in jeopardy of being doomed to what one headline writer has called "bimbo limbo," the actress was convinced all along that she would transcend this stigma. "Even from the beginning, when I was doing like junk television, I still had this focus," she told *Vanity Fair.* "I knew I wasn't going to be doing that forever."

Pfeiffer waited a full year before taking on her next role, as Elvira, the haughty cocaine-addicted gangster moll in Brian De Palma's typically gripping film *Scarface.* Next was the lead in *Ladyhawke,* a medieval flight of fancy costarring Matthew Broderick and directed by Richard Donner. While Pfeiffer has the reputation of being every film crew's dream on the set—to the point that Jonathan Demme told *Vanity Fair* that she "treats everyone with tremendous respect. She's the only actor I've ever heard of who received an extremely special, costly gift from the film crew at the end of a shooting"—she admits that she and Donner were frequently at odds during *Ladyhawke.* Apparently Donner had wanted her to play the part of "a beautiful princess romping through the woods," Pfeiffer told Peter Stone of *Interview,* which was not her idea of a role with substance. What appeared in the picture, then, was a modified version of Donner's vision that seemed to satisfy both director and actress. But why did Pfeiffer agree in the first place to do a film in which her character didn't please her? Because, she explained to Stone, "it was the most charming script I'd ever read."

It was during Pfeiffer's next film, *Into the Night*, in which she played a fast-lane party girl pursued by Iranians through the streets of Los Angeles, that, according to *Newsweek*, "her sense of comedy emerged, along with something both haunting and heartbreaking." No longer in danger of being offered roles that capitalized only on her good looks and, in fact, praised by the critics for her talents, Pfeiffer still had not starred in enough of a commercial success to capture the attention of movie audiences. Alan Alda's box-office flop *Sweet Liberty* in 1986 proved more of the same. In this comedy about a history professor whose award-winning book on the American Revolution has been bought by Hollywood, Pfeiffer's character brought what *Vanity Fair* called "a satiric bite to a sugary movie." She played a leading lady who exudes demureness and purity while the camera's rolling, and turns tough and career-driven when it stops, harboring not the slightest confusion about the distinction between make-believe and reality. The *New Yorker* commented that Pfeiffer has "the enchanting prettiness of a pink-and-white flower; she has no dark tones yet and no mystery." But the plight of her career to this point was best summarized by the magazine's parenthetical remark that "maybe her roles just haven't given her the opportunities to show them."

Made career with Witches of Eastwick

The career-launching break came in 1987, when Pfeiffer landed a lead role in *The Witches of Eastwick*, based on John Updike's novel of the same name. As a small-town single mother with supernatural powers, Pfeiffer teams up with fellow witches Cher and Susan Sarandon to will an eligible bachelor into their lives. Their collective efforts are enough to lure the lecherous Darryl, played by Jack Nicholson, from New York City, and from there the story begins. Pfeiffer not only held her own against these cinematic big-leaguers, but came through with what the *New Yorker* called "a soft and fluid" comedy style "that blends right in with the others." While the movie received mixed reviews and contained one of Pfeiffer's more forgettable roles, it became a commercial hit and succeeded in transforming her career.

Pfeiffer, who had been out of the country when *Witches* opened, later told *Newsweek*: "I came back and everyone had seen it. It was the first time I had been in a really successful movie. And I noticed a tremendous change, in the scripts that were being offered to me, people recognizing me on the street." It seems that being conscientious finally paid off for this actress. Susan Sarandon recalled that on the first day of rehearsals Pfeiffer had all four or five drafts of the script on hand for quick reference, and Cher, the movie's other female lead, told *Vanity Fair*: "When I met [Michelle], I thought she was very soft and maybe too sweet, too nice. But, you know, it's all part of someone who has a definite purpose, who is a lot stronger than even she knows sometimes." Most who have worked with Pfeiffer have praised her technical facility—a seemingly innate awareness of the camera—but what really propels her is a sense of perfectionism and a genuine enthusiasm for her work. A Hollywood rarity, Pfeiffer has won the respect of colleagues, critics, and moviegoers alike.

Yet least impressed by all the kudos is Pfeiffer herself. She enjoyed her character's bedraggled appearance in *The Witches of Eastwick* and scoffs at the appraisals of her beauty. "Meryl Streep, Dianne Wiest, they're beautiful," the actress said in an interview with *Time*. "I think I look like a duck.... I should have played Howard the Duck." Another point of contention between Pfeiffer and her supporters regards her personality. "I'm always amazed at how consistent people find me and my behavior," she told *Interview*'s Peter Stone, "when in fact I do feel different all the time." Pfeiffer attributes this to the intensity of her personality, which, she confided to Stone, "gets me into trouble ... I don't know the word balance." Pfeiffer is shy and modest, an avoider of Hollywood social scenes. For her, celebrity is a mixed blessing, an invasion of her habitually private nature. "I didn't become an actress so that my life could be exposed," she told *Vanity Fair*. "It's really the only thing that makes me contemplate [not] acting. I would give it up because I hate it that much."

A former tomboy

As one of four children born to a heating and air-conditioning retailer and his wife, Pfeiffer enjoyed a fun-in-the-sun childhood in Midway City, California. Her quietness apparently evolved later in life, for she recalled to *Time*: "I was a tomboy, always beating somebody up. The comments on my report card said I needed to work on my mouth." But one thing that has remained constant is Pfeiffer's work ethic. At age 14, she took a job in a clothing store and has not stopped working since, compiling a list of occupations that include checking out customers at a Vons supermarket and operating a printing press. Pfeiffer admits that her father, a strict conservative, urged her to save money, but she told *Interview* that she realized the importance of financial independence when she went into acting, as "someone told me that being able to turn down a part was the only thing that would ever give me power."

Brief enthusiasms for painting and dance during Pfeiffer's high school years proved fleeting, and it was not until she attended drama class that her interest in acting emerged. "It was the first thing that made the work and commitment effortless," she said in a *Newsweek* interview. Following graduation from Fountain Valley High School, Pfeiffer enrolled in a junior college, which she soon left to study court reporting. But the desire to act persisted and, at the urging of her friends, she entered and won the Miss Orange County pageant. Her first agent and appearances in a few commercials were the upshot of this victory, and from there Pfeiffer was cast in two short-lived TV series, *Delta House* and *B.A.D. Cats.*

New to Los Angeles and subject to the cattle-call auditions that most struggling actors must endure, Pfeiffer became involved in a cult devoted to "vegetarianism and metaphysics," according to *Newsweek.* Although she remembers little about the cult's philosophy, Pfeiffer does acknowledge that those were difficult years. Deliverance came in an acting class when she met Peter Horton. Horton helped free her from the cult, and the two were married in 1982. Although she dislikes admitting it, Pfeiffer told *Newsweek*: "I don't believe in women being saved by men, but I think it was true. I was very lucky."

Unlike its storybook beginning, however, the marriage ended after seven years. Despite a painful breakup, Pfeiffer and Horton have remained friends, evident in her conversation with *Interview*: "We've always been close even up to the separation, which was very difficult for both of us because we never stopped caring for each other.... [Now] we're like best friends when we see each other."

Professionally Pfeiffer seems very much in control, achieved in part through her rigorous selection of roles and ability to milk them for all their subtleties. She has worked almost continuously since *The Witches of Eastwick* came out and 1988 proved a pivotal year for her careerwise. As the lead in Jonathan Demme's *Married to the Mob,* she played Angela DeMarco, a suburban mobster's wife who is tired of living the nightmarish parody of middle-class existence. After her husband is killed, Angela flees with her young son to New York's Lower East Side, where she is pursued by her husband's boss and murderer, stalked by his jealous wife, and eventually falls in love with an FBI agent, played by Matthew Modine. Pfeiffer received rave reviews for her portrayal of the tender-hearted heroine. "She gives an extraordinary performance ... [making] Angela's toughness and her goodness believable, funny, and touching," remarked the *New Yorker,* and *Newsweek* commented on Pfeiffer's "stunning mix of comic agitation and haunted vulnerability."

Pfeiffer closed 1988 starring opposite Mel Gibson and Kurt Russell in Robert Towne's *Tequila Sunrise* and opened 1989 with Stephen Frears's *Dangerous Liaisons*. While Pfeiffer found the latter film's compressed schedule demanding and her own part emotionally draining, the project proved a success from all viewpoints. Costarring with Glenn Close and John Malkovich, she played Mme. Tourvel, an alluring and notoriously pious woman trapped in a tragic web of sexual intrigue. While *Vanity Fair* claimed that her performance "unravels with an intensity that is almost too painful to watch," *Interview* hailed Pfeiffer for possessing "a wild and rare combination of attributes: the varied skills of a character played with the demeanor of a real star." Her director, Frears, according to *Vanity Fair*, found her "extremely centered," adding that "you can't get [Michelle] to do a false thing."

Her next series of accomplishments included Pfeiffer's first foray into the theater in a performance of Shakespeare's *Twelfth Night* and the portrayal of lounge singer Susie Diamond in Steve Kloves's film *The Fabulous Baker Boys* (1989), for which she received an Oscar nomination and won critical acclaim for her singing. In 1990 Pfeiffer was paired with Sean Connery in *Russia House*—a movie based on John LeCarré's best-selling spy novel of the same name. And in *Frankie and Johnny* (1991) she downplayed her extraordinary looks in order to play the ordinary-looking waitress Frankie to Al Pacino's Johnny.

Purrs as Catwoman

It was her performance as Catwoman in the 1992 sequel to *Batman, Batman Returns*, that guaranteed her superstardom. In a role that many had sought, Pfeiffer purred, hissed, and clawed her way into the hearts of critics and fans alike. With her help, *Batman Returns* became a blockbuster that grossed over $100 million.

Pfeiffer's most recent work includes *The Age of Innocence* (1993) and *Wolf* (1994). The former is director Martin Scorsese's adaptation of Edith Wharton's novel of the same name. Set in the New York society of the 1870s, the movie sets up a conflict between duty and passion when the noble Newland Archer (Daniel Day-Lewis) must choose between his commitment to his fiancée and his love for the scandalous Countess Olenska (Pfeiffer). Critics were enamored, with Richard Corliss of *Time* declaring: "[Scorsese's] faithful adaptation of *The Age of Innocence* is a gravely beautiful fairy tale of longing and loss." At the other end of the extreme was *Wolf*, a modern-day werewolf tale with Jack Nicholson as the man who turns into a wolf and Pfeiffer as the romantic interest. While the reviews were primarily positive, attendance was somewhat disappointing.

Pfeiffer weds

On November 13, 1993, Pfeiffer surprised friends and family by turning what they thought was a christening into a wedding ceremony. She married David Kelley, a producer and the creator of the Emmy-winning CBS series *Picket Fences.* The couple currently has two children.

Sources

Interview, August 1988; February 1989.

Maclean's, August 29, 1988.

Newsweek, August 22, 1988; November 6, 1989; June 20, 1994.

New York, October 16, 1989.

New Yorker, June 2, 1986; June 29, 1987; August 22, 1988.

New York Times, January 1, 1989.

People, July 13, 1992; September 20, 1993; April 25, 1994.

Rolling Stone, September 3, 1992.

Time, June 21, 1982; August 16, 1988; January 16, 1989; September 20, 1993; November 29, 1993; February 14, 1994.

Vanity Fair, February 1989.

Sidney Poitier

Born February 20, 1927
Miami, Florida

"I want to take risks, and I want to be my own man—as I have been—to the extent of saying, 'I'll work at what I want to work at.' ... I think that after all these years and after this life, I'm entitled to make choices on a purer basis than people are generally afforded. It's not for financial reasons. It's for reasons that have to do with an honest look at my life."

ACTOR AND DIRECTOR

Notable for his perseverance in acting during a particularly racist period in American history, Sidney Poitier began his stage career as an understudy at the American Negro Theatre (ANT) in 1945. Poitier had been working as a janitor at the ANT in exchange for acting lessons from director Frederick O'Neal. After losing an audition due to his thick Bahamian accent and limited reading ability, Poitier learned to control the accent by imitating radio announcers and to read by studying newspapers with an elderly Jewish waiter. Eventually he won a place in the theater as an alternate in the lead role of the 1945 production of *Days of Our Youth,* and with the experience of several roles onstage, he was cast in 1950 in Joe Mankiewicz's film *No Way Out.*

Reviewing Poitier's 1980 autobiography *This Life,* Mel Watkins of the *New York Times Book Review* summed up the actor's early career in this way: "Despite favorable critical reaction to his initial film work, the early 1950s were lean years.... After Mr. Poitier's performance in the television production of *A Man is Ten Feet Tall* ... the NBC switchboard was deluged with calls from irate viewers protesting the interracial drama." Besides being a target for racist audiences in the 1950s, he was perceived as an "Uncle Tom"—a black man who is too uncritical of whites—by militant blacks in the 1960s.

Poitier was tremendously successful in films such as *Something of Value* and *A Raisin in the Sun,* and he became the first black actor to win an Academy Award, in 1964, for his role in *Lilies of the Field.* While the characters he played in these films were free of previous Hollywood black stereotypes like the sweet, singing maid or the happy-go-lucky jazz musician, he was part of a new convention—the serene, almost "tamed" black hero who masked anger with patience. Perhaps in those decades of riot and confrontation during the fight for civil rights, white audiences could not be entertained by an angry black face, which would be associated with the events of the time, but preferred a more complacent portrait. But while Poitier's characters supposedly increased his commercial appeal for white audiences, black audiences resented a black character image that seemed to cater to Hollywood stereotypes by adapting a Cary Grant-type reserve. Poitier responded to that criticism in his autobiography, *This Life,* as quoted in the *New York Times Book Review*: "I knew that however inadequate my steps appeared, it was important that we make it ... I also understood the value system of a make-believe town [Hollywood] that was at its heart a racist place."

A premature baby

Sidney Poitier was born two months prematurely on February 20, 1927, while his parents were in Miami, Florida, to sell a tomato crop. Only his mother, Evelyn, expected him to live (he weighed only three and a half pounds), but after he was brought home to Cat Island in the Bahamas, he flourished alongside his six brothers and sisters. While in some ways idyllic, life on Cat Island was an economic struggle for Poitier's parents. In his autobiography he recalled a child who, until the age of ten, didn't know about ice cream, forks, or electricity, and spent most of his time fishing, swimming, and catching turtles.

The Depression settled into the United States when Poitier was still in school, and the demand for fresh fruit from their farm decreased. His father's worsening rheumatism and arthritis interfered with his ability to work, and eventually Poitier dropped out to help him, after only four years of school. Poitier described his perspective on his father's life on the island to Aljean Harmetz of the *New York Times*: "He had no power, no influence except with his children. To be poor and black in the Bahamas was demeaning. I saw the humiliation of a well-intended, hard working honest man categorized as a surplus entity. My mother dressed me in flour sacks because she couldn't afford clothing.... She taught me that the only undignified thing about wearing such clothes was if they were dirty."

Poitier went to New York in 1940 after encountering segregation and the Ku Klux Klan in Miami, where he had moved in with one of his brothers. Looking back on his first days in New York City, Poitier attributed his survival to his mother's lessons in respect and good manners. These were not lessons in subservience, but in honesty and a dignified regard for others. These qualities, he said in his book, "carried me to a white policeman in New York City when I had gone downtown to look for a dishwashing job and I had no money and I said, 'I wonder if you could loan me a nickel for the subway and if you'll tell me where you're working tomorrow, I'll return the nickel.' And he did."

Joined the army at 16

Before his acting career of 40 years was launched, he joined the army at 16. Poitier had apparently lied about his age to get in, and after a brief stay of nine months, he was discharged in 1945 because of faked insane behavior. Sources other than his autobiography, however, report that Poitier was a physiotherapist, and do not mention a Section Eight (a discharge because of mental illness). Despite this negative experience, Poitier returned to New York with renewed ambition and resolve.

Once there, he happened to read an article in the *Amsterdam News* reporting on the American Negro Theatre and its need for actors. Poitier's Bahamian, singsong accent proved so untenable that despite the shortage of male auditioners and his matinee-idol good looks, he was actually thrown out of the theater before he had finished three lines. When he went back for another tryout after six months of disciplined self-education, the improvement in his diction was enough to win him the understudy role to the male lead, Harry Belafonte. This particular casting call was answered by only one man, Poitier; his recitation for the directors was read directly from *True Confessions* magazine.

Onstage, Poitier quickly adapted to many different dramatic genres, portraying a butler in *Strivers Road,* Boris Kolyenkov in *You Can't Take it With You,* Polydorus in *Lysistrata,* and Rudolph in *Anna Lucasta.* Adjusting as quickly to film with Mankiewicz's "message" movie (*No Way Out*), in

Poitier with Lilia Skala in a scene from *Lilies of the Field*, March 8, 1964.

which he played a doctor, Poitier would follow the role with a priest, a trucker, and a basketball player in his search for positive black role models. His landmark role came in *Blackboard Jungle*. An adaption of an Evan Hunter novel, the 1955 film chronicles a New York teacher's frightening experience teaching in a high school. Poitier portrays a violent student who eventually sides with authority during a switchblade confrontation. Leonard Maltin described the movie in his *Television and Video Guide* as "hard-hitting entertainment." Poitier won critical recognition for his role in this popular movie, the first to use rock music in the soundtrack. In another groundbreaking role, Poitier played the father in the movie version of *Raisin in the Sun*, about a Chicago family struggling with impoverished living conditions and fading hopes. Although the characters drawn from Lorraine Hansberry's play are generally considered trite in retrospect, a portrait of a black family that was not steeped in prejudice and white myth was remarkable for 1961.

Wins Oscar for Lilies of the Field

Maltin described Poitier's subsequent movie, *Lilies of the Field,* as "a 'little' film that made good, winning Poitier an Oscar as a handyman who helps build a chapel for ... German-speaking nuns." The critic called it "quiet, well-acted and enjoyable." The Academy Award was a huge leap forward for minority equal rights in the entertainment industry, and substantially boosted Poitier's professional reputation, bringing him work with ever more celebrated actors.

In 1967 Poitier appeared in *To Sir, with Love,* in which he struggles to educate a classroom of toughs in an East End London school. His performance was both skillful and warm and helped further his status as an appealing leading man. Also that year, Poitier had what he called the "awesome" experience of acting with Katharine Hepburn and Spencer Tracy in the movie *Guess Who's Coming to Dinner.* The movie's material was considered somewhat risky, dealing with an interracial marriage, but the real issues are treated with dialogue that borders on the flimsy and sentimental. The title character, a black man who meets his white fiancée's parents for the first time, seems conventional, static, and lacking in development. A new trend in Hollywood would soon reject three-dimensional black characters even more thoroughly.

In response to the "blaxploitation" movies of the 1970s, such as *Shaft* and *Superfly,* Poitier served up the western *Buck and the Preacher,* the first movie of his directorial career. This debut met with generally good reviews, and he and his costar, Harry Belafonte, added genuine human qualities to what Colin L. Westerbeck, Jr., called "the latest word in self-reliant, soft-spoken, straight-shooting cowboys." Vincent Canby of the *New York Times* agreed with Westerbeck in calling the movie an attempt to desegregate American myth and history. Instead of the hip, violent urban cowboys of the blaxploitation movies, Poitier and Belafonte played, said Canby, "black wagonmasters [who] bravely tried to guide ex-slaves to homesteads in the West after the Civil War"—in other words, old-fashioned, moral heroes. Joseph McBride praised the movie in a 1972 *Rolling Stone* article, saying: "*Buck and the Preacher* is saved from being a mere stunt like the black *Hello Dolly* by its creative use of the conventions it turns inside out. It mocks them at the same time it allows black audiences (and vicariously, whites) the pleasure of usurping the mythology which the Western has long used to keep minorities in their place."

Poitier followed *Buck and the Preacher* with *A Warm December,* which was received as only mediocre by the critics. *New York*'s Judith Crist called it a "dashing, slick old Hollywood romance—and the sort of movie that the popcorn-and-Kleenex crowd ... can really wallow in."

Directs Stir Crazy

Perhaps Poitier's most popular movie was the smash hit *Stir Crazy,* which teamed Gene Wilder with Richard Pryor, the pair having successfully worked together in *Silver Streak.* Poitier's directorial contributions were not always noted, but Richard Combs of the *Monthly Film Bulletin* admired the "genial, wide-open spaces of [his] direction." Wilder and Pryor play two New Yorkers who tire of the city and head west, only to be mistaken for bank robbers; they soon land in jail. As Pryor strides loosely down the barred prison halls saying, "We bad, we bad," Wilder spastically imitates him like an un-hip shadow. When Wilder's character is brought out of solitary confinement, he pleads for more time to "find himself." With *Stir Crazy,* critics agreed that Poitier had found his strength, in comedy that appealed to a large and varied audience; they cited his knack for directing films that combined mild social commentary with broad slapstick humor. In an earlier review, Combs touched on the movie's reception: "The populist nerve that Poitier seemed to be playing towards in [the earlier film] *A Piece of the Action* has been a resounding hit."

Stir Crazy was released four years after Poitier temporarily retired from acting, at first solely to compose his 1980 autobiography. Because of his success and sound financial management, Poitier extended his leave of absence to spend more time with his second wife and all six daughters. Leonard Goldberg, Poitier's friend and former president of Twentieth Century-Fox, suggested another reason for the sabbatical: quoted in the *New York Times,* Goldberg remarked, "I think he got bored. Sidney found the parts he was being offered were the same kind of parts he had already played." Poitier reasoned in his book that the hiatus was necessary for such things as "writing, reading, walking on the beach, thinking about the earth and the stars and listening to other drums."

When Poitier returned to acting in 1988, he insisted that he was not interested in the technical and financial headaches of producing and directing. For now, he prefers to concentrate on acting. "As an actor, I can do my stint before the camera and then go relax in my trailer while the director is out there in the rain setting up the next scene," he said to Herbert Nipson of *Ebony* magazine.

One of the parts that brought him in front of the cameras again was the lead in *Little Nikita,* a role originally written for a white man. This may have been a sign of increased flexibility in Hollywood's casting, but opportunities for blacks are still less than ideal. In David Ansen's *Newsweek* review of *Little Nikita*, Poitier reported that "you find almost a complete shutout of black actresses, which is unforgivable." The movie concerns an air force agent who befriends the troubled teenage son of a husband-wife spy team. Poitier found *Little Nikita* an attractive acting prospect because "some of the scenes were wonderfully well drawn," he told Aljean Harmetz in the *New York Times*.

Shoot to Kill, the second movie of Poitier's 1988 doubleheader, is an adventure picture that proved a physical challenge for the actor, whose character tracks a psychopathic murderer through the mountains of the Pacific Northwest. On the way, he scales cliffs, almost freezes to death, saves a guide's life, and leaps on a ferryboat's hood. Lawrence O'Toole of *Maclean's* admired Poitier's poise in his review, saying, "The man is a marvel—probably the only actor who could shoo away a grizzly by making faces at it and yet somehow manage not to seem like a fool." David Ansen found the role unworthy of Poitier, but Janet Maslin, a *New York Times* movie critic, enjoyed a return to the old-fashioned suspense movie. "For anyone who thinks they don't make spine-tingling detective films the way they used to, good news: they've just made another." She singled out Poitier for special praise: "The main attraction is Mr. Poitier, still an actor who conveys immense star quality without resorting to much small talk."

In 1992 Poitier appeared in *Sneakers,* a thriller that teamed technology and politics. The film follows a group of high-tech security experts as they try to steal a gadget that can enter and decode any computer program it encounters. Although it garnered mixed reviews, the movie did well at the box office.

In a 1957 *Newsweek* interview, Poitier said: "I have no politics, but I am a Negro. For this reason, I try to do and say nothing that might be a step backwards.... Two years ago I had ulcers, a worry bug about my future, the future of my race ... but ... I found I could learn to accept what I had to accept and to try to change what I wanted to change. Now? I 'dig' my work." Such a statement reflects his role in Hollywood at that time. Poitier bore a solitary burden in being the only black leading man, and was then perceived as a symbol for all black people. He might, for instance, have been the most familiar black person to white suburbanites in the 1950s. He had a tremendous opportunity to help black people, and he helped by staying calm and collected, satisfied to be himself.

Sources

American Film, September 1980.

Commonweal, May 26, 1972.

Ebony, May 1988.

Jet, June 21, 1993.

Maclean's, February 22, 1988.

Maltin, Leonard, *Leonard Maltin's Television and Video Guide,* Signet, 1990.

Monthly Film Bulletin, April 1981.

New Republic, May 10, 1980.

Newsweek, May 13, 1957; December 15, 1980; February 22, 1988.

New York, May 28, 1973; December 15, 1980.

New Yorker, June 2, 1980; September 21, 1992.

New York Times, April 29, 1972; May 4, 1987; February 12, 1988.

New York Times Book Review, August 17, 1980.

People, August 4, 1980; March 30, 1992; September 14, 1992.

Poitier, Sidney, *This Life,* Knopf, 1980.

Rolling Stone, July 20, 1972.

Elvis Presley

Born January 8, 1935, Tupelo, Mississippi
Died August 16, 1977, Memphis, Tennessee

Elvis Presley is "a complex figure of American myth: as improbably successful as a Horatio Alger hero, as endearing as Mickey Mouse, as tragically self-destructive as Marilyn Monroe."
—*Jim Miller*

SINGER AND ACTOR

Admired as one of the most successful recording artists and performers of all time, American singer Elvis Presley exploded onto the music scene in the mid-1950s. With a sound rooted in rockabilly and rhythm and blues, a daringly performing style, and a magnetic charm, the pioneer rock 'n' roller became an idol for an entire generation of music enthusiasts. Adoring fans remember him as The Father of Rock 'n' Roll, The King, and Elvis the Pelvis, and he is widely credited with introducing a new era in popular culture. His influence can hardly be overestimated, for many of the greatest names in modern music—including the Beatles, the Rolling Stones, and Bob Dylan—were inspired in one way or another by his enormous energy, magnetism, and talent.

Elvis spent his earliest years in his hometown of Tupelo, Mississippi, where he and his family shared a two-room house. And as a teen he lived in Memphis, Tennessee, where his family relocated when he was in the eighth grade. Shortly after finishing high school in 1953, the unknown artist began driving a delivery truck for the Crown Electric Company. He fooled around with the guitar in his free time.

The year he graduated, however, the young hopeful also made an amateur recording at the Memphis Recording Studio. He followed it with a second in 1954 and captured the attention of Sam Phillips at Sun Records. As a result, Elvis created the now-legendary Sun recordings, hailed by many as among his finest. With a musical career in the offing, the future star quit his truck-driving job in 1954 and began performing professionally, mostly in rural areas where he was billed as The Hillbilly Cat. He also saw his first Sun recording, "That's All Right Mama," rise to number three on the Memphis country-and-western charts. Thus, despite some disappointments, including discouraging words from the Grand Ole Opry and rejection by New York City's Arthur Godfrey Talent Scouts, Elvis persisted. By the end of 1955, after making a six-state southern tour with Hank Snow's Jamboree that piqued considerable interest, the up-and-comer had negotiated the agreement with RCA that would bring him stardom.

Creates sensation with "Heartbreak Hotel"

Elvis's very first RCA single, "Heartbreak Hotel" (written by Presley, Tommy Durden, and Mae Boren Axton, mother of country star Hoyt Axton), was wildly successful and became his first gold record. "From the opening notes of the song," wrote Jim Miller in a *Newsweek* review, "the air is electric." The air remained electric as the singer scored hit after hit with such tunes as "Don't Be Cruel," "Hound Dog," "Blue Suede Shoes," and "Love Me Tender." His sound, which had evolved from his roots in the Deep South and combined elements of country and western, rhythm and blues, and gospel, was new, and it was instantly popular. Though not the inventor of rock and roll, Elvis, reflected John Rockwell in the *New York Times*, "defined the style and indelible image."

Voice alone did not comprise the star's appeal. He was also a remarkable showman. Advised by Colonel Tom Parker, whom he signed as his manager early in 1956, Elvis began making films, appearing on television, and otherwise keeping himself in the public eye. Though reportedly shy and disinclined to be interviewed, the upstart musician gave performances that drove audiences mad. His smoldering good looks and captivating smile, coupled with the pelvic "bump-and-grind" rhythm that earned him the name Elvis the Pelvis, projected an exciting sexuality that was unprecedented in the music world. He prompted moral outrage from the older

Presley won numerous awards, including three Grammys. He earned *Billboard* magazine's Vocal Single of the Year Award for "It's Now or Never" in 1961; was named Las Vegas entertainer of the year in 1969; was honored by RCA for setting the highest record sales in the company's history (275 million) in 1970; received the Bing Crosby Award from the National Academy of Recording Arts and Sciences in 1971; and was posthumously named Male Musical Star of the Year for 1977 by the Academy of Variety and Cabaret Artists. In 1971 the city of Memphis, Tennessee, named a street for him: Elvis Presley Boulevard.

generation and hero worship from the younger to become, in Rockwell's words, an entertainer "parents abhorred, young women adored and young men instantly imitated."

Elvis was already a legend by the time he was drafted into the U.S. Army in 1958, and during his two-year hitch, most of it spent in West Germany, his recordings continued to sell well. But by the time he returned from his tour of duty, the music climate in the United States had changed. There was a notable downturn in his career, and The King of Rock and Roll devoted most of the 1960s to making movies that were entertaining but undistinguished. In 1968 the rocker staged a successful, if short-lived, comeback and during the seventies he concentrated on playing nightclubs.

Elvis dies

At approximately 2:30 p.m. on August 16, 1977, Presley's body was found in the bathroom at Graceland, his Memphis, Tennessee, mansion. Although the local medical examiner reported that Presley died of heart failure, rumors of the star's amphetamine use flourished. For a number of years prior to his death, in fact, Elvis looked as if he had passed his prime. Apparently though neither a drinker or a smoker, The King was known as a junk-food addict (reputed to favor fried peanut butter and banana sandwiches) and had gained considerable weight. He also had a history of hypertension.

Despite the circumstances, The King continued to grow in stature after his death. Indeed, in a piece for the *Saturday Evening Post,* Jay Stuller even suggested death "lent [him] a tragic aura." Whatever the reasons, grief-stricken fans remained fiercely devoted and scrambled to preserve their idol's memory. In the process, they spawned an entire industry. More than 15 years later, memorabilia abounds and hundreds of new products pay tribute to the Presley legend—everything from slippers and shampoo to porcelain dolls and grandfather clocks. There are more than 200 active Elvis fan clubs, the city of Memphis hosts an annual Elvis Week, and at one time a bill was put before the U.S. Congress that advocated making the recording giant's birthday a national holiday.

The King's achievement has yet to be duplicated. He picked up more than 100 Top 40 hits as well as more than 40 gold records, and sales of his recordings exceed one billion copies. He also influenced an entire generation of rock musicians, including Bob Dylan, John Lennon, and Bruce Springsteen. Trying to unravel the mystique, Stuller quoted Graceland Enterprises marketing director Ken Brixey: "I guess the best answer is that he was a blue-collar worker who in spirit never tried to rise above his roots. He's the epitome of a man who started out with nothing, became something and never lost his attraction to the masses. He's a true folk hero."

Sources

Dunleavy, Steve, Red West, Sonny West, and Dave Hebler, *Elvis, What Happened?*, Ballantine Books, 1977.

Escott, Colin, and Martin Hawkins, *Catalyst: The Sun Records Story*, Aquarius Books, 1975.

Esquire, December 1987.

Goldman, Albert, *Elvis*, Avon Books, 1981.

Gregory, Neal, and Janice Gregory, *When Elvis Died*, Communications Press, 1980.

Newsweek, November 12, 1984; August 3, 1987; June 6, 1988.

New York Times, August 17, 1977.

People, March 4, 1985; August 17, 1987.

Saturday Evening Post, July/August 1985.

Time, July 20, 1987.

Leontyne Price

Born February 10, 1927
Laurel, Mississippi

OPERA SINGER

"You need common sense as much as you need talent in the career.... Common sense, which means your own vibes, and going with them. I'm just homespun. I am still homespun. It's sort of down home, very country. I think of myself as a strange mixture of collard greens and caviar."

When Leontyne Price's angelic voice trailed off that night at New York's Lincoln Center in 1985, signaling the end of her final performance of the title role in Guiseppi Verdi's opera *Aida*—a role that has become synonymous with her name—the applause that embraced the great diva's farewell echoed widely, not only through the famed home of the Metropolitan Opera but through Price's heart as well. "That moment, I was a sponge, and I'll have all that moisture the rest of my life," Price told Robert Jacobson of *Opera News.* "I soaked that in. It's the most intense listening I've ever done in my life. For a change, *I* listened. I have every vibration of that applause in my entire being until I die. I will never recover from it. I will never receive that much love as long as I live, and I would be terribly selfish to expect that much ever again."

Seldom has an artist received applause that was so genuine and so deserved. After all, Price was 57 years old that evening, performing one of the most demanding roles in opera, and yet her voice was as full as the day she first performed *Aida* in 1957 and literally set the standard for its execution. But then Price's voice, her instrument, was so rare and special to her that she had taken great pains throughout her career to guard it from overuse, and to not destroy it performing roles that she thought she couldn't handle.

If the time was not right or she didn't think she could handle a certain part, Price was known to reject the invitations of such great conductors as Herbert von Karajan, Rudolf Bing, or James Levine with the wave of a hand. For this, she became known in music circles as arrogant and "difficult," but for the fiercely independent Price it was a matter of survival to be selective. "The voice is so special," she told *Opera News*. "You have to guard it with care, to let nothing disturb it, so you don't lose the bloom, don't let it fade, don't let the petals drop."

Whether she was known as "the girl with the golden voice" or "the Stradivarius of singers," Price is, without question, one of the great operatic talents of all time. The fact that she was the first black singer to gain international stardom in opera, an art form until then confined to upper-class white society, signified a monumental stride not only for her own generation, but for those that came before and after her.

Musical studies

Price was born in Laurel, Mississippi, on February 10, 1927. Her father, James Price, worked in a sawmill, and her mother, Kate, brought in extra income as a midwife. Both parents were amateur musicians, and encouraged their daughter to play the piano and sing in the church choir at St. Paul's Methodist Church in Laurel. Price graduated from Oak Park High School in 1944, then left home for the College of Education and Industrial Arts (now Central State College) in Wilberforce, Ohio. There, she studied music education with the idea of becoming a music teacher, but Price's professors realized that there was something special about her abilities and advised her to change her major to voice. When the prestigious Juilliard School of Music in New York offered her a four-year full-tuition scholarship, Price leapt at the chance and arrived in the big city in 1949.

With living expenses so high in New York City, Price for a time feared that she would have to follow the path of some of her friends and take a job singing in blues clubs and bars, which would have been a little like the great Renaissance painter Michelangelo working as a house painter.

But Elizabeth Chisholm, a longtime family friend from Laurel, came to Price's rescue with financial support, and the young singer was free to study full-time under vocal coach Florence Page Kimball. "It was simply the Midas touch from the instant I walked into Juilliard," Price told *Opera News*. "I learned things about stage presence, presentation of your gifts, how to make up, how to do research, German diction, et cetera." From Kimball, she went on to add, Price learned the steely control which would allow her to perform at top voice over so many performances, "to perform on your interest, not your capital. What she meant was, as in any walk of life, there should be something more to give."

Price thrived at Juilliard, and her role as Mistress Ford in a student production of Verdi's *Falstaff* caught the eye of composer Virgil Thomson, who cast her in a revival of his opera *Four Saints in Three Acts*, Price's first professional experience. This in turn led to a two-year stint (1952-54) with a revival of George Gershwin's *Porgy and Bess*, which toured the U.S. and Europe. During this time Price married her costar in that opera, William C. Warfield. The marriage was a disappointment, however, and the two divorced in 1973 after years of separation.

Began professional career

In 1954 Price made her concert debut at New York's Town Hall, where she exhibited great skill with modern compositions; a magnetic performer, she enjoyed the concert format and continued to tour regularly throughout her career, much to the chagrin of opera purists. Fast becoming a darling of the New York critics, Price soon saw her career take off. In 1955 she appeared in Puccini's *Tosca* on NBC television, thus becoming the first black singer to perform opera on television. And she was so well received that she was invited back to appear on NBC telecasts of Mozart's *Magic Flute*, Poulenc's *Dialogues of the Carmelites,* and Mozart's *Don Giovanni.*

One of the most fruitful associations of Price's career began in 1957, when she was invited by conductor Kurt Herbert Adler (he had seen her NBC *Tosca*) to make her American operatic debut as Madame Lidoine in *Dialogues of the Carmelites* with the San Francisco Opera. In later years, San Francisco seemed to be the place where Price returned to challenge herself with new roles, thus expanding her repertoire.

In fact, Price first performed *Aida* there under quite unusual circumstances. "The first *Aida* I did, period, anywhere, was on that stage, by accident," Price said in *Opera News*. "I've always threatened to give two wonderful medals to two wonderful colleagues who happened to have two wonderful appendectomies and gave me two wonderful opportunities to sing *Aida*. They are Antonietta Stella in San Francisco in 1957 and Anita Cerquetti at Covent Garden in 1958. The year I did *Dialogues*, Stella had an emergency appendectomy. Adler walked into the room and asked if I knew *Aida*. I told him yes, and I was on. I went through the score with Maestro Molinari-Pradelli, and I knew every single, solitary note and nuance. I had it ready to travel. After that *Aida* was definitely part of my repertoire. That was being in the right place at the right *time*."

Achieved international acclaim

In the following years, Price expanded her repertoire significantly on American soil, with such distinguished companies as the Chicago Lyric Opera and the American Opera Theater as well as the San Francisco Opera. She credits the great Herbert von Karajan with introducing her to European audiences. Price's debut on that continent came at Vienna's Staatsoper in 1958 as Pamina in *Zauberflote,* not in *Aida* as has been commonly written. Her second European performance was in *Aida* at the same theater, and she quickly forged a reputation in Europe with a string of appearances on such venerable stages as London's Covent Garden, Verona's Arena, the Salzburg Festival, and Milan's historic La Scala, where her *Aida* won the respect of Verdi's native audience.

Her international prominence now secure, Price returned home to make her debut at the mecca of American opera, New York's Metropolitan Opera, and thus began a long, often controversial, but always glorious association with that revered institution. Her Leonora in *Il Trovatore* on January 27, 1961, brought a standing ovation of 42 minutes, the longest ever given at the Met. Over the next several years Price was a staple in Metropolitan productions. When the company moved its home to the impressive new Metropolitan Opera House at Lincoln Center, director Rudolf Bing extended Price the ultimate honor of opening the house in the world premier of Samuel Barber's *Antony and Cleopatra.*

Although the opera itself was not well received, Price was magnificent, having dedicated herself to the role with total commitment. *"Antony and Cleopatra* was the event of the century, operatically speaking," Price told *Opera News.* "I was there! I lived the life of a hermit for a year and a half, so as not to have a common cold. From the moment I was asked to do this, I simply did everything I possibly could to have it be right. I accepted that responsibility with the greatest happiness. This was the greatest challenge of my life."

Since 1958, Price has recorded almost exclusively for RCA Victor. Her records include Negro spirituals, pop tunes, Christmas carols, hymns, American, French, and German art songs, and complete operas.

Clearly on top of the opera world, Price appeared in 118 Metropolitan productions between 1961 and 1969, when she drastically cut back her appearances not only in New York but elsewhere. It was here that she began to strike some opera insiders as ungrateful, vindictive, and arrogant, but Price insists that she was merely protecting herself from overexposure. "If I don't want to do something, I don't do it—nothing against anyone or the institution," she told Jacobson. "If you say yes to something that may not go, you are discarded—not the people who asked you to do it. They have something else to do. You are part of a unit, and they need your expertise to make the unit better.... The thing that's been misunderstood is that I don't give a lot of rhetoric before I say no. I just say no. It saves everybody time, and maybe because I don't give a reason, it's taken in a negative way."

In the 1970s Price drastically cut her number of opera appearances, preferring to focus instead on her first love—recitals—of which she enjoyed the challenge of creating several characters onstage in succession. Her career credits include countless recordings, many of them for RCA, which enjoyed an exclusive 20-year contract with the diva. She has won 13 Grammy awards, the Presidential Medal of Freedom (the nation's highest civilian award) in 1965, the Kennedy Center Honors for lifetime achievement in the arts in 1980, and the First National Medal of Arts. She has appeared on the cover of *Time* magazine, and she performed at the White House in 1978. In 1990 Price wrote *Aida: A Picture Book for All Ages*, and in May 1991 she sang at the celebrations marking the one-hundredth anniversary of Carnegie Hall in New York. Price has lived alone for years in a townhouse in New York's Greenwich Village.

Sources

Baker, Theodore, *Baker's Biographical Dictionary of Musicians,* Schirmer, 1984.

Hitchcock, H. Wiley, *The New Grove Dictionary of American Music,* Macmillan, 1986.

Opera News, July 1985; August 1985.

Southern, Eileen, *The Biographical Dictionary of Afro-American and African Musicians,* Greenwood Press, 1982.

Public Enemy

RAP GROUP

Public Enemy is one of the most important groups of the rap/hip-hop world. Both the sound they create and the message they deliver are uniquely intense. These "prophets of rage," as they call themselves, make music that is unquestionably arresting, danceable, and entertaining. At the same time, they constantly exhort the young black men and women in their audience to be proud, to be aware of their culture, to fight the forces of oppression, and to take responsibility for themselves and their race. The group's phenomenal success was summed up by a *New Statesman and Society* contributor who wrote, "Public Enemy have interlocked noise, rage, hype, glamour, and the raising of a new African-American political consciousness more effectively than anyone in the history of popular music."

The band that seems so politically driven

Public Enemy "has jerked rap music into an active political sphere. The music outdistances other political pop with both its urgency and its visionary approach to the dance floor. And the group has made pop music that is vital in the contemporary debate about race in American culture for the first time since the 1960s."
—Peter Watrous

began in a casual, party atmosphere at Adelphi University on Long Island—home turf to most of the members. Lead rapper Chuck D was the nucleus around which Public Enemy took shape. He started out at Adelphi as Carlton Ridenhour, a graphics arts major and the author of *College Madness,* the first comic strip by a black student to appear in the college newspaper, *The Delphian.* When Ridenhour began working at WBAU, Adelphi's influential radio station, he adopted the name Chuckie D and began playing the latest rap and hip-hop music long before it was anywhere near mainstream airwaves. In fact, so little of this music was being released that Chuckie D found he was unable to put together a whole show without playing some records twice. In response to that situation, he began contributing his own raps over prerecorded rhythm tracks. He told Scott Poulson-Bryant in *Spin* magazine that he wasn't political at first, but that as time went on and his confidence increased, "I would say things on the radio and in my raps about the community. As I saw it, I was just being a responsible adult."

At this point in his life, Ridenhour thought that he'd probably parlay his love of music and his interest in graphic design into a career designing album covers. He certainly didn't guess that the foundations of Public Enemy were being laid when Hank Shocklee, a deejay friend, asked him to emcee a few parties. Their collaboration was so successful that they soon formed a deejay collective known as Spectrum. Other members included rapper William Drayton ("Flavor Flav"), Hank Shocklee's brother Keith, Carl Ryder, Eric Sadler, and Norman Rogers ("DJ Terminator X"). They played countless parties around Long Island, publicizing the events with posters designed by Ridenhour. In 1983 Spectrum took over WBAU's Saturday night airwaves with the Super Spectrum Mixx Show, and they also hosted a local video show, WORD (World of Rock and Dance).

Bill Stephney was a peripheral member of Spectrum who had become a record company executive after graduating from Adelphi. He believed that the group could be transformed into a record company's dream—"a combination of Run-D.M.C. and [politically outspoken punk group] The Clash. Funky beats paired with polemics [argumentation]," he told Poulson-Bryant. He reported the group's potential to entrepreneur Rick Rubin, who had done much to widen rap's popularity by launching the careers of Run-D.M.C. and LL Cool J. Rubin was convinced after "Public Enemy Number One," a Spectrum creation, became WBAU's most requested song. Chuckie D and the others avoided Rubin's overtures, however, believing that rap artists were targets for victimization by record companies.

"I'd say to my Moms, 'Tell him I'm not here' [when he called on the phone]," Ridenhour recalled to Poulson-Bryant. But Rubin's persistence, coupled with Stephney's reassurances, finally won out. In 1986 Flavor Flav, DJ Terminator X, and Chuckie D (now "Chuck D") signed a contract with Rubin's Def Jam, Columbia Records' newly created rap division.

Music with a message

From the first, Public Enemy sought to grab the attention of young blacks and send them a series of pointed messages. Their first album, *Yo! Bum Rush the Show,* attacked the mindless materialism that they saw as the hallmark of the mid-1980s. "Everybody was into 'Let's get dumb, let's get crazy, let's get stupid,'" Lewis Cole quoted group producer Hank Shocklee as saying in *Rolling Stone.* "That was the thing of 1985, '86. So we decided, 'Let's put something together that will give people something to think about as well as listen to.'" Their second album, *It Takes a Nation of Millions to Hold Us Back,* was "hittin' hard to make people understand how corrupt the white system is," Chuck D told Poulson-Bryant. And *Fear of a Black Planet* "was about the problems white people have with themselves," while their fourth, *Apocalypse '91: The Enemy Strikes Black* "is the one where we deal with the problems we've got with ourselves. Black accountability."

"Musically, we wanted to make something obnoxious," Hank Shocklee told Lewis Cole. "When people are asleep, you have to take drastic means to wake them up." He elaborated in *Spin:* "We wanted to put certain hooks in the sound so that when you heard it coming out of a car, you knew what record was on. It was Noise [with a] capital N.... We wanted to submerge you in sound, a thunderstorm of sound. And Chuck's voice would come out of it like the voice of God." Each band member's contribution is an integral part of the Public Enemy product, Shocklee concluded: "What you hear, lyrically and musically ... is the sound of a collage of ideas being rejected and accepted." *Detroit Free Press* writer Gary Graff described Public Enemy's "noise" as "an aural assault of buzzes, sirens, knife-edged guitar riffs, turntable scratches and a bass-drum attack that pummels like uppercuts to the chin." Scott Ian, member of the heavy metal group Anthrax, related to Graff his first reaction to Public Enemy; he was overwhelmed by "Chuck's voice, the heaviness of the beats, all the crazy noises. It wasn't so much musical—just all this stuff going on.... When Public Enemy came out, they just stole the show. There was nothing like it ever before."

Public Enemy's sound may be absolutely original, but many of the ideas expressed in their lyrics are not. Most of the members are admirers of past and present black leaders and revolutionaries, including Nat Turner, Marcus Garvey, Malcolm X, Huey Newton, and Nation of Islam leader Louis Farrakhan. Their raps echo the rhetoric of the 1960s Black Power movement, and they underscore the parallel between themselves and the Black Panther party with their back-up group, S1W (Security of the First World).

S1W, which originated as Public Enemy's security force, is a troop of men, clad in military uniforms and toting plastic Uzi machine guns, who stand at attention throughout the performance—except for occasional breaks into martial-arts-style moves that Lewis Cole called in *Rolling Stone* "an ironic variation of the synchronized steps of Sixties Motown groups."

Group generates controversy

Not surprisingly, many people find Public Enemy threatening. The group has been criticized by people of all races for their often violent imagery and their strident opposition to the existing power establishment. Media fire almost forced them to disband in 1989 after adjunct member Richard Griffin ("Professor Griff"), leader of S1W and Public Enemy's "minister of information," made anti-Semitic remarks in an interview with the *Washington Times*. In it, he laid the blame for the socioeconomic plight of contemporary blacks at the feet of Jews, who, he said, had financed the slave trade, and are "wicked ... [and responsible for] the majority of the wickedness that goes on around the globe," including "what's happening in South Africa." The interview contained several other inflammatory remarks—including praise for deposed Ugandan dictator Idi Amin—and it gained an even wider audience when it was reprinted in the June 20, 1989, issue of the *Village Voice*. Public Enemy came under attack from many quarters, and the Jewish Defense Organization even sent a group armed with chains and clubs to Public Enemy's offices.

Chuck D responded to the furor with a confused series of announcements, stating first that Public Enemy was going to disband, then that it would continue but would refuse to deal with the record industry, and finally, in a press conference, giving notice that Griffin was no longer a part of the group. "The black community is in crisis. Our mission as musicians is to address these problems. Offensive remarks by Professor Griff are not in line with Public Enemy's program. We are not anti-Jewish. We are pro-black, pro-black culture, and pro-human race," Chuck D said, as quoted by *Nation* writer Gene Santoro. Following this announcement, he was silent; but "Fight the Power," the Public Enemy song that served as the theme for Spike Lee's racially charged movie *Do the Right Thing*, climbed the charts and spoke eloquently for the band. Griff eventually returned to the group, and Public Enemy later stirred up more controversy with a single inspired by their media trial, "Welcome to the Terrordome." Far from being apologetic or conciliatory, it brought new charges of anti-Semitism because of the lines "Crucifixion ain't no fiction/ so-called chosen frozen/ Apology made to whomever pleases/ Still they got me like Jesus."

Chuck D philosophized to the *Los Angeles Times:* "We're not liked because never before has the black man or so many black males spoken their opinion on so many things." While decrying the black racism that Public Enemy sometimes seems to encourage, Gene Santoro agreed with Chuck D that the group has been unfairly defamed because of the unpleasant truth they speak; Santoro wrote: "There's no denying that blacks, especially young black males, are stuck at the bottom of the socioeconomic heap. That remains Public Enemy's main point, and it's been validated over recent months by the barely submerged racism in print and television discussions about hip-hop in the wake of the P.E. controversy."

The world portrayed by Public Enemy is not pretty or appealing, but it is reality for many Americans. *Detroit Free Press* writer Graff praised the group for refusing to duck the hard issues: "Public Enemy has walked as dangerous an edge as any rap group has traversed.... As [the group] confronts racism, oppression, cultural genocide and self-destruction in the black community—touching on drugs, gangs, education and interracial relationships—Chuck D charges through each topic without apology or diplomacy.... [Public Enemy has] brought the Big Picture to modern rap."

After having remained in the forefront of rap from their inception, Public Enemy seemed to be succumbing to the dominance of West Coast "gangsta rap" in 1994. Their release of that year, *Muse Sick-N-Hour Mess Age,* debuted at Number 14 on *Billboard*'s Top 200 album chart, but it had fallen to Number 126 after six weeks. Reviews of the disc were mixed, with one stirring some controversy with its seemingly personal nature. Still, the burgeoning popularity of California's Long Beach Sound owed much to the groundbreaking work of Public Enemy.

Sources

Chicago Tribune, April 15, 1990.

Commentary, March 1990.

Detroit Free Press, October 2, 1991.

Detroit News, May 14, 1990.

Ebony, January 1989; June 1990.

Interview, September 1990.

Los Angeles Times, February 4, 1990.

Mother Jones, February/March 1990.

Nation, June 25, 1990.

New Statesman & Society, February 23, 1990.

Newsweek, March 19, 1990.

New York Times, April 22, 1990.

People, March 5, 1990.

Rolling Stone, August 10, 1989; October 19, 1989; November 16, 1989; May 17, 1990; October 3, 1991.

Spin, October 1991.

Time, February 5, 1990.

Village Voice, June 20, 1989.

Washington Post, April 15, 1990.

Washington Times, May 22, 1989.

Queen Latifah

Born 1970
East Orange, New Jersey

"I can have fun and still show I'm on the ball."

RAPPER AND ACTRESS

Queen Latifah is one of the hottest rap artists in America. As a female who often dresses in African-print outfits, she certainly distinguishes herself from the male-dominant, sweatsuit-clad rap establishment. But it's not only because she physically stands out from the rest that she is significant. Latifah's genius lies in intelligent lyrics that promote female self-respect, African American cultural pride, and the virtues of being positive. She also has a charming personality that impresses her audiences. With her albums, Latifah has won a multicultural, multigenerational following, bringing rap to larger listenership than many of her fellows.

Named "Latifah"

Latifah was born in New Jersey around 1970 and given the name Dana Owens. When she was eight, a Muslim cousin nicknamed her Latifah, which means "delicate and sensitive" in Arabic. She added "Queen" when she got her first record contract. It wasn't to denote rank, but to remind black Americans know they are descendants of African kings and queens. "She is very culturally oriented," commented Latifah's mother, Rita Owens, to Peter Watrous in the *New York Times.* "And there are a lot of kings and queens from Africa."

Both of Latifah's parents had musical talent. Her father played drums, and frequently held jam sessions in the house. Latifah and her older brother would hit pots and pans to join in the mood. She also sang in the church choir. Her parents separated when Latifah was still young, and they were eventually divorced. She, her mother, and the rest of the family moved into a housing project in East Newark, New Jersey. Now a single parent, Latifah's mother worked full-time during the week, held a part-time job on the weekends, and attended college. She eventually earned a degree in education, and within two years of that she moved the family out of the projects.

A Rap artist is formed

In 1980 Owens was teaching art at Irvington High School while Latifah was a student there. Latifah was very active in high school, playing on the girls basketball team, earning a high grade point average, and being voted Most Popular, Best All Around, Most Comical, and Best Dancer in her senior year. She also hung out with a group of girls who would do rap music in the school bathrooms. Latifah learned how to do the human beat box (making rhythm noises by blowing into a cupped palm)—much like the improvised rhythm of her father's jam sessions. She and her friends heard that there was another female rap group in the area. They joined together to form the group Ladies Fresh and tried out their act at the Irvington High School talent show. Soon, the ambitious group was performing in any venue they could land.

When Mark James, who was known as D.J. Mark the 45 King, performed at one of the high school dances, Latifah and her friends began hanging around James, listening to music in his parents' basement and doing some original demos. After high school, James took a demo of Latifah's called "Princess of the Posse" to Fred Brathwaite, host of *Yo! MTV Raps.* Brathwaite played it for some people at Tommy Boy Records, and they signed up Latifah immediately.

In 1988 Latifah released her first single, "Wrath of My Madness," which sold an acceptable 40,000 copies. With the video production of "Ladies First," which showcased Latifah and other female rappers in an anti-apartheid message, Latifah had arrived. An exciting European tour and the release of her first album, *All Hail the Queen,* followed.

All Hail the Queen was a smash. It hit the Number 6 spot on *Billboard*'s rhythm and blues charts and sold more than one million copies worldwide. Latifah was praised for breaking "the male-dominated boundaries of the business with her Afrocentric, woman's point-of-view rhyming and lyricizing," the Detroit *Metro Times* noted. She was also hailed for her courage in mixing rap with straight singing—something other rappers didn't do.

The album established her not only for her music ability, but also for her intelligent lyrics. Her theme song, "Ladies First," promoted both chivalry and the idea that women must take a stand for themselves and display self-respect. Other songs looked at the issues of homelessness and African American pride. Within a short time, *All Hail the Queen* proved that Latifah was not just a novelty act in the virtually all-male world of rap. She had established herself as a talented, intelligent musician with something important to say.

Embraces womanism

As a consequence of her debut effort, according to Watrous, "the Queen became a spokesperson for ... young black women—and for a media hungry for someone articulate, political and savvy about feminism but not confrontational." Fans all over the world looked up to Latifah. Twice she was invited to air her views on feminism at Harvard University. However, in spite of the topics of her songs, Latifah has shrugged off the label of feminist. "I have a fear of feminism," she told Dinitia Smith in *New York.* "To me, feminists were usually white women who hated men.... I don't want to be classified with them." What she prefers her ideology to be about is "womanism—feminism for black women, to be natural, to have our sisterhood."

Latifah has also become known for her graciousness and generosity toward other female rappers. This is unusual in the rap world, where infighting and competitiveness runs rampant. "I'm proud of everybody, and I feel there's room for everybody," she told Alan Light in *Rolling Stone.* "So I don't feel threatened when other girls put out good records— I feel motivated to make a good record as well."

Maintains control in male-dominated business

In terms of the other controversies in the world of rap, Latifah still remains supportive of her fellows. She has defended other rappers who use obscenities and see women as playthings in their music. Although she disagrees with their style, she defends their right to artistic expression. "A lot of what these guys are saying needs to be heard.... They're bringing reality—the reality of the black culture—to a lot of people.... I have to defend their right to say these things—even things I don't like," Latifah told a *Los Angeles Times* reporter.

Latifah released her eagerly awaited follow-up album, *Nature of a Sista,* in 1991. Again, critics commended the rapper's intelligent lyrics as well as her musical ability, and the album spawned two hit singles, "Latifah Had It Up 2 Here" and "Fly Girl." Following the album, she launched a concert tour of the United States with reggae star Ziggy Marley.

Despite all the success, Latifah's life has not been without sorrow. In the spring of 1992 her brother, Lance, an East Orange policeman, was killed in an off-duty motorcycle accident. To deal with her grief, she threw herself into working on her third album, *Black Reign,* released in the fall of 1993. "*Black Reign* is about the past year of my life, the hardest year I've ever lived through," Latifah told *Essence.*

During that difficult year Latifah also landed a role in the well-received Fox television sitcom *Living Single* as well as a part of a nurse in the Michael Keaton film *My Life.* Latifah was not a stranger to the silver screen; she had appeared in *Jungle Fever, Juice,* and *House Party 2.* Latifah managed to branch out in the music industry as well. Using her growing clout, she formed Flavor Unit Records and Management Company to launch the careers of rising rap artists. Already, Latifah has been responsible for the rise of many artists, including Naughty by Nature and Apache, and promises to continue to be a queenly force in the music industry.

Sources

Chicago Tribune, July 4, 1990.

Ebony, October 1991; December 1993.

Essence, May 1991; August 1991; October 1993.

Los Angeles Times, January 28, 1990; September 8, 1991.

Metro Times (Detroit), August 23-September 3, 1991.

New York, December 3, 1990.

New York Times, August 25, 1991.

People, September 30, 1991; November 29, 1993.

Rolling Stone, February 22, 1990; January 10, 1991; October 17, 1991.

Time, Fall 1990; May 27, 1991.

Robert Redford

Born August 18, 1937
Santa Monica, California

ACTOR AND DIRECTOR

R obert Redford is one of America's favorite film stars, a leading man with movie credits spanning three and a half decades. Instantly recognizable for his all-American good looks, Redford has never felt comfortable as a matinee idol and has refused to settle into preconceived notions of how a movie star should look, act, or conduct a career. Indeed, Redford's most important achievements in recent years have come behind the camera: as director of films such as *A River Runs Through It*, *Milagro Beanfield War*, and *Quiz Show* and as founder of the prestigious Sundance Institute in Utah. "Robert Redford has been famous for nearly thirty

"The world has grown up fast, it's become a very serious place, and I think I want to spend my time more wisely."

years, the equivalent, in an age of kindergarten attention spans, of a geologic epoch," wrote Philip Caputo in *Esquire*. "But if fame's horrors confirm the blessings of anonymity, then Robert Redford has provided precious little tabloid pleasure over the years. It is a testament to the power of Redford's home-on-the-range aura that he seems to have slipped out of Hollywood without paying the requisite celebrity check that is normally handed to matinee idols. He retains a reputation for not making compromises, for maintaining his integrity, for not bowing to the craven demands of the Industry." This self-imposed independence from Hollywood has given Redford an unprecedented degree of control over his work both on–and off–screen, as well as a standard of privacy unknown to most superstars.

Esquire correspondent Mike Barnicle noted: "Redford ... is a lock, a guarantee, a walk to the teller's window. He is larger than life and more bankable than any bond, stock, or piece of beachfront property that all the people in his business, all those smarmy, well-tanned and worked-out people, pressing iron and doing wrist curls with one-hundred-dollar bills, could ever dream of purchasing. Robert Redford is a star. A huge star. He is a guy who can change your life just by returning your phone calls." Fame has never sat easily on Redford's shoulders, however. He has always been uncomfortable with his celebrity, feeling that it creates a stumbling block in his championship of important political and environmental causes. "People have been so busy relating to how I look, it's a miracle I didn't become a self-conscious blob of protoplasm," he told *New York* magazine. "It's not easy being 'Robert Redford.' Sometimes it even makes people angry. They think you're getting paid a lot of money for just sort of floating through something. But it's never been that. Ever. It's always agony."

In *New York* magazine, Neal Gabler observed that Redford might have been just another Hollywood star with a winning smile, except for the fact that he used his looks as a metaphor. "In character after character," Gabler wrote, "Redford explored the idea that we are all trapped as he is, that we can never quite bring into phase who we are with what we represent to others." Redford agreed that what he calls the "handsome thing" might have ruined his life if he had been conscious of it at an earlier age. "As a kid, I was anything but handsome," he said in *New York.* "Freckles. Totally unruly hair. Barbers used to put a CLOSED sign on the door when I walked up. This 'handsome thing' kind of came later on. I don't think I would have had the perceptions I have about life, the feelings I have about life, had I honestly believed that I was handsome all my life."

Grew up in working-class neighborhood

Redford's was an ordinary childhood in a stable, if struggling, California family. He was born in 1937, the oldest of two sons of Charles and Martha Redford. In his early youth, the family lived in a mostly Hispanic, working-class neighborhood in Santa Monica. His father, a mail carrier and later an accountant, was a rigid disciplinarian who tried to discourage high-blown ambitions in his children. "It was schizophrenic," Redford remembered in *Esquire* of his childhood. "Here I was, being told to toe the mark, take it on the chin, accept things, but I was in America, where you could dream and fulfill your dreams." The idea of being a movie star never entered young Robert Redford's head, even though he lived close to the seat of the movie industry. Instead, he read books and played sports, especially baseball. He also got into trouble.

Sometimes with a gang and sometimes alone, the teenaged Redford engaged in petty crimes of vandalism, trespassing, and theft. At 15 he vowed to climb every tower and belfry in town, and once he and a friend broke into a convent school just to prove they could do it. They were caught and reprimanded by the police. "I had so many restraints on me as a kid, being told, 'Don't do this, don't do that.' I'd just go out and do it to show it ain't so," Redford told *Esquire*. "And I was aware of the fear you could generate in others through your behavior. You know, going out to the edge."

Never an honor student, Redford still managed to earn sufficient grades to land a baseball scholarship to the University of Colorado in Boulder. He began classes there in 1955 but found himself challenged more by the ski slopes and painting than by the college curriculum. Eventually he lost his scholarship when he skipped baseball practice and engaged in excessive drinking. The stay at the university was not fruitless, however; Redford discovered there that he wanted to be an artist, and a friend suggested he move to Paris to study painting. He worked in the Los Angeles oil fields until he had earned enough to fly to Europe. He wandered from country to country before settling in art school in Florence, Italy.

By late 1957 he was back in California looking for a job. In his Los Angeles apartment building he met a young Mormon woman, Lola Van Wagenen, who encouraged him to try again as an artist. The couple married in 1958 and moved to New York City, where Redford studied painting at the Pratt Institute in Brooklyn. Redford thought he might like to try theatrical set design, so he enrolled at the American Academy of Dramatic Arts in hopes of gaining contacts in the New York theater world. "I'd never been in a play in my life," he told the *New York Times*. "Acting seemed ludicrous to me, but people kept telling me I could do it." Redford's professors at the Academy were impressed by his budding ability. One of them recommended him as a replacement actor for an ongoing Broadway show, *Tall Story*, and in 1959 Redford became a full-time performer.

Works in television

After short stints in *Tall Story* and another Broadway play, *The Highest Tree*, Redford quickly found lucrative work in television dramas. In the early 1960s he appeared on such important programs as *Playhouse 90*, *Route 66*, *Alfred Hitchcock Presents*, *Bus Stop*, and *Twilight Zone*. He also continued to earn significant roles on Broadway, including the lead in a romantic comedy called *Sunday in New York*. His movie debut came in 1962, with a low-budget anti-war film called *Warhunt*.

In 1963 Redford was cast in a new Neil Simon comedy, *Barefoot in the Park*. He took the role of Paul Brattner, a proper attorney married to a free-spirited young woman with radical ideas about propriety. The show was an immediate hit on Broadway, but Redford remained with it only six months. "My perversity came out," he explained in *Newsday*. "I created accidents and problems to break the monotony.... If you came on with one shoe off one night, at least it made life happen on stage. Otherwise, it got pretty plastic after a while."

His experience with theater convinced Redford that he would rather do movies and television. He moved back to Hollywood and shopped his talents around. A series of lackluster movies such as *Inside Daisy Clover* and *This Property Is Condemned* did little to boost his career, and he considered leaving acting. Then, in 1967, he was asked to reprise his *Barefoot in the Park* role on film, with Jane Fonda in the female lead. The movie was a hit, and the "handsome thing" brought Redford the attention of prestigious producers and directors.

Becomes superstar with Butch Cassidy and the Sundance Kid

The film that established Redford as a superstar, however, was *Butch Cassidy and the Sundance Kid*, released in 1969. A comedy/drama about a pair of gunslingers in the waning Wild West, *Butch Cassidy and the Sundance Kid* earned six Academy Award nominations and was one of the top-grossing movies of the year. The film paired Redford with Paul Newman, and the duo showed an uncanny screen chemistry that would be repeated in 1973 in the Oscar-winning *The Sting*. The success of *Butch Cassidy* brought Redford numerous offers, but he decided to choose subsequent film work carefully to avoid being swept into meaningless "good guy" roles. Late 1969 brought *Downhill Racer*, a cynical look at an Olympic hopeful, and *Tell Them Willie Boy Is Here*, a western anti-hero film.

Redford deserves credit for defying attempts to pigeonhole him as one year's matinee idol. Still, his fame—dictated though it was by his high standards—caused him problems. "A funny thing happened," he told *Newsweek*. "Somewhere along the line I ran into this fellow out there.

Redford as Sundance with Paul Newman as Cassidy in *Butch Cassidy and the Sundance Kid*, 1969.

This other me. He seemed to be somebody who just got his Eagle Scout badge. It's not someone I can relate to real well. In the beginning I was sort of amused by it. And then it began to be a slightly panicky feeling. And I began to be more obsessive about privacy."

Ironically, superstardom brought a certain relief from the rigors of Hollywood. Redford felt free to deny interviews about his private life. He also used his muscle to bring projects he liked into production. Two of these, *Jeremiah Johnson* (1972) and *The Candidate* (1972), did slow box-office business initially but have since reaped substantial profits. Other films from that period—*The Way We Were* (1973), *The Sting* (1973), and *Three Days of the Condor* (1975)—were profitable from their release and have become popular classics. *New York*'s Gabler, suggesting that Redford filled

Redford bought land in rural Utah for a family retreat and then began buying huge tracts around it to ensure that it would not become overdeveloped. The land now hosts his Sundance Institute, a training facility for independent filmmakers and other artists, as well as a few environmentally sensitive homes.

a superstar niche created specifically by the times, wrote, "Redford was a different star for a different America. There was no saber rattling his soul, no fuse snaking to some internal bomb. Like John F. Kennedy, he was cool and ironic. There was a detachment that perfectly matched the spirit of national complacency.... And yet it was not just Redford's good looks that staked a claim on his audience but a suspicion that his characters were always resisting the burden of those looks."

Politics consumes Redford's life

Politics, especially environmental issues, began to consume Redford. In 1976 he convinced Warner Bros. to produce *All the President's Men,* a drama about the two reporters who covered the Watergate scandal for the *Washington Post.* The material did not necessarily lend itself to high drama, but the film was a critical and commercial success, winning best picture of the year honors from the National Board of Review and the New York Film Critics Circle. Another Redford-initiated production, *The Electric Horseman* (1979), offered a similarly jaundiced view of politics and its press coverage as empty posturing. "What Redford has always captured best is the flawed American hero," *Newsweek*'s David Ansen observed. "These are characters ripe for packaging and corruption, exploited American Fausts who put their souls on the auction block.... The rebounding irony is that no matter how marred the characters he plays, it is Redford's 'perfection' the audience carries home. He is a comfort who would rather be a thorn."

As early as 1970, Redford told the *Toronto Globe & Mail* that he would not spend his entire career as an actor. "I'll stay in acting until I get bored with myself or until I no longer enjoy it," he said. "Then I'll get into something else." Truth to tell, Redford has never become bored by acting, but he has found challenges as a film director that fulfill his artistic nature. In 1980 he directed his first feature-length film, *Ordinary People,* a bitter tale about a dysfunctional upper-class family. Redford won an Academy Award as best director for his debut work, but the implications of his achievement were more lasting for him. He told *Esquire* that film direction brought him back to his first love—painting. "Bang! It was a big flash," he said. "I haven't lost it as an artist. Designing a scene, the two, acting and painting, came together."

At the very pinnacle of his career, Redford became even more guarded about his personal life—and even more particular about the films in which he would appear. *Esquire*'s Caputo claimed that the reclusive Redford "began to earn a reputation as a loner and a maverick." That reputation did little to erode the star's popularity, however. After a hiatus of almost four years, he returned to the screen as baseball player Roy Hobbs in *The Natural* (1984). Ansen explained that the film "casts Redford as a secretive athlete with a magical prowess at bat. It's a combination of player and part that can only brighten the golden image Redford disowns." The critic added that in *The Natural* Redford "grounds the movie's bolts of fancy like a lightning rod." In 1986 Redford took the role of hunter Denys Finch Hatton in *Out of Africa,* yet another film that earned multiple Academy Award nominations, including best picture of the year. Redford told *New York* that his work in *Out of Africa* ranks among the least satisfying of his career. He called Finch Hatton "the most purely symbolic character I've ever played.... The toughest. He isn't given any purpose, really, any professional purpose, other than to exist like a bird would."

Perhaps in response to his casting in the shallow role of Finch Hatton, Redford appeared in two subsequent films that offered very different characters. In *Legal Eagles* (1986) he appeared as a lighthearted attorney, and in *Havana* (1991) he played an aging gambler in the last days before the Cuban Revolution. *Havana* frankly exposed Redford as a man in midlife, and the actor relished the chance to move away from typecasting. "It wasn't a question of whether I'm now going to play 'age,'" he told *New York.* "It was a fact of not trying to do anything about what I am.... That's one of the things that drew me to [the character]. Something in him that he can't articulate knows he's gone as far as he's going to go with this life."

Draws critical praise with A River Runs Through It

Redford's words may have been prophetic. *Havana* did not perform well at the box office, and its star retreated behind the camera to direct again. One of his most notable projects as a director was the adaptation of Norman Maclean's novella *A River Runs Through It.* Filmed in the gorgeous wilds of Montana, *A River Runs Through It* follows the fortunes of a pair of brothers and their minister father, who communicate best while fly-fishing. "Robert Redford obviously fell in love with Maclean's craggy, lyrical American voice, and you can feel his affection in his voice-over reading of big chunks of the text," wrote Ansen in *Newsweek.* "Redford puts Maclean's story into straightforward chronological form (spanning 1910 to 1935) and does an honorable job emulating the author's unsentimental, laconically witty style." Caputo praised Redford's daring for overseeing "such an aggressively thoughtful movie," adding that the film is "a slap back at Hollywood's delight in telling its stars that they can't have everything their way."

After *A River Runs Through It* Redford turned back to acting. He appeared in *Sneakers* (1992) as a high-tech security analyst who leads a group of talented misfits in a plan to steal a gadget that can enter and decode any computer program. In *Indecent Proposal* (1993) Redford played a millionaire who offers a financially strapped architect $1 million in exchange for sleeping with the architect's wife. While both films received mixed reviews, critics generally credited Redford's performance.

In 1994 Redford re-emerged as a gifted, bankable director; his film *Quiz Show,* about the cheating scandals that plagued television game shows in the 1950s, opened to sold-out houses and rave reviews. In exploring the themes of greed, the inherently deceptive nature of entertainment, and class differences in America, Redford created what many called an instant classic, one that was sure to dominate at the 1995 Academy Awards.

Hollywood has never been able to crush or even bruise Redford. If, as Gabler noted, some film critics have found him "wooden and passive," he has never languished long without a chance to shine. If the machinations of the industry are distasteful to the star, he simply turns to his own Sundance Institute, where premiums are placed on creativity and innovation. One constant in either arena is Redford's enduring need for privacy, his reluctance to talk about his family or his most personal feelings. *McCall's* correspondent Natalie Gittelson contended that Redford "has stubbornly refused to shape an image and adopt an attitude, with all the artifice that implies, to present to a world hungry for Redford himself the man behind the star. As does every true artist, he prefers that we know him through his work. And if his often astounding artistry as an actor is sometimes overwhelmed by his equally astounding good looks (which grow only more so as he mellows and matures with time), it just increases his determination to be respected for his talents rather than adored for his physical beauty."

As for the future, Redford has indicated that he will probably appear in fewer movies and direct more. Much of his time is consumed by involvement in environmental causes—he is a strong supporter of the Natural Resources Defense Council, the Environmental Defense Fund, and the National Wildlife Federation, and in 1989 he was awarded a medal by the Audubon Society. "I'm into middle age, and I'm more mature in many ways," he told *McCall's.* "My kids are grown up now, and I care what they think; before, they were children, and it didn't matter that their father wore makeup and cavorted on the screen with actresses in designer outfits, but now I have a need for more personal commitment and personal dignity." He added: "The world has grown up fast, it's become a very serious place, and I think I want to spend my time more wisely."

Sources

The Detroit News, September 17, 1994.

Esquire, March 1988; September 1992.

Globe & Mail (Toronto), September 14, 1970.

McCall's, February 1988.

New Republic, April 18, 1988; November 16, 1992.

Newsweek, May 28, 1984; October 12, 1992.

New York, December 10, 1990; April 26, 1993.

New York Times, October 26, 1969.

People, January 20, 1986; July 21, 1986; May 4, 1992; September 14, 1992; May 9, 1994.

The Red Hot Chili Peppers

"What this band is about is helping your brothers."—John Frusciante

ROCK BAND

The Red Hot Chili Peppers emerged in the mid-1980s as one of the trailblazing bands in the world of alternative rock and spearheaded the wave of groups that fused hard rock and punk thrash with 1970s funk. Although this heady musical brew earned them a loyal underground following, the band didn't begin to reach mass audiences until videos from their 1989 album *Mother's Milk* began to appear regularly on MTV. The Peppers' hard-edged style wasn't the only thing standing between them and mainstream success, however; the tumultuous offstage lives of the band members generated a great deal of controversy as well.

The band's frenetic tempos, churning guitar chords, and onstage mania owe a great deal to the punk movement of the late seventies and early eighties. On the other hand, the slapping bass and funky drums that grace much of their material come out of the band's devotion to funk and soul, especially the various projects of George Clinton, the father of what became known as "P. Funk." Clinton's bands, most notably Parliament and Funkadelic, fused psychedelic rock and dance music in the early seventies and exercised a huge influence on the next generation of rock musicians. According to former Peppers guitarist John Frusciante, "The truest, heaviest metal is on early Funkadelic records." Clinton's style no doubt influenced the band's self-description as a "hardcore, bone-crunching, mayhem, psychedelic sex-funk band from heaven."

The band that would become the Red Hot Chili Peppers began in the early 1980s. Singer Anthony Kiedis and bassist Michael Balzary, who calls himself Flea, were classmates at Hollywood's Fairfax High School. Kiedis, a child of divorced parents, had moved from his mother's home in Michigan to live with his father, actor Blackie Dammett, in Los Angeles. Kiedis did some film acting in his teens, playing Sylvester Stallone's son in the 1978 movie *F.I.S.T.* Flea was born in Melbourne, Australia, and arrived in the United States in 1967, moving to Los Angeles in 1972. He was a trumpet prodigy in his childhood, but grew up to play bass for the punk band Fear. "I only had one bass lesson," he told *Guitar Player*'s Joe Gore. "The teacher gave me an Eagles song ... but I just wasn't into it, so I decided to figure things out on my own." Flea added that he played in a band with the Peppers' first two guitarists, Jack Sherman and Hillel Slovak. "Actually," he confided, "it was Hillel who taught me how to play bass."

The band takes the name Red Hot Chili Peppers

The Peppers' earliest incarnation appeared at a Hollywood club in 1984. Kiedis and Flea joined up with Slovak and drummer Jack Irons for an impromptu jam. The quartet called itself Tony Flow and the Miraculously Majestic Masters of Mayhem; when asked to return for a second performance, they adopted the name The Red Hot Chili Peppers, which Kiedis claims to have seen on "a psychedelic bush in the Hollywood Hills that had band names on it."

The band's debut, 1984's *The Red Hot Chili Peppers,* which was released on EMI Records, broadened the band's cult appeal. The record, according to *Interview*'s Dimitri Ehrlich, "established the Peppers as prophets of a type of music whose time was about to come: not rock that you could dance to, but rock that you must dance to." In addition to accelerating rockers like "True Men Don't Kill Coyotes" and "Mommy Where's Daddy," the LP featured the first in a series of distinctive cover versions of classic songs, a funk-rap rendition of Hank Williams's country standard "Why Don't You Love Me." Neither Slovak nor Irons played on the first album, but Slovak returned for their 1985 follow-up *Freaky Styley,* produced by none other than the band's idol, George Clinton. *Freaky* continued in the vein of the first album, featuring a cover of funk master Sly Stone's "If You Want Me to Stay" and emphasizing the band's lewd side a bit more with such numbers as "Sex Rap" and "Catholic School Girls Rule." In fact, the group's crowing about sex would get louder with each record, just as their onstage exhibitionism and aggressiveness with female fans would cause band members trouble.

Irons took over drum duties on the Peppers' next effort, 1987's *The Uplift Mofo Party Plan.* Though it yielded no hits, this record featured a number of solid funky originals and a rap version of folkrocker Bob Dylan's sixties hit "Subterranean Homesick Blues." The Red Hot Chili Peppers remained a cult band, and reviews like the following from *Stereo Review* didn't help: "I want to like an album as aggressively bad as *The Uplift Mofo Party Plan.* But I just can't. The Red Hot Chili Peppers do everything in their power to chafe, outrage, and sicken, cranking out with truly dizzying energy a goulash of electrified funk, chest-thumping rap, and vaguely suggestive nonsense lyrics." The reviewer concluded that this was "an album that recreates the sensation of being seventeen and drunk on cheap wine." Whether the Peppers would consider this a negative sensation was unclear. The group released *The Abbey Road E.P.,* a mini-collection of earlier favorites, in 1988. This record, too, failed to generate major sales.

Slovak dies of overdose

In 1988 tragedy struck the band: Slovak died of a heroin overdose. Up until this point the band had been cavalier about its drug use, but Slovak's death changed everything. For a time it looked as if the band would fall apart completely. Irons was devastated by the loss of Slovak; he left and eventually joined the band Eleven. Kiedis and Flea decided to carry on. At first they recruited former Funkadelic guitarist Blackbyrd McKnight and drummer D. H. Peligro from the San Francisco punk band the Dead Kennedys, but the chemistry didn't work. Finally Frusciante, a guitar player in his late teens influenced equally by funk and hard rock, left his band Thelonius Monster to play with the Peppers. The group auditioned a number of drummers, settling finally on Detroit native Chad Smith, whom Kiedis described in *Interview* as "a molten core of sheer power."

The new Red Hot Chili Peppers released the album *Mother's Milk* in 1989. The original songs were a mix of more serious tunes like "Knock Me Down," inspired by Slovak's death, and "Johnny Kick a Hole in the Sky," which continued the band's use of Native American themes, as well as straight-out sex songs. The band broke through commercially, however, with its cover of funk and soul legend Stevie Wonder's "Higher Ground." The video began to appear regularly on MTV, and suddenly the band had the national visibility it had sought all along. The band scored again with the videos for "Knock Me Down" and "Taste the Pain," and *Mother's Milk* quickly scored half a million sales. *Guitar Player* remarked, "The current edition of Red Hot Chili Peppers may be the most intense yet."

In 1990 the band moved into a Hollywood Hills mansion to begin recording its next album. Its contract with EMI had run out, and Warner Bros. signed them. Producer Rick Rubin suggested the move to the mansion, and though the band claimed that the house had a few ghosts, they had no complaints. Flea had married and his wife, Loesha, and daughter, Clara, shared the mansion's festive atmosphere. The band wasn't free of controversy, however. Kiedis was convicted of exposing himself at a performance in 1989 and had to pay a substantial fine. In March, during an MTV broadcast, Flea and Smith grabbed a female fan and spanked her. They narrowly escaped prison sentences for battery, disorderly conduct, and solicitation to commit an unnatural act. Slovak's death had affected the band members' outrageous behavior in some ways, however; they swore off hard drugs and began to talk a lot about spiritual values in their music. "It's a matter of unity," Flea told *Guitar Player,* "of four guys listening to each other and playing together."

This new sense of unity found its way into the Peppers' 1991 release, *Blood Sugar Sex Magik,* which was written and recorded in the mansion. As Flea disclosed in a Warner Bros. press package, "The whole house was really just a big, warm, beautiful, peaceful place. Not for one minute did we feel any negative energy. Even living together, which could really create tension, turned out perfectly." The album catapulted them as close to the mainstream as they have ever been, hitting music stores at the same time the Peppers kicked off an extensive United States tour. Suddenly, it was impossible to tune into alternative and even some classic-rock radio stations without hearing the funky new hit "Give it Away" or the touching ballad "Under the Bridge"—an emotionally raw account of Keidis's own struggle with drugs—playing at least several times a day.

Despite the group's overwhelming success in 1992, John Frusciante abruptly left the band. Finding a successor was not easy. The band first hired Arik Marshall, then Jesse Tobias, before finally recruiting guitarist Dave Navarro, who was formerly of Jane's Addiction. In early 1994 the band was set to begin preproduction for their new album, which is to be produced by Rick Rubin, who produced *Blood Sugar Sex Magik.*

Sources

Guitar Player, December 1989; April 1990; December 1993.

Interview, August 1991.

People, April 16, 1990.

Rolling Stone, May 17, 1990; April 7, 1994.

Spin, October 1991.

Stereo Review, February 1988.

Additional information obtained from a Warner Bros. press release on *Blood Sugar Sex Magik,* 1991.

Julia Roberts

Born October 28, 1967
Smyrna, Georgia

ACTRESS

T he breathtaking ease with which Julia Roberts has captivated Hollywood and legions of fans is a throwback to that Golden Age of Clark Gable and Vivien Leigh—a time when movie stars had that unmistakable star quality that could light up the screen with a larger-than-life glamour. Many actors today have either one or the other—a predominant beauty or talent—but Roberts has that rare and formidable combination of both gorgeous looks and an instinctive and versatile dramatic ability, which perhaps explains her quick rise to the heights of both popular and critical success. Ever since the release of only her third major film, *Pretty Woman*—the blockbuster that pulled in sales of over $400 million worldwide—Roberts has wielded the power of being the number one female box-office draw.

"There is a nonthreatening quality to Julia. She's boldly vulnerable. It's unbelievable that someone so physically beautiful could also have this 'everyperson' quality about her, but that's exactly why she's a movie star."—Joe Roth

In *Pretty Woman* Roberts plays a down-on-her-luck prostitute who is whisked off the streets into the lap of luxury by a wealthy Prince Charming, played by Richard Gere. This modern-day Cinderella story has parallels to Roberts's real-life rocket to fame—a rather swift trip accomplished with a minimum of dues-paying and no formal training. Three days after her high school graduation, Roberts left her hometown of Smyrna, Georgia, for New York City. Almost immediately she was offered a modeling contract by the Click agency, and shortly thereafter secured a role in her first feature film. Never mind that prior to this her sole acting credits were a couple of high school plays.

Having family connections didn't hurt. Roberts's older siblings, brother Eric and sister Lisa, are actors as well. It was at Lisa's apartment in New York that Roberts made her home away from home at age 17, and it was Eric who secured the novice actress her first movie role playing his on-screen sister in the still unreleased 1986 western *Blood Red.*

The theatrical seeds were sown early in Roberts's childhood. In the 1960s, her parents operated a workshop for actors and writers in Atlanta, and young Julia spent her toddler years taking in family productions of Shakespeare in the park. Although the theatrical workshop was a financial disaster and disbanded after her parents' divorce in 1971 (her father subsequently sold vacuum cleaners until his death five years later, and her mother became a church secretary), it served to infect all the Roberts children with what matriarch Betty calls "the family disease." While siblings Eric and Lisa pursued acting singlemindedly throughout their growing-up years, Julia's acting bug remained latent. She long harbored the dream of becoming a veterinarian, but remarked to *Rolling Stone* that the interest in acting was, all the same, "just kind of there in my mind all the time." Of the three adult Roberts children (there is also a younger sister, teenager Nancy), Eric has had the most formal training. He studied at London's prestigious Royal Academy of Dramatic Art and finished up at New York's American Academy of Dramatic Arts, while Lisa trained at the Neighborhood Playhouse in New York.

Moves to New York

When Julia Roberts moved to New York, her initial plan was to study acting. However, she soon found that the academic route just didn't work for her. As she told *American Film,* "I never really made it to acting school. I went to acting classes a few times, but it never seemed very conducive to what I wanted to do, somehow. I never really decided, I'll go to school, I won't go to school—things just sort of happened. Sometimes people seem kind of disappointed by that; they want to hear about all these grueling years." She did bounce around for a year, on the one hand enjoying the bohemian life in Greenwich Village with her sister Lisa, and on the other, plunging herself into auditions for commercials and film and TV work, but coming up empty. As she reflected on that time in *American Film*, "I don't think I really impressed anyone. I didn't get called back a lot, just enough to keep on going." That's when her brother Eric stepped in to pave the way for her film debut—her first professional job. As *Blood Red*'s director Peter Masterson recalled in *People*: Eric "just said, 'I've got this sister. Is it okay if she's my sister?' He just said that she was good."

That was just the push Julia Roberts needed to get her career rolling. Shortly after *Blood Red*, she landed a role in an episode of TV's *Crime Story*; then, in the summer of 1987 she had the good fortune of shooting three movies back to back. The first two were rather inconsequential: the shallow teen dud *Satisfaction*, in which Roberts portrayed a bass player in an all-girl rock band; and the little-seen HBO movie *Baja, Oklahoma*, where she played Lesley Ann Warren's free-spirited daughter. But it was the coming-of-age, girl-buddy feature *Mystic Pizza* that finally provided the showcase for Roberts's star presence to shine. Well received upon its release in 1988, this unpretentious, gentle little film became the beginning of the big time for the actress. Portraying a feisty Portuguese American waitress in a performance charged with sexuality, Roberts became a darling of the critics and the new find atop every casting director's list. As good as the other actresses were who shared the screen with her, they tended to fade from view—all eyes were hypnotically focused on Roberts as she proceeded to singlehandedly steal every scene. As Nancy Mills wrote in *Cosmopolitan*, "Her gutsy, sultry Daisy Araujo, eager to escape the confines of a Connecticut fishing village, struck many as a reminder of those forties sirens who had oomph as well as intelligence."

Among those taking notice of her magnetic *Mystic Pizza* performance was director Herbert Ross, who sought out Roberts to join the star-studded cast of his *Steel Magnolias*. Working alongside such stellar company as Sally Field, Shirley MacLaine, Olympia Dukakis, Daryl Hannah, and Dolly Parton—on only Roberts's second major film—was a heady and enlightening experience for Roberts. "I learned so much from those women," she told *American Film*. "I owe them a lot more than I could ever articulate. Just watching five tremendous women do what they do close to perfectly." With her intensely moving portrayal of Shelby, Sally Field's dying, diabetic daughter, Roberts demonstrated remarkable range for someone so new to film acting. The understated sweetness and sorrow of *Steel Magnolias'* Shelby was worlds away from the lusty, wisecracking bombshell of *Mystic Pizza*. With *Steel Magnolias* Roberts secured her place among Hollywood's elite. In a cast filled with Oscar-winning veterans, it was only newcomer Roberts who walked away with accolades: a Golden Globe Award and an Academy Award nomination.

Becomes household word with Pretty Woman

With her next film—the enormously successful *Pretty Woman*—Roberts became a household word and picked up best-actress honors with an additional Golden Globe Award and another Oscar nomination. Although zealous fans made it the number two box-office smash of 1990 and the highest-grossing romantic comedy in cinematic history, *Pretty Woman* was more often than not condemned by the critics for being insultingly simplistic and sexist. Richard Corliss of *Time* felt that it came "close to finding the least admirable characters [a prostitute and a greedy tycoon] to build a feel good movie around," and that it pandered to the lowest common denominator with its "mechanical titillation and predictable twists." Many critics, however, were quite smitten by Roberts's sexy comedic charm, and addressed their objections to the ho-hum script. "As a sexy, free-lance hooker who wins the heart of a cool and powerful corporate raider ... Roberts exudes a melting warmth, a well-honed wit and a smile so disarming it's dangerous," extolled *Newsweek*'s David Ansen, declaring that her "delectable comic performance in *Pretty Woman* turns an all too familiar romantic formula into a surprising treat." Even the *New York Times* gushed that Roberts "is so enchantingly beautiful, so funny, so natural and such an absolute delight that it is hard to hold anything against the movie." The *Times* further pronounced that Roberts "is a complete knockout, and this performance will make her a major star."

That it did. A tremendous publicity storm descended upon Roberts when *Pretty Woman* was released in the spring of 1990, and her phone rang off the hook with endless requests for photo sessions and interviews. Her comely image was splashed across countless magazine covers (she even became the first woman to grace the cover of *Gentlemen's Quarterly*), and she made every "most beautiful women in the world" list that was compiled that year. For while *Pretty Woman* displayed the actress's comedic flair, it also trumpeted her sex appeal to full advantage. The movie never could have reached the heady heights it did without the considerable aesthetic attributes of its star. Audiences and critics alike fell in love with a unique beauty marked by the enormity of its features—the mile-wide smile set off by a pair of supple, voluptuous lips, deep, cocoa-brown eyes framed by a set of expansively arched eyebrows, a wild mane of auburn hair, and what *Pretty Woman* director Garry Marshall described in *Rolling Stone* as "possibly the longest legs since Wilt Chamberlain."

Her box-office appeal assured, Roberts became a hot property with a jam-packed schedule. Ever honing her versatility, she immediately switched gears from romantic comedy to shoot two films in the thriller genre, *Flatliners* and *Sleeping With the Enemy*, both of which went on to enjoy financial success. *Flatliners*, released in the summer of 1990, saw Roberts as a cerebral medical school student intent on experiencing temporary lab-induced death, while *Sleeping With the Enemy*, released the following winter, proved Roberts's ability as a serious dramatic actress with her portrayal of a housewife seeking refuge from an abusive husband. The directors of both films had nothing but praise for Roberts. *Flatliners* director Joel Schumacher was particularly impressed with her complexity, while *Sleeping With the Enemy*'s Joseph Ruben noted in *Rolling Stone* that Roberts has two things going. There's something that happens photographically with her, that star quality you hear about. And she's got this emotional vulnerability that lets you see and feel everything that's going on with her. And the two of them together bam."

Roberts's next two projects were a serious film about death, as well as one that took her into never-never land. The first, *Dying Young*, cast Roberts as a hired companion to a terminally ill leukemia patient with whom she falls in love. The second project had her suspended in wires as Tinkerbell in *Hook*, Steven Spielberg's big-budget adaptation of Peter Pan. When asked in *Vanity Fair* why she chose to play Tinkerbell, Roberts responded: "Well ... I've always loved Tinkerbell, first of all. I thought it would be nice to be in a movie that was more focused toward children."

Takes time off

Because Roberts became so hot, so fast, she found herself exhausted and badly in need of some time off. So after *Hook* she essentially took two years off, during which she could relax away from the spotlight. As Joel Schumacher revealed in *Vanity Fair*, "[Roberts] needed this time off. Deserved it. If she had kept up her professional pace, then people would have accused her of being a workaholic. You can't win. I mean, though she's very sophisticated in many, many ways now, she's still so very young, and needed some time so she could grow up a bit."

She also needed to get away from the public scrutiny of her private life. In a short period of time Roberts left a string of broken hearts. When filming *Satisfaction*, she met and began living with costar Liam Neeson, who was 16 years her senior. The next year on the set of *Steel Magnolias* she was teamed with Dylan McDermott, who played her husband on-

Among Roberts's hobbies are needlepoint, knitting, and collecting furniture.

screen and her fiancé off-screen. Her most notorious love interest was *Flatliners'* costar Kiefer Sutherland, with whom she broke her engagement in 1991—three days before they were to wed. Soon thereafter, she flew off to Ireland with Sutherland's friend and fellow actor Jason Patric.

Returns to Hollywood

While a two-year hiatus might have proved disastrous for other actresses, Roberts was able to command $8.5 million when she returned to the screen in the 1993 movie *The Pelican Brief.* Based on John Grisham's bestseller, *The Pelican Brief* centers on a law student (Roberts) who discovers the man responsible for the murder of two Supreme Court justices. The movie scored well at the box office, though some critics were less than impressed. The 1994 romantic comedy *I Love Trouble,* in which she costarred with Nick Nolte, was neither a critical nor popular favorite.

While filming *The Pelican Brief,* Roberts shocked media and fans alike by secretly marrying the offbeat country music star Lyle Lovett. After the intense scrutiny given her previous relationships, Roberts pulled off a coup by keeping not only the wedding, but also their very relationship, a secret. In an effort to keep their lives private while dating, the two developed a secret code—Lovett would dedicate songs to Fiona (Roberts's middle name) or to his "very special friend." The marriage is unorthodox in many ways, with their busy schedules often keeping them apart for weeks at a time. Yet Roberts maintains that the separations have not hurt their marriage, which remains "blissful." Roberts described her feeling in a *Rolling Stone* interview: "I think that when you have a great love, and you're secure in that, it doesn't matter how far apart you are. Lyle and I actually spend a lot more time together than people imagine."

Robert's most recent projects include the film *Mary Reilly,* a take on the Dr. Jekyll and Mr. Hyde story, in which she plays a chamber maid opposite John Malkovich, and a remake of the 1939 film classic *The Women,* in which she will costar with Meg Ryan. Although Roberts takes her work very seriously, cultivating a close, supportive base of family and friends is the top priority for her. "I mean, acting is a true love of mine," she told *Rolling Stone,* "but it's not the true love. There are times when I get so bogged down by the politics of this business that I just have these great domestic fantasies. Being at home, and being quiet, and reading, and having a garden, and doing all that stuff. Taking care of a family.

Those are the most important things. Movies will come and go, but family is a real kind of rich consistency."

Sources

American Film, July 1990.

Cosmopolitan, November 1989.

Harper's Bazaar, February 1989; September 1989.

Newsweek, March 26, 1990.

New York Times, March 18, 1990; March 23, 1990.

Parade, February 24, 1991.

People, Summer 1990; September 17, 1990; December 31, 1990; January 7, 1991; February 25, 1991; March 4, 1991; July 1, 1991; July 12, 1993; May 9, 1994; May 16, 1994.

Premiere, December 1990; December 1991.

Rolling Stone, August 9, 1990; July 14-28, 1994.

Star-Ledger (Newark, NJ), February 24, 1991.

Teen, December 1990.

Time, April 2, 1990; February 18, 1991; December 20, 1993; May 2, 1994.

USA Weekend, February 8-10, 1991.

Vanity Fair, October 1993.

Vogue, September 1988; April 1990.

The Rolling Stones

Often billed as "the world's greatest rock and roll band," the Rolling Stones have earned the title—if not for their musical prowess, then certainly for their longevity.

ROCK GROUP

O ften billed as "the world's greatest rock and roll band," the Rolling Stones have earned the title—if not for their musical prowess, then certainly for their longevity. The roots of the group go back to 1949, when Keith Richards and Mick Jagger, both from Dartford, England, went to school together. It would take another 11 years, however, before their paths would cross again. To their amazement, they discovered that both of them had grown up listening to the same great American bluesmen and rockers like Chuck Berry and Bo Diddley. The two formed a friendship that was based around one common interest: music.

The band forms

At the time, Jagger was attending the London School of Economics while Richards was struggling at Sidcup Art College. Soon they found out about a local musician named Alexis Korner who held blues jams at the Ealing Club. After Jagger began to sing for Korner's Blues Incorporated, he decided to join a group that Richards was putting together. Other members included Ian Stewart, Dick Taylor, Tony Chapman, and a guitar play-

The Rolling Stones—Richards, Wood, Jagger, and Watts.

er named Brian Jones. While Richards was more into the Berry school of rock guitar, Jones was pure blues and often referred to himself as Elmo Lewis (in reference to the slide guitarist Elmore James).

Charlie Watts was already making a fair living drumming for a jazz combo when he was persuaded to replace Tony Chapman. The oldest member, a rocking bassist named Bill Wyman, hooked up immediately thereafter to complete the rhythm section. With the shrewd talents of manager/publicist Andrew Loog Oldham, they began opening for Blues Inc. at London's Marquee Club in 1963, billed as "Brian Jones and Mick Jagger and The Rollin' Stones" (after a Muddy Waters tune). Dick Taylor was no longer in the band at this time.

With hair longer than any other group and an attitude that made the Beatles look like choirboys, the Stones took full advantage of their image as "the group parents love to hate." "That old idea of not letting white children listen to black music is true," Jagger told Jonathan Cott, "cause if you want white children to remain what they are, they mustn't." Their negative public image was constantly fueled by Oldham, who also decided that Stewart's old-fashioned presence did not fit in with the rest of the band and so delegated him to the background. His tenure with the band from then on was brief.

Sign contract with Decca Records

Oldham quickly secured the Stones a contract with Decca Records and in June 1963 they released their first single, a cover of Chuck Berry's "Come On" backed with "I Want to be Loved." Reaction was good and it would only take another six months for the group to make it big. Continuing their eight-month residence at the Crawdaddy Club in Richmond, they released their version of the Beatles' "I Wanna Be Your Man," followed by Buddy Holly's "Not Fade Away," which made it to Number Three in Great Britain. Their fourth single, "It's All Over Now" by Bobby Womack, would climb all the way to the top in their homeland. Their next hit, "Little Red Rooster," likewise reached Number One but was banned in the United States because of perceived lewd content.

They already had two albums out in England by the time they broke the U.S. Top 10 with "The Last Time," written by Jagger and Richards. And in the summer of 1965 they had a worldwide Number One hit with "Satisfaction." Propelled by Richards' fuzz-tone riff and Jagger's lyrics about a man who couldn't get enough, the song immediately secured a seat in rock history. Oldham had played up the outlaw image of the band to the point where they became his creation, and he was no longer needed.

Allan Klein took over as manager and in 1966, after having relied on other artists' songs, the Rolling Stones released their first all-originals LP, *Aftermath*. The band was plagued by drug busts during the mid-sixties psychedelic era and in 1967 the Stones recorded their reply to the Beatles' *Sgt. Pepper's Lonely Hearts Club Band*, titled *Their Satanic Majesties Request*. The album paled in comparison to the Beatles masterpiece and is noted mainly as the last album Brian Jones actually worked on, later becoming too involved in drugs.

Richards shoulders Jones's part

Picking up Jones's slack, Richards met the challenge with 1968's *Beggar's Banquet*. His acoustic guitar work sounded as full as an orchestra on "Street Fighting Man," and one of the most deadly electric solos ever recorded appears on "Sympathy for the Devil." It was obvious the Stones didn't need Jones anymore and he officially quit (or was booted out) on June 9, 1969. Less than one month later he was found drowned in a swimming pool, with the official cause listed as "death by misadventure."

Two days later, the Stones had their replacement in former guitarist for John Mayall's Bluesbreakers Mick Taylor. His first gig was a free concert in memory of Jones at Hyde Park. Taylor's influence would bring the level of musicianship up a few notches until he quit in 1975. Their first album after he joined was still mostly a Richards album, however. *Let It Bleed* was released to coincide with an American tour and contained two particularly haunting tunes, "Midnight Rambler" and "Gimme Shelter." The latter became the title of the Stones' movie of their free concert at Altamont, California, which became a disaster when Hell's Angels members (hired as security guards) stabbed a youth to death right in front of the stage.

In 1971 the Stones formed their own label, Rolling Stones Records, and began to expand their musical horizons. *Sticky Fingers* contained jazz with "Can't You Hear Me Knockin" and the country-flavored "Dead Flowers" continued the trend of "Honky Tonk Women." Their next album, *Exile on Main Street,* oddly enough, was passed over by critics when it came out, but over the years has come to be regarded as probably their finest recording. With Richards hanging out with singer-songwriter Gram Parsons, the country influence was stronger than ever but the album—four sides of vintage Stones at their tightest, and loosest—also contains gospel ("I Just Want To See His Face"), blues ("Shake Your Hips"), and full-tilt rock ("Rip This Joint").

Their next two albums, *Goat's Head Soup* and *It's Only Rock and Roll,* contain both outstanding tracks and what some critics considered real dogs. "Time Waits For No One," with a beautiful solo by Taylor, shows just how much the Stones had changed, yet tracks like "Star Star" reveal just the opposite: the bad boys of rock just couldn't grow up. Five years was enough for Taylor and he decided to walk away from one of the most sought-after positions in rock. "The fact is I was becoming stagnant and lazy with the Stones. I really got off on playing with them, but it wasn't enough of a challenge," he told *Rolling Stone* magazine. Many guitarists were rumored to be taking his place (Roy Buchanan, Jeff Beck, Peter Frampton, and Rory Gallagher among them).

Ron Wood joins band

The obvious choice, though, was Rod Stewart's right-hand man, Ron Wood. Wood pinch-hit for Taylor on the 1975 tour of America, bounding

The Rolling Stones on *The Ed Sullivan Show*, July 10, 1966.

back and forth with the Faces before finally settling with the Stones. The first full album he contributed to was *Black and Blue* in 1976. Once again the Stones stretched out by dabbling in reggae ("Cherry Oh"), disco ("Hot Stuff"), and a smoky lounge lizard treatment on "Melody." Wood fit the Stones mold perfectly, almost a carbon copy of Richards both physically and musically. The group's future was in doubt in 1977 when Richards was busted in Toronto for dealing heroin, but his sentence did not include any jail time. Save for 1978's *Some Girls,* the next four Stones records seem indistinguishable from each other. The songs are vehicles for Richards's guitar hooks with nothing equaling the emotion of previous hits like "You Can't Always Get What You Want" or "Moonlight Mile."

Richards was reportedly not too happy when Jagger took time off to work on his first solo album (even though Wyman and Wood both had records outside the group). Jagger refused to tour to support the Stones' *Dirty Work* LP, instead hitting the road to promote his own *She's The Boss.* Richards had toured with Wood's New Barbarians in 1979, but he was outraged that Jagger would make the Stones a second choice. "I felt like I had failed. I couldn't keep my band together," he told the *Detroit Free Press.* He stated that the Stones will "have to wait for me. They kind of pushed me into this solo thing, which I really didn't want, and now they're paying a price." Richards released his own album, *Talk Is Cheap,* with plenty of barbs for Jagger. "I'm enjoying myself too much to all of a sudden stop," Richards said.

Rumors of the band's breakup were quieted in 1989, when the Stones announced plans for a new album and a world tour. A favorite with critics, *Steel Wheels* quickly sold over two million copies; the tour, sponsored by Anheuser-Busch, drew barbs from many for being so blatantly commercialized. Despite the criticism, however, the Steel Wheels Tour—which reportedly raked in over $140 million—was a hit with music reviewers and fans. The 1990 *Rolling Stone* readers and critics polls selected the Stones as best band and artist of the year, and cited Steel Wheels as 1989's best tour.

The group's ability to overcome internal dissention and the toll of more than 25 years in rock and roll's fast lane to put together the industry's success story of the year surprised some observers, but not the Stones themselves. "The Stones, it's a weird thing, it's almost like a soap opera," Richards told *Rolling Stone.* "We needed a break to find out what you can and can't do on your own. I had to find myself a whole new band.... But then I realized maybe that's the way to keep the band together: leaving for a bit.... I never doubted the band personally—but I'm an incredible optimist where this band is concerned. It never occurred to me that they might not be able to cut it. Absolutely not."

In July 1994 fans eagerly awaited the newest Stones album, *Voodoo Lounge,* which rose nearly to the top of the album charts in its first week of release—selling 153,000 copies. This success came despite the fact that founding member Bill Wyman had left the band in 1992. As reported in the *Detroit Free Press,* Richards said he was at first "ready to murder" the bassist, but the band found working without Wyman "a lot easier than we thought it would be." After auditioning a number of bassists, the band let Charlie Watts choose his counterpart in the rhythm section, and the result was Darryl Jones. Jones had previously worked with such greats as Miles Davis and Sting.

The name for *Voodoo Lounge* was inspired by a kitten that Richards picked up in Barbados. He named the cat Voodoo, and when the Stones started recording in Ireland, Woods put up a sign in the studio that said "Voodoo Lounge."

In addition to the tremendous popular response *Voodoo Lounge* has received, the critical response was also enthusiastic. Most praised the breadth of the album, which at times delves into such disparate traditions as Celtic folk, country, funk, and blues. According to Gary Graff of the *Detroit Free Press*, "This time the Stones provoke with their music, and the array of approaches on *Voodoo Lounge* makes each listen fresh proof that the Stones are far from a spent musical quantity."

Sources

Detroit Free Press, December 4, 1988; July 10, 1994; July 22, 1994; August 3, 1994.

Detroit News, September 27, 1988.

Guitar Player, February 1980; April 1983; May 1986; January 1987.

Guitar World, March 1985; March 1986.

Metro Times (Detroit), December 7, 1988.

Oakland Press (Oakland Co., MI), December 4, 1988.

Rolling Stone, May 6, 1976; May 20, 1976; May 5, 1977; November 3, 1977; November 17, 1977; June 29, 1978; August 10, 1978; September 7, 1978; March 8, 1990.

Axl Rose

Born in 1962
Lafayette, Indiana

SINGER, SONGWRITER, AND
BANDLEADER

Axl Rose, lead singer and songwriter for the heavy metal band Guns N' Roses, has mined his dark moods and hellbent-for-destruction attitude to produce some of the most riveting rock music in recent years. Controversy swirls around Rose almost constantly; his lyrics have offended blacks and gays, his quarrels with fellow band members and other artists are legion, and his drug-and-alcohol-fueled lifestyle has raised concerns among parents of the teenagers who flock to his shows. Rose refuses to apologize for either his message or his methods, both of which have propelled Guns N' Roses to the front rank of modern rock bands. "This is ... art; this is how I feel," he said of his music in *Spin*. "You don't like it—don't ... listen. It's real easy."

"We need Guns N' Roses.... If everyone on the planet 'just said no' tomorrow, our culture, our society, would still need someone to celebrate and act out the great [self-sacrificing] trip. It's as old as our civilization."—Danny Sugerman

Spin correspondent Dean Kuipers described Axl Rose as a "rust belt punk" who "has built an empire from the chips constantly falling from his shoulder. It appears that since a very young age he has had a singular mission: to prove to himself that some piece of America would accept his mind, his obvious talent, and even his rage, without any compromise." Rose seems to have found his piece of America. The Guns N' Roses debut album, *Appetite for Destruction*, has sold in excess of 13 million copies; the 1991 releases *Use Your Illusion I* and *II* were shipped platinum (a million copies), and lingered long on the *Billboard* charts. Their 1993 release, *The Spaghetti Incident?*, also met with success.

The challenge facing Rose, who has drawn such gut-wrenching emotion from his own anger and frustration, is to adopt a path that will allow him to be true to his vision without falling prey to self-destruction. Author Danny Sugerman put it this way in *Spin*: "Axl [is] in the perfect position to be the first of the Too Fast to Live, Too Young to Die set to avoid the early death which seems to be an occupational hazard of the artist whose sensitivity connects and enriches all who listen—yet eats away at the artist."

The making of Axl Rose began in Lafayette, Indiana, a town squarely divided between the "haves" and the "have nots." Kuipers offered a poignant description of Rose's hometown: "Lafayette, Indiana, is a blue-collar town about 65,000 small, the eastern part of the city separated by the rank Wabash River from west Lafayette and Purdue University. Not unlike many small towns, the river is a demarcation zone. One side doesn't mix with the other, and for kids the rivalry is obsessive. The lower-middle-class residents of east Lafayette work at A. E. Staley's corn syrup plants, out at the Subaru-Isuzu factory, or at Eli Lilly Pharmaceuticals. They fix their own cars at curb-side."

Grew up angry

Rose was born into this environment as William Bailey, in the early 1960s. He grew up holding his own in a violent world, the quintessential "angry young man" who felt put upon by every authority figure in his path. At a 1991 concert in Indianapolis, Rose began the show with a few observations about his home. "I grew up in this state for two-thirds of my life," he said. "It seems to me that, basically, there are a lot of ... scared old people in this ... state and for two-thirds of my life those ... old people tried to hold [me] down." Friends of the teenage Bill Bailey remember him as a sensitive boy with a hair-trigger temper that got him into fights with police, girlfriends, and other teenagers.

Monica Gregory, who runs a rock clothing shop in Lafayette, told *Spin* that the future rock star was as often a victim as a perpetrator of violence.

"He got hassled a lot for a variety of reasons," Gregory said. "It happened to him in Chicago once—he was with my ex-husband at the time—and for very little reason, these guys started hassling them: 'Who do you think you are? Bon Jovi?' It was like: 'No, leave me alone.' The guys with the ties and short hair were yelling obscenities at Axl and Dana 'cause they got long hair. All the cops came in and basically beat the crap outta Axl.... Just because."

By the time he was 20, Rose had been jailed on numerous occasions for battery, contributing to the delinquency of a minor, public intoxication, criminal trespass, and mischief. A high school dropout, he spent much of his time with a small group of friends in his bedroom in his grandmother's house. Rose brought a piano into the bedroom and the gatherings became musical happenings that spawned bits of songwriting or impromptu composing. "The creative side he had was so intense," Gregory told *Spin*. "And I think it grounded the little group of people that was there for I don't know how many years." One of that group was guitarist Izzy Stradlin, born Jeff Isabelle. After Stradlin graduated from Jefferson High School in 1979, he decided to move to Los Angeles and try to find work with a rock group there.

Leaves for L.A.

Rose followed, but the two had little luck at first. In the summer of 1982, according to *Spin*, Rose returned to Lafayette and girlfriend Gina Siler. After some idyllic months, Rose persuaded Siler to finish high school early and join him in Los Angeles. They left Lafayette together that year and drove across the country to Hollywood, where they rented a cheap apartment.

"The people back in Indiana, they missed out on something that I got to experience," Siler told *Spin*. "I lived with him during that period of 'Bill' to 'Bill Axl' to 'Axl.' It was the strangest thing, because some days he'd be Bill, some days he'd be Axl, some days I didn't know who the hell he was.... For a long time he tried to dispel the fact that he had ever lived in the Midwest. He was trying to build an image, and a persona of a musician he thought he wanted to be."

The relationship between Rose and Siler fizzled, but Rose and Stradlin were able to form a workable band and find gigs at local clubs in the Los Angeles area. From the very outset of their career, Guns N' Roses capitalized on the "party hard" image. Club ads for their shows often read "FRESH FROM DETOX" or "ADDICTED: ONLY THE STRONG SUR-

VIVE." Singer Rose and rhythm guitarist Stradlin recruited lead guitarist Slash, bass player Duff McKagan, and drummer Steven Adler. For a time the group members lived together in a studio apartment. Most of the money that came in was spent on drugs and alcohol; heroin became the drug of choice and has since proven a difficult habit to break for Rose, Stradlin, and Adler, who finally split with the band over tension stemming from his addiction. Slash too has battled the drug.

In 1986 Guns N' Roses signed a contract with Geffen Records, but their wild antics alienated producers and managers. Eventually, with the help of engineer Mike Clink, the band produced its first full-length album, *Appetite for Destruction,* in 1987. Rose wrote the album's lyrics and sang lead on all the songs, revealing one of the strongest male voices in rock since the early days of Robert Plant, lead vocalist of the 1970s heavy metal juggernaut Led Zeppelin. However, the release's frank portrayal of violence and its pro-white-male bias found little airplay on radio or MTV. The album languished in sales at first until one of the cuts, "Sweet Child o' Mine," got grass-roots word-of-mouth support from fans.

Guns N' Roses gain exposure as opening act for Aerosmith

Guns N' Roses reached just the right audience when they became the opening act for Aerosmith on a 1987 tour. By the end of the tour *Appetite for Destruction* had gone platinum in sales and was topping the *Billboard* rock charts. *Philadelphia Inquirer* contributor John Milward wrote: "No law says that rock and rollers have to be good role models, but the blue-noses of the Parents Resource Music Committee couldn't have dreamed up a group with such exploitative bad attitudes as Guns N' Roses. *Appetite for Destruction* unspools like a cheesy movie about the Hollywood lowlife ... [portraying] a wicked, corrupting world and [suggesting] that it only makes sense to have some fun on the way to hell."

Life at the top has done little to improve Axl Rose's legendary temper. Some sources say that during production for the group's second full-length album he threatened to quit the band almost every other day. Kuipers noted: "Axl and the rest of G N' R remain as conflicted, hair-trigger, and tight in everyone's face as ever. In the midst of wild success they have been variously drug addicted, paranoid, homophobic, racist, xenophobic [afraid of foreigners], ruthless, violent, a threat to the liberty of the press, and a pain in the ass to almost everyone." Several of their songs drew protests from numerous fronts; live shows were performed after long delays by band members visibly under the influence of drugs.

If the songs and the artists offended some, they also found sympathetic followers. "There's always an audience for wild-eyed hellions with electric guitars," wrote Milward in the *Philadelphia Inquirer*. "The Guns N' Roses difference is that youths somehow sense that these guys' raucous sounds are more genuine than those of their heavy-metal peers. They're reckless kids who have stumbled onto a career, and they seem so out of control that you can't help believing the most scandalous stories. They're stupid enough to live out each and every rock-and-roll cliche but talented enough to spike their best songs with that same 80-proof energy."

Society may have "hired" Axl Rose to act out his personal self-destruction onstage—and in the tabloids—but his talent is not to be taken lightly. "Some years ago, rock became a very big business," declared Dave DiMartino in *Entertainment Weekly*. "That Guns N' Roses are now a part of that business is a given; that their behavior goes so much against its grain provides many with hope, inspiration, and, best of all, in the view of more than one Guns N' Roses fan, [a] sorely needed kick in some very complacent behinds." Rose's perfectionism delayed the releases of *Use Your Illusion I* and *II* for almost a year; he was determined not to put anything but the best product on the shelves for his fans. Rose told *Musician:* "One of the reasons why Guns N' Roses is successful and people are into it as much as they are [is that] the truth comes through and you can feel it in the music. We're being as honest as we can. Whether you like the opinions or not is another story. But it's real."

Rose's antics offstage made headlines a number of times in 1991. First he was accused by a neighbor of battery; the charges, well covered by the press, were eventually dropped. Tabloids also printed lurid details of his brief marriage to Erin Everly, including allegations that he physically abused her (she sued him for this treatment in 1994). The most highly publicized incident, however, occurred in St. Louis in the late summer of 1991. In the midst of a live concert, Rose became infuriated when a fan near the stage continually photographed him. After repeated requests to security guards to remove the fan, Rose leaped into the crowd and tried to wrest the camera from the man's hands. Then Rose and the other band members left the stage. The crowd in turn became ugly and surged toward the stage, breaking the barrier that might have held them back. A riot ensued, during which police and security guards battered people with nightsticks while other concertgoers damaged or stole Guns N' Roses' equipment, speakers, and microphones. Ultimately, 60 people required hospitalization, a brand new concert hall suffered $500,000 in damages, and the band found itself in the middle of a tour without any equipment. Critics pointed fingers at Rose for starting the riot and St.

Louis authorities actually lodged charges against the singer, which were eventually settled.

Rose defended himself in *Musician.* Noting that he "wasn't Mother Theresa that night," he added that the band has to contend constantly with bootlegged videotapes and audiotapes of their work. "I have to enforce that there's no cameras, no videotapes and no tape-recorders because I don't want crappy material out there," he said. "I want to approve tapes before they go out. If we did a [weak] version of a song one night for whatever reasons and we had technical difficulties, I don't want that being a representation of me out there. There's things done to protect the fans and there are things done to protect the artist. In St. Louis there was no respect for fans or the artist." Rose primarily blamed shoddy security measures for the incident in St. Louis. The singer told *Musician:* "As of right now we are considered the most dangerous band in the world. That's kind of a good reputation to have as far as a rock band is concerned. That means you're doing great and you're going to do better." Still, that reputation can be a personal liability. Rose has undergone intensive psychotherapy to try to root out the source of his frustrations and self-destructive behavior. "I was told that my mental circuitry was all twisted," he said in *Entertainment Weekly.* The magazine also suggested that Rose had been diagnosed as a manic depressive and placed on lithium carbonate, the maintenance treatment for that disorder. Unnamed sources quoted in the magazine claim, however, that Rose does not always take the medication, and that after some periods of calm a torrent of rage and mayhem is entirely predictable.

Rose told *Musician* that objectionable crowd behavior at Guns N' Roses concerts is a byproduct of the "bad guy" image he has been handed by the press. "It's really hard to handle the frustration I get, and the anger, at being portrayed consistently so negatively," he said. In fact, Rose is known among those closest to him as a devoted artist who means well and who is committed to pleasing his fans. "To view this band merely as hard-rockin' bad boys is a big mistake," wrote Janiss Garza in *Entertainment Weekly.* "They also write songs that are complex, structurally and emotionally." In concluding, Garza asked: "When a group is so openly willing to bare its soul ... does anyone have the right to play the role of judge and jury?"

The band's 1993 release, *The Spaghetti Incident?*, has none of the blatantly racist lyrics of their earlier work. *Time* reported that, instead, Guns N' Roses "present a collection of tributes to the 70s punk rock that inspired them—from the Sex Pistols' 'Black Leather' to the Stooges' 'Raw Power'— and in doing so they find a way not only to display superb musicianship but also to express anger without their characteristic crassness.... Several of the songs contain obscenities directed at society in general, but not at any specific group. The Gunners could learn a lesson from that. Their musical heroes were able to create great vitriolic songs without letting their rage spill over into bashing minorities. Punks don't have to be jerks."

Sources

Entertainment Weekly, August 9, 1991; September 20, 1991.

Musician, September 1991.

New Yorker, November 11, 1991.

People, December 30, 1991; September 13, 1993.

Philadelphia Inquirer, February 16, 1989.

Rolling Stone, November 17, 1988; December 9, 1993.

Spin, November 1990; September 1991.

Time, December 6, 1993.

Roseanne

Born in 1953
Salt Lake City, Utah

"Nobody gets more out of [Roseanne] than me.... It helps me remember the humanity in everybody. I try to have that in every show every week—some redeemable kernel so that I know that it's there, too. I'm watching the show just like everyone else."

ACTRESS AND COMEDIAN

Roseanne is one of the most powerful women in Hollywood. Her comedy has been called new wave, feminist, and revolutionary, yet her subject matter—marriage, kids, housework—is conventional. Critics have found her both "dangerous" and irresistible. Her hit show, *Roseanne,* is entering its seventh season and shows no sign of stopping. It is the only television show that has retained its top-10 rating in its original run, as well as in syndication. Tom Shales, the television critic for the *Washington Post,* praised *Roseanne* in *Vanity Fair*: "When I watch the show, I not only enjoy it, I marvel at it—the way [Roseanne] avoids all the pat answers and sappiness of most sitcoms. The show stands alone. It always has. And she has been able to retain the high quality. Sometimes it's very dark and bitter, and it scares me a little, but the audience seems to go right along with it."

Raised among Mormons

Born and raised in Salt Lake City, Utah, Roseanne, who is Jewish, was one of the few non-Mormons at her school. At Christmas, her teachers would ask "our little Jewish girl" to sing about the dreidel (a Top brought out at Hanukkah). "So I would sing the dreidel song, and then explain why I didn't believe in Jesus," she told Gioia Diliberto of *People*. The rest of the time, she recalled to Stu Schreiberg in *USA Weekend*, "I'd sit in the back of classrooms and had very few friends." At the age of 16, Roseanne was hit by a car and knocked unconscious. She came out of the coma several days later and experienced a "grotesque personality change," quoted the *New York Times'* Joy Horowitz. Roseanne was hospitalized for nearly a year, and her experience there was so painful that she still refuses to discuss it in detail.

After her recovery, Roseanne became pregnant and gave up the baby for adoption. (Eighteen years later, she was reunited with her daughter. The two now share a close relationship.) She later left high school and moved to Colorado. There she met and married a local postal clerk, had three children, and worked at a variety of low-paying jobs. For entertainment, she frequently went to comedy clubs, most of which were dominated by male comics doing what Roseanne considered sexist material. She decided it was time to even the score.

Breaks into stand-up comedy

In 1981 she delivered a five-minute monologue at a Denver club. Soon after, she was playing clubs throughout the West and Midwest. Her career took off after performing at the Comedy Store in Los Angeles. From there she appeared on network and cable television specials and was a frequent guest on *The Tonight Show*. Her routines included jabs at men—married and single—motherhood, and housekeeping. "Listen to her bag the bachelor ethos," wrote *Vogue*'s Tracy Young. "Get a relationship and face the *real* danger. Look at a mortgage for thirty years, you skydiving *wimps*." Helpless husbands and demanding children also drew her comic wrath. Young continued: "If husbands take a beating from [Roseanne], kids don't fare much better.... [She] reads the instructions on a bottle of aspirin as, 'Take two and keep away from the children.'"

In 1988, amid much publicity and fanfare, ABC-TV introduced *Roseanne*, a half-hour situation comedy starring Roseanne as a married mother of three. With few exceptions, *Roseanne* was instantly declared a hit. One critic called it a "grungy-funny sitcom" and "a standup *tour-de-force* with plot and dialogue." Some critics compared it to the classic television series *The Honeymooners,* which ran in the 1950s. They said Roseanne played Ralph Kramden to her television husband's composite portrayal of Alice and Norton. Unlike other television wives and mothers, as Horowitz noted, "Roseanne is flawed." Though she loves "her romantic sop of a husband," she never hesitates to point out his faults. In one episode, according to the critic, Roseanne tells him: "I put in eight hours a day at the factory, and then I come home and put in another eight hours.... And you don't do NOTHIN'!"

Wanted to create a more "honest" show

Roseanne set out to create a show that did not whitewash the difficulties of raising a family in late–twentieth–century America. She criticized typical family sitcoms for ignoring the real world. "Nothing in reality is ever addressed on sitcoms," she explained to Schrieberg. "Will Junior go out with the smart girl or the good-looking girl?' I want to deal with being broke, with the implied violence of family life." She told Horowitz, "I want to do real revolutionary TV.... I want to do a show that reflects how people really live. Telling the truth at any point in time is really revolutionary. I want this show to tell the horrible truth rather than parody the truth. When you tell the truth you don't insult anyone's intelligence."

Because Roseanne's vision for her show was so complete and unwavering, she ran into trouble with network management. The first season, in particular, was plagued with battles over artistic control. Roseanne felt that the show's producer, Matt Williams, wanted to portray feminist comedy as coarse and insulting. In an effort to produce the kind of show she wanted, Roseanne fired Williams, and a host of other producers, writers, and directors, until she found a group of people that could articulate her viewpoint.

Six years later, most critics and viewers would agree that she has admirably accomplished her goal. Robert A. Iger, the president of the ABC Television Network Group, shared his theories for the show's continued success with *Vanity Fair*: "In her own special way, [Roseanne] really speaks the truth to people through the voice of Roseanne Conner [her television character]. Roseanne Conner is probably the most honest character on network television. The credit there belongs largely to Roseanne Arnold, who just has an ability to speak to the people on an equal level. It's an amazing quality.... She may push the envelope in terms of television, but she doesn't push the envelope in terms of *life.*"

Controversial personal life

While her career has soared, Roseanne's personal life has been riddled with drama and controversy. She has published two autobiographies—*Roseanne: My Life as a Woman* (1989) and *My Lives* (1994)—that reveal a traumatic past and troubled present. With complete candor, she described the poverty and hurt she experienced while growing up. According to Roseanne, her parents subjected her to sexual, emotional, and physical abuse—charges they vehemently deny. She also tells of working as a prostitute in order to help support her kids, and of her battles with drugs. Speaking of *My Lives*, she told *Vanity Fair*, "I don't know why I did it." She continued, "Sometimes I think I wrote it as a cleansing thing, and sometimes I think I did it because I got involved with the recovery movement and wanted this to be inspirational. I've read a lot of recovery books. It took a long time to write this book. It was very painful. It cost me a lot."

Roseanne has a collection of 200 dolls and each doll represents one aspect of her personality.

Her troubled past has also affected her relationships with men. In 1989 Roseanne divorced her first husband, Bill Pentland, in order to marry Tom Arnold. She and Arnold met when both were doing stand-up comedy, and after sharing a close relationship for years, the two were married in January 1990. In May 1994 Roseanne filed for divorce from Arnold, citing irreconcilable differences. In the court papers Roseanne claimed that she suffered abuse during their marriage: "I now realize that I have been a classic battered and abused wife. Throughout our marriage [Arnold] hit me, struck me, has thrown objects at me, pinched me and verbally abused me." In response Arnold told *People*, "The allegations made against me are false." Whatever the truth, the two have moved on with their lives and each is involved in a new relationship.

When asked by *People* what she would like to do after her series ends, Roseanne responded: "First, I want to make my own movies—documentaries of interesting people I have met. Two, have an Oprah-type talk show. Three, read my poetry and set it to music. Four, move to a beach in Spain and become a nudist."

Sources

Detroit News, October 18, 1988.

Newsweek, October 31, 1988.

New York Times, October 16, 1988; May 15, 1994.

People, April 28, 1986; March 21, 1994; May 2, 1994.

USA Weekend, September 23-25, 1988.

Vanity Fair, February 1994.

Vogue, April 1987.

Arnold Schwarzenegger

Born July 30, 1947
Graz, Austria

"I never start evaluating how I do this. For me it's a total waste of time. Totally. I don't want to analyze yesterday. Tomorrow. Period. Because that's what counts."

ACTOR

With a heavy accent and a distinctive bodybuilder's physique, Arnold Schwarzenegger seemed an unlikely candidate for box-office superstardom. But that is exactly the position Schwarzenegger has achieved since his humble beginnings in the movie *Hercules Goes to New York*, in which he used the pseudonym Arnold Strong to mask his identity. Although he was already known for his bodybuilding titles, including Mr. Universe, and for his appearance in the documentary *Pumping Iron*, Schwarzenegger did not become a success in feature films until he landed the lead role in *Conan, The Barbarian* in 1982. That movie, which grossed more than $100 million worldwide, propelled him to international stardom. During the 1980s, his films grossed more than $1 billion, earning him the title "Superhero to the World." Schwarzenegger's success has not been limited to the movie world, however; he is also a real estate tycoon, owning property in southern California and Denver; and he married Maria Shriver, a successful national TV news anchor and one of the Kennedy clan.

Grew up in humble surroundings

Schwarzenegger came from very humble beginnings. He was born in a small village outside of Graz, Austria, where his house was not equipped with a telephone, flush toilet, or refrigerator until he was 14 years old. "With that kind of upbringing," commented Schwarzenegger in *Vanity Fair*, "you learn not to take anything for granted." Schwarzenegger's father was a policeman, and his only sibling, a brother, died in an auto accident.

Schwarzenegger claims that it was precisely this lack of material goods that served as his motivation to be successful. He began to look for a way out of his village when he was very young. Schwarzenegger would "daydream about success when I was ten years old. I would dream about America." At age 15, he committed himself to bodybuilding. He was soon winning competitions throughout Europe, and by age 20 he won his first Mr. Universe title.

In 1968 Schwarzenegger realized it was time to make a move on his dreams, and he came to America to participate in a Miami Beach bodybuilding contest. He was disappointed to lose in a contest he thought he could win easily, but the trip turned out to have a positive result. The well-known bodybuilder Joe Weider was impressed by Schwarzenegger, and asked him to come to Los Angeles. "I decided to move," said Schwarzenegger. "There was no alternative. The thought of going back to Austria or Germany was not an option. My vision of where I wanted to be in life was forward, and Austria would have been backward."

Settles into L.A.

The move marked a turning point in his career. Schwarzenegger, who was already known for his strictness and self-discipline, began to increase his training regimen. He attended school and studied English and business. Weider encouraged him to write articles on bodybuilding and pose for photographs. In the years from 1968 to 1980 Schwarzenegger climbed to the peak of his professional bodybuilding career, eventually accumulating an unheard-of seven Mr. Olympia titles.

Schwarzenegger, however, had his eyes on a bigger goal—he wanted to reach a larger audience, a movie audience. At a Mr. America contest in 1972, he met George Butler and Charles Gaines, who were interested in making a bodybuilding documentary called *Pumping Iron.* They were duly impressed by Schwarzenegger's physique. "Arnold is like the Matterhorn," Gaines commented. "We didn't discover him, we just noticed him first."

The notoriety he gained in *Pumping Iron* had an unusual side effect—it put Schwarzenegger at the forefront of the high-society crowd. He posed for artist Jamie Wyeth; was part of a living-art exhibit at the Whitney Museum; and he modeled for Andy Warhol pieces. Schwarzenegger used his increased visibility to promote his sport. "The whole thing was to make bodybuilding hip," he claimed, "to take it out of the sports page or the circus page or whatever and have it covered in the regular press."

Looks for success on own terms

Popularizing bodybuilding wasn't the only goal in Schwarzenegger's career. Before *Pumping Iron,* he had made a disastrous feature movie called *Hercules Goes to New York* under a pseudonym. Despite the movie's poor showing, the experience had an effect on defining Schwarzenegger's career goals. "Everyone in the business told me to lose my name, my accent and my shape," he commented in the *Chicago Tribune.* "But, far from limiting me, I think all that helped me to be unique. No one could ever tell me I looked just like another actor or sounded like someone else. So after using another name in my first movie, I decided to just go with my real name and be myself. I wanted to be successful on my own terms."

Not wanting to star in another flop, Schwarzenegger got to know producer Dino De Laurentiis and was eventually cast in De Laurentiis's adaptation of the story of comic-book hero *Conan, The Barbarian.* Conan became a big hit, making $100 million around the world. Schwarzenegger's successive action/adventure movies—*The Terminator, Conan, The Destroyer, Commando,* and *Raw Deal*—were also hugely popular, marketing the Schwarzenegger image and propelling him to international superstardom in the course of a few years.

As a departure from the strongman role, Schwarzenegger starred in the film *Twins,* a comedy adventure that paired him with diminutive actor Danny De Vito, with whom he formed a couple of mismatched and misplaced twin brothers. The film was a big success, proving that Schwarzenegger could be just as popular in lighter roles as he was playing superheroes. Schwarzenegger admits that this kind of role may be more in tune with his real personality: "I feel much more comfortable with gentle scenes than violent ones," he said in *Premiere.* "When I studied with [acting coach] Eric Morris, I was always much better with lovey-dovey talk than with dialogue when I'm mad and angry. I had the most trouble where I had to scream and hit everyone, because I'm not that way myself."

Since *Twins,* Schwarzenegger claims to have retired from one-dimensional strongman parts. In *Total Recall* he plays instead an interesting dual role: that of a simple construction worker with a hidden identity in this science fiction psychological thriller. About the film, Schwarzenegger commented in the *Chicago Tribune:* "It's very strange and bizarre, and as much about the nature of reality and dreams as it is an action film. It's definitely got a Hitchcock feel to it, and having to play two totally different characters was a big challenge for me."

It was Schwarzenegger's hard work, spanning the course of several years, that got *Total Recall* released. He purchased the script from Dino De Laurentiis and found the right production team and cast. He did most of this simply because he liked the plot and was intrigued by the lead role. About Schwarzenegger's performance, Georgia Brown wrote in the *Village Voice* that his portrayal of the character was well intentioned, if flawed: "In the beginning, when he's supposed to be a slightly thick, memory-erased construction worker, Schwarzenegger conveys a gentle, passive pathos. But as his character expands and grows potent, there's need for interior growth."

Only "perfect" will do

Schwarzenegger's discipline and hard work showed during the production of this movie, which was made under difficult conditions in Mexico. The star expressed his feelings about the hard work involved in moviemaking in *Premiere:* "I don't care what it takes. You can scream at me, call me for a shot at midnight, keep me waiting for four hours. As long as what ends up on the screen is perfect." This is an attitude Schwarzenegger learned from sports: "You go back to the gym and you just do it again and again until you get it right," he said in *Vanity Fair.*

In 1991 Schwarzenegger appeared in *Terminator 2: Judgment Day.* The film was a huge box-office draw—selling $54 million worth of tickets in its first weekend. This success was followed by a major flop the next year. The much-publicized and eagerly awaited Schwarzenegger film *The Last Action Hero* was a bitter disappointment. Most recently *True Lies,* released in the summer of 1994, has gathered critical kudos and big ticket sales. Schwarzenegger plays a secret agent whose wife (Jamie Lee Curtis) thinks he's a boring salesman. She learns otherwise, however, when her life is threatened as she becomes mistakenly involved in her husband's latest assignment. Schwarzenegger followed up *True Lies* with *Junior,* a comedy about a man (Schwarznegger) who becomes pregnant.

Schwarzenegger's personal life has been as high-profile as his career. In 1986 he married television news anchor Maria Shriver, and became part of the Kennedy clan. He and Shriver frequently appear at charity functions near their Pacific Palisades, California, home. "I love to schmooze," said Schwarzenegger in *Vanity Fair* about his many social appearances. In 1990, the couple's first child, Katherine, was born. "Becoming a father for the first time has definitely changed me, and for the better," he admitted in the *Chicago Tribune*: "Having a baby really does make you aware of how others depend and rely on you. A new baby is so helpless and so vulnerable and you feel protective and want to make sure it grows up the right way and is well loved and looked after." Since then the couple has had another daughter and a son.

Schwarzenegger's non-movie pursuits include real estate investing and politics. He has parlayed his movie income and some shrewd real estate speculating into a fortune of over $50 million. He campaigned for Republican presidential candidate George Bush during the 1988 elections, in spite of his relationship with the Democratic Kennedy clan. Bush named him chairman of the President's Council on Physical Fitness for his help, a position Schwarzenegger called "a fun challenge." Schwarzenegger tackled this appointed post with the tireless zeal and salesmanship that he displays in the rest of his career. After Democrat Bill Clinton was elected to the White House Schwarzenegger withdrew from his post.

Overall, Schwarzenegger seems to be the embodiment of the American Dream ideal that if you work hard and are disciplined, you will be successful. He wakes up every morning at 6:00 a.m. and goes to the gym. "I do not miss a day. It keeps me in check," Schwarzenegger indicated. "Bench-pressing three hundred pounds will always be bench-pressing three hundred pounds. That will never change, no matter how much money I have or how famous I am." The actor is also supremely self-confident, and kind and tolerant of his adoring fans. "Arnold's confidence is not surprising, if you consider what he's accomplished," said *Total Recall* director Paul Verhoeven. "After all, he did what seemed impossible. He was not a logical choice for fame. But Arnold's drive and his charm made him different. It made him a star."

Sources

Chicago Tribune, May 27, 1990.
Premiere, June 1990.
New York Times, July 14, 1991.
Time, October 4, 1993; April 11, 1994.
Vanity Fair, June 1990.

Jerry Seinfeld

Born in 1954

COMEDIAN AND ACTOR

H e never wanted just a piece of chocolate cake," Jerry Seinfeld's mother, Betty, told *People* magazine's Mark Goodman. "It was the whole cake. And he always waited until he got what he wanted." For Seinfeld, that wait took some 15 years, from his post-college days as a traveling stand-up comic to network television as the star of a sitcom that bears his name.

Mr. Generic

As a fledgling comic, Seinfeld remained focused on his career; he reportedly earned money by selling light bulbs by phone, taking no more-interesting job that might distract him from his goals. By 1990 Seinfeld had entered the ranks of stand-up stardom, frequenting *The Tonight Show* and *Late Night with David Letterman*, getting his own cable TV special—and reinforcing his own brand of mild-

"I love everything about being famous. You hear so many celebrities talk about the price of fame. As I see it, there's no price. It's all free. You get special treatment everywhere. You can talk to people if you want, and if you don't want to you don't have to. Why are celebrities always whining? What's the problem?"

mannered humor. For many comics, such steady work would be reward enough for more than a decade of plugging away. But Seinfeld's own stage persona could have cost him his stardom, as Stephen Randall, in a *Playboy* article, noted: Just one appearance on *Tonight* sent the careers of fellow comics Steven Wright and Garry Shandling soaring, while Seinfeld kept playing small venues even after several network gigs. Randall described a probable reason: Seinfeld, he said, "is a hookless comedian. He has no gimmick. Unlike Shandling's single-guy lament or Richard Lewis' autoneuroticism, there's nothing unique about Seinfeld's material.... He's as well suited for the hip and cynical [*Late Night*] as he was in 18 appearances on the cornball *Merv Griffin* show. He's Mr. Generic." However, Randall continued, "talk with Seinfeld's friends and colleagues and they'll point out the up side to his generic comedy. He wears well. There's no gimmick to get tired of. He's as funny the tenth time you see him as he was the first."

Fortunately for Seinfeld, audiences found his quiet dependability more appealing than, say, the rantings of such flashes in the pan as Andrew Dice Clay. His "casual observational humor," remarked Randall, "causes rollicking waves of laughter. It's middle-of-the-road stuff—about his neighbors with the pet monkey ('If you need a pet that roller-skates and smokes cigars, it's time to think about a family. You're so close'), about commercials ('They say Tide cleans bloodstains. I say if you've got a T-shirt with bloodstains, then maybe laundry isn't your biggest problem')." The difference in Seinfeld, Randall added, is that the comic's "delivery and timing are honed by constant practice, taking the material up several notches. There's nothing shocking here—not even a stray four-letter word—nor anything that could conceivably go over the head of anyone with even a moderate television education."

A show about "nothing"

The same sensibility can be found in the sitcom *Seinfeld*. The NBC series, which debuted as a summer replacement show in 1990, "takes place in a recognizable Manhattan, not some generic city, and the city's more amusing perils give the show its edge," as James Kaplan wrote in *Mademoiselle*. The plotting of Seinfeld is sometimes so minimalist that it can be called nonexistent. In a nutshell, the show follows stand-up comic Jerry Seinfeld and his friends as they approach city life and love in the 1990s.

Jerry's fictional sidekicks include George, a nervous ne'er-do-well; Kramer, the hyperactive next-door neighbor; and Elaine, who conducted a precurtain romance with Jerry but now retains best-pal status. All four characters are drawn as believably as network sitcom standards would allow, and much of the credit for that goes to Seinfeld coproducer and key writer Larry David, who admits that he's the inspiration for George. David and Seinfeld are old friends and writing partners whose contrasting styles complement one another, according to *New York* magazine reporter Chris Smith. "Where Seinfeld is a serene, clean-mouthed comic with an eye for detail, David is a high-strung, pessimistic cynic given to extremes of insecurity."

"All comedians are cranky. I never met a funny person who wasn't. To be funny, you've got to be cranky. Now, I'm a contented person, but a thousand and one things irritate me. That's what I love about New York. I thrive on all the craziness. That's why New York produces good comedians. It's that constant chafing. If you've got a comedic bent, New York is going to provide you with plenty of ammo. The place is a gymnasium of irritation."

"I'm no big-deal actor," the comic admitted to Randall, but the series capitalizes on Seinfeld's strengths; each episode is framed by segments of the stand-up Jerry performing routines based on the events of that evening's show. But even the events mirror real life in their ability to be ordinary. In a now-famous episode, Jerry, George, and Elaine spend a half-hour in real time waiting for a table at a Chinese restaurant. None of them can take the pressure of the wait, because each is distracted by outside forces—Jerry wants to catch an early movie, George is sweating out the aftereffects of an unsuccessful date, and Elaine is just too famished to be quiet. The biggest plot twist occurs when Jerry runs into his uncle's receptionist.

What also separates *Seinfeld* from the crowd is its almost clinical emotional center, especially when compared to the bulk of sitcoms for whom caring-and-sharing sentimentality is the order of the day. At the *Seinfeld* set, noted Smith, the motto is "No hugging, no learning." In a typical scenario, as Seinfeld himself related in a *Gentlemen's Quarterly* article, "George and Elaine had scenes where they realized that, after knowing each other a few years, they were totally uncomfortable around each other unless Jerry was present. They weren't friends; they were friends-in-law."

For all its laughs, "a lot of people don't understand that *Seinfeld* is a dark show," as Larry David told Smith. "If you examine the premises, terrible things happen to people. They lose jobs; somebody breaks up with a stroke victim; somebody's told they need a nose job. That's my sensibility." "If one wanted to make one major complaint about Seinfeld," Kaplan remarked conversely, "it would be that it tickles without cutting. Jerry gets that mad look in his close-set eyes but never does anything truly outrageous. This is pretty safe comedy, which also happens to be very, very good. So what? Seinfeld is like a delicious, airy confection, spun out of next to nothing."

Success has not gone to Seinfeld's head. The performer does indulge certain quirks, however; for instance, he will line up, "with military precision," 11 pairs of brand-new designer basketball shoes, according to Smith. "As soon as a pair develops one smudge, he donates it to the Salvation Army." Seinfeld follows a strict health-food diet, practices yoga daily, and studies Eastern philosophy. About the only trapping of stardom is Seinfeld's collection of Porsches.

Work is Seinfeld's motivator. When not shooting the sitcom he still makes stand-up appearances across the country. In the 1990 *Playboy* piece, Randall commented that for reasons not even Seinfeld understands, "he's wedded to the idea of doing live, stand-up comedy. 'It's a life's mission,' he says. 'I don't know what the hell I'm trying to accomplish.'" Randall added that the performer "took a vacation once. He and a girlfriend went to Barbados for a week, drinking pineapple juice with a little umbrella in it. He hated it. 'I guess it's great if you have a job you can't stand and you live in a place you don't like. For me, that kind of relaxation is a hairsbreadth away from stultifying boredom.'"

Dates much younger woman

In May 1993 Seinfeld was walking in New York City's Central Park when he became captivated by a dark-haired woman who was also walking in the park. After asking for her phone number the two began to date. Their relationship caused quite a stir, however, because of their age difference—Seinfeld was then 38 and the woman, Shoshanna Lonstein, was only 17 and still a senior in high school. Despite some harsh media attention, Lonstein and Seinfeld continued their relationship until November 1994.

Seinfeld recently added the book *Seinlanguage* to his long list of successes. Published in late 1993, this collection of monologues and one-liners quickly became a national best-seller. His success is further documented by Emmy Award nominations and by taking Comic of the Year honors. Still, the performer considers one kind of accolade to stand above the rest. "I'd rather say something that people would quote as a great line that I said, that I thought of, than win an Oscar," he told Randall. He relates how one night he was in a car going to New York, listening to the radio, and the host of a post-game show quoted him in describing what a great sports day it had been: "He said, 'It's like Jerry Seinfeld says, How are we ever going to impress our kids? What stories will we have? How can the world change that much again that we can blow kids away with stories like the ones our parents told us, about the war and the Depression, when milk was a nickel and cars were a quarter? What will we say? When I was a boy, dogs didn't have the vote. They had no say in the world at all. In fact, we kept them on leashes.' When I heard that on the radio, that was the biggest boost I'd ever had. That, to me, is the coolest thing you could do on this planet."

In the *New York* interview, Seinfeld's managers told Smith that they think Jerry will be playing Billy Crystal-type movie roles in the next few years. Until that day comes, Seinfeld will have to contend with television stardom and the type of fan letter he quoted in the *Gentlemen's Quarterly* article: "Dear Sirs: The *Seinfeld* show is the greatest. It is so naturally funny, the cast is great. I'm embarrassed to say that I don't know the name of the comedian who plays the leading character, but he is great too." As Seinfeld commented: "And we're told the research indicates we're getting a more educated audience."

Sources

Cosmopolitan, May 1994.

Gentlemen's Quarterly, November 1991.

Life, October 1993.

Mademoiselle, September 1991.

New York, February 3, 1992.

People, December 2, 1991; October 11, 1993; March 28, 1994.

Playboy, August 1990.

USA Weekend, February 14, 1992.

Sinbad

Born November 10, 1957
Benton Harbor, Michigan

Sinbad "never tells jokes.... He doesn't deliver payoff lines; he slam-dunks them. His comedy is large, physical, impetuous. Psychologically, he jams us, poking holes in our lifestyles. His stories mirror our foibles."—David Ritz

COMEDIAN AND ACTOR

Known for his "clean comedy," stand-up comic Sinbad pulls off a rare feat of delivering stage monologues that are funny and outrageous without being profane. The son of a Baptist minister, Sinbad strongly feels that stories of life itself are the stuff of humor, and that profanity is not necessary to make people laugh. As he told Aldore Collier in *Jet*: "Life unedited is funny."

Sinbad's family always demonstrated support and love for each other. In an interview with *Essence* Sinbad recalled growing up as one of five children: "[We had] a daddy with tremendous integrity, a genuine Christian, and a mother with boundless love. I remember Mama coming to my elementary school to talk about Harriet Tubman. Early on, I loved Black history. We had a family unit strong as steel. Still do. That's why they're around me every day and in every way." In fact all five of Sinbad's siblings work with him.

Early in his career Sinbad found that getting rid of profanity in his act was a way of trusting his own comic instincts. "I'll never forget it," he related to *Collier*. "I was on stage and I was dying. I didn't really know how to do comedy and I was trying to write stuff rather than just be what I am. And I remember I cursed on stage. And it was the worst feeling I ever had. People were laughing, but I said I would quit comedy before I had to do that.... I went home and learned how to be myself. I learned that your life is funny."

Draws comedy from real-life experiences

The follies of male-female relationships are often the focus of Sinbad's monologues. "Relationships are just plain funny," he was quoted as saying by Collier. "Only a wife or girlfriend could make a man act the way he does. Only a husband or boyfriend could make a woman act the way she acts." Sinbad frequently draws upon stories of his own family in his act. He commented in *Ebony* that such "comedy really works because it's about being on a stage and talking about everything that is wrong with all of us. And we realize, 'Man, I'm not the only one who's messed up like this.'"

Being funny has always been part of Sinbad's life. The native of Benton Harbor, Michigan, was always "the goofy kid," as he told a contributor to *People*. At 6'5", Sinbad originally aspired to be a basketball player, and thought that someday he might mix comedy and sports by being one of the Harlem Globetrotters. Basketball was his first real passion and it had a very positive influence on his life. "[Basketball] is why I never smoked or drank," Sinbad commented in *Essence*. "When I came up, my idols advertised Ovaltine. Never even thought they dated girls. I took my ball to the movies and sat it down next to me. Basketball was my date, my romance. I was afraid girls would take away my game."

While attending the University of Denver on a basketball scholarship, a knee injury forced him to give up the sport, and he left in 1978. Sinbad later joined the U.S. Air Force, and began working at stand-up comedy after he won a talent contest. "Inspired," as the contributor to *People* related, "[Sinbad] set out to get himself discharged by walking off duty in his underwear. 'Just kick me out,' he begged. 'Let's work as a team.'"

Begins career as stand-up comic

After he left the air force in 1983, Sinbad became a success on the comedy nightclub circuit in Los Angeles, and eventually appeared seven times on the television talent show *Star Search.* He also performed as an opener for

Sinbad commented on his name, which he took from Sindbad the Sailor, a character found in *The Arabian Nights' Entertainments* who had seven wonderful voyages: "I renamed myself Sinbad because Sinbad is bad. He could hang with rogues and with kings. He didn't have the strength of Hercules, but he could outwit anyone. He was loyal to his men and always held his head high. Every time I was down, I'd think of my name and Sinbad would give me a lift."

such music groups as the Pointer Sisters and Kool and the Gang, and was a regular on the short-lived *The New Redd Foxx Show.* Eventually, he did warm-ups for studio audiences of *The Cosby Show,* during which time his idol, Bill Cosby, helped land him a role on the hit NBC-TV series *A Different World.*

Sinbad's role on *A Different World*—which humorously depicted the lives of students and faculty at an all-black college—was the irreverent dormitory director and gym teacher Walter Oakes. A reviewer in *Variety,* who commented that the show's strength was its "likable and energetic cast," added that "dorm antics are infectiously led by the single-named Sinbad, who is delightful as the big guy struggling to keep order in a nonstop party house." In 1990 Sinbad's character on the show was broadened to become a counselor. According to co-executive producer Susan Fales, as quoted in *Jet,* the move to make Sinbad's character more serious was to increasingly "address social problems, like sex education, teen pregnancy, and drugs" and to have the popular Sinbad become "the voice of what's happening in the Black community."

Sinbad chose to leave *A Different World* at the end of its 1990-91 season. After a number of successful television specials, Sinbad returned to the weekly format in 1993 with *The Sinbad Show.* In the show he plays a 35-year-old computer game designer whose carefree bachelor lifestyle is disrupted when he takes on two foster children. David Hildbrand of *People* had this to say of Sinbad's performance: "Given more room to maneuver than he had on *A Different World,* Sinbad proves to be an engaging and vigorous, if at times overbearing, presence." The show has performed well and been especially praised for its positive depiction of African American manhood—a viewpoint that Sinbad feels has been lacking in television up to this point. "Black men are already responsible, already take care of our duties, but nobody emphasizes that," Sinbad tells *Jet.* "I hear all this bad talk against men and their children. I just got so tired of it."

Sinbad has recently had to fight the impression that fathers are second-rate caretakers when it comes to raising children. In 1993 Sinbad and his wife of seven years were divorced and he felt that the courts were biased when considering to whom the custody of his children, Royce and Paige, should be awarded. "I had to fight in court and make the court realize I could take care of my kids. They (the court) actually tried to make me a weekend father," Sinbad told *Jet.* "I'm not here just to enjoy them and buy them toys. I want to discipline them, I want to help them in

Sinbad in a scene from *The Sinbad Show,* 1993.

school and that doesn't come from once a week." The court listened to Sinbad and he and his ex-wife currently share custody of their children.

Despite the recent turmoil in his personal life, Sinbad continues to gain professional success. In addition to his new show, Sinbad has signed a contract with Walt Disney Pictures to star in and co-produce a number of feature films.

Sources

Ebony, April 1990.

Essence, November 1992.

Jet, February 12, 1990; August 13, 1990; May 6, 1991; November 22, 1993.

People, September 29, 1986; October 18, 1993.

TV Guide, November 27, 1993.

Variety, October 4-10, 1989.

Will Smith

Born c. 1970

"It's always been fun for me to tell a story and make people laugh. I've always been a show-off, and uncomfortable when people weren't looking at me."

RAPPER AND ACTOR

Will Smith is one of the hottest young performers in Hollywood today. He began his career as a rap musician and soon branched out into acting. The television sitcom in which he stars, *The Fresh Prince of Bel-Air,* has been a solid hit since its introduction in 1990, and it shows no signs of slowing down. Smith has recently turned his attention to motion pictures, attaining a small part in the comedy *Made in America* and starring in *Six Degrees of Separation.*

Smith was raised in Philadelphia, Pennsylvania, one of three children born to Will, a refrigeration engineer, and Caroline, a school board employee. It was Caroline who taught her family that education could be found outside the classroom. "When I was about seven, we drove cross-country and saw Yellowstone and Mount Rushmore and the Alamo and the Grand Canyon," Smith told *People.* "You see something beautiful, bigger than you, it mellows you, changes your attitude for life."

Gains fame as rapper

Smith discovered music early and became a rapper by the age of 12. In 1981 Smith met Jeff Townes (Jazzy Jeff) at a friend's party. While they immediately liked each other, it took a few weeks for the friendship to find common ground. "I bought this canned fart spray and sprayed it at a party," Townes told *People*. "We just cracked up. When I found Will had the same humor, that was when we really clicked." Townes was a DJ and it was he who dubbed Smith the "Fresh Prince." In 1987 Jive Records released the pair's debut album, *Rock the House*. Their brand of rap was lighter than most—rapping about moms wanting to buy their kids' clothes and problems with girlfriends. The album was a big hit and the following year the pair won a Grammy Award for the song "Parents Just Don't Understand." By 1989 Smith and Townes had recorded two more albums—*He's the DJ, I'm the Rapper* and *And in This Corner*. Both albums went platinum (selling one million copies), and they appeared in concerts all over the world. "We weren't as big as Hammer," Smith told *TV Guide*, "but we did very well."

When asked about the biggest influence on his rap style, Smith responded: "Kids' books. I was really into Dr. Seuss stories. Read them a certain way, and all that rhyming sounds like rap."

So well in fact, that the duo made millions of dollars. Smith was overwhelmed by his new wealth, and he spent lavishly. He bought a mansion in suburban Philadelphia, jewelry, expensive clothes, and seven cars equipped with stereos. He also had plenty of "friends" to help him spend his cash, but when he found himself broke in 1989, his friends deserted him. "*That* was a big lesson," Smith told *TV Guide*.

Quincy Jones, who produces *Fresh Prince,* was initially responsible for Smith's entry into television. He was impressed by Smith and sent NBC Entertainment president Warren Littlefield Fresh Prince's music videos from *Yo, MTV Raps*. Littlefield told *TV Guide*, "It was clear to me right away that this guy [Smith] was a natural. I would go up and down the halls saying that we had to do something with him."

Stars in The Fresh Prince of Bel-Air

In the fall of 1989 Smith found himself wanting to try something new (though he ultimately would continue his music career, calling music his true love). He ran into Benny Medina, a Warner Bros. Records executive, and told him that he was interested in acting. Coincidentally, Medina had been trying to sell a new series to NBC management that was based on his own background. Medina was a street-smart kid from a poor neighborhood, who was taken in as a teen by a wealthy family in posh Beverly Hills,

California. He arranged for Smith to audition for the network executives. Medina recalled the audition in *People*: "Will read the script, put some of his personal nuances in it, and right after that everybody was shaking hands, hugging and kissing."

So *The Fresh Prince of Bel-Air* was born. Smith basically plays himself: a cool, smooth-talking Philadelphia youth, who suffers culture shock when he is sent to live with his wealthy relatives in California. Smith is serious about his work on the show—he seeks advice on how to improve his performance and checks the script to make sure he's not asked to do anything out of character. Feeling he's progressed in terms of his acting ability, Smith recalled his first year on the show for *People*: "I was trying so hard. I would memorize the entire script, then I'd be lipping everybody's lines while they were talking. When I watch those episodes it's disgusting. My performances were horrible." His performances rapidly improved, however, and in 1993 he was nominated for a Golden Globe Award for best TV comedy actor.

Begins to work in movies

In 1993 Smith had a small but pivotal role in the movie *Made in America*, which starred Ted Danson and Whoopi Goldberg. Smith credits Goldberg for helping him on the set. "Whoopi taught me how to behave between scenes," Smith told *TV Guide*. He made the most of his role, and Michael Segell of *Cosmopolitan* wrote, "[Smith's] performance in a small part nearly stole ... *Made in America* from Ted Danson and Whoopi Goldberg."

His real breakthrough, however, came when he won the starring role in *Six Degrees of Separation*, which was released in late 1993. The film is an adaptation of an award-winning play by John Guare, in which a gay, African American con artist passes himself off as actor Sidney Poitier's son. The story is based on a real-life incident in which a smooth-talking young man conned his way into the homes of two wealthy Manhattan couples by convincing them that he was a Harvard classmate of their children and the son of Poitier. He also persuaded them that he had no money because he'd been mugged. (In fact, the con artist never went to Harvard and Sidney Poitier has no son.) While Smith felt comfortable playing the part of a con man, he had problems with his character's homosexuality. "That was really difficult," Smith told *Cosmopolitan*. "I had enough innate charm for the audience to make them buy that this guy could put one over on people. But the gay part—just the concept of looking at a man the way you'd look at a woman—was really hard. I don't have anything against homosexuals—I'm just not one. So there was nothing I'd learned as an actor or done in my life that I could draw on." The last scene in the movie called for Smith's character to kiss another man, but Smith was so uncomfortable that the director had to rework the scene so there'd be no kiss. (Smith later regretted his behavior, remarking that his refusal to play the scene as written was unprofessional.) The movie received mixed reviews and only performed moderately at the box office, but critics were generally very impressed by Smith's performance.

Smith is currently working on *Bad Boys*, a buddy action film in which he costars with Martin Lawrence. Smith has a wife, Sheree, and a son, Willard Smith III. Smith credits his wife with keeping his ego in check. They met while sitting in the audience of the TV series *A Different World*. Smith began to pursue Sheree, but it was six months before she would date him and two years before she would agree to marry him. When *TV Guide* asked Smith why such a hot young star would want to settle down, he replied: "I've always been a one-girl guy. I was never a playboy. I don't know why, but I just really prefer to be with one person."

Sources

Cosmopolitan, November 1993.

Mademoiselle, December 1993.

People, September 24, 1990.

TV Guide, October 13, 1990; January 23, 1993.

Wesley Snipes

Born July 31, 1962
Orlando, Florida

"I know that I still have to perfect my craft ... so I can be twice as good and twice as fast, be able to change personalities and be fully committed and believing at the drop of a dime. I have to do the work. At some point in time, the work will be so strong that you won't be able to deny me."

ACTOR

Before reaching the age of 30, actor Wesley Snipes was already recognized as an important new figure in his field. His picture graced the cover of *Newsweek* and *Jet* magazines, the *Washington Post* called him the most celebrated new actor of the 1991-92 season, and *New Yorker* magazine critic Pauline Kael dubbed him one of the most impressive members of a new generation of American actors. By 1994 Snipes, with a variety of memorable roles to his credit, appeared on the verge of becoming one of the key players in the film industry.

The secret to his success seems to be an astounding versatility coupled with a striking intensity that renders his characters sharp and unforgettable. Snipes is also keenly aware of the obstacles that have hindered the advancement of black actors in cinematic circles. "You will never hear me say I don't see myself as a black actor but just an actor who happens to be black," he told *Ebony* magazine's Laura Randolph. "Every chance I get I'm going to tell you I'm an African-American man who is acting.

Snipes was born on July 31, 1962, in Orlando, Florida. His father, an aircraft engineer, and his mother, Marian, then a teacher's aide, divorced a year after his birth. His mother then moved him and two of his seven siblings to the South Bronx section of New York, where he spent his childhood honing negotiating skills. Snipes stood 5 feet 5 inches tall when in high school—he eventually grew 6 more inches—and substituted bravado, boldness, and charm for height at that time, which in turn served as a solid foundation for his adult life.

Snipes's aunt Della Saunders entered him in talent shows when he was a child. One of those led to a minor role in the off-Broadway play *The Me Nobody Knows* when Snipes was 12 years old. Frequent auditions and basketball practice kept him busy in high school, and his competitive nature helped ensure that he would fare well academically. His keen interest in dance led him to enroll at New York's High School of Performing Arts, known for its strong dance department. Snipes was content there, so two years later, when his mother decided to move the family back to Orlando, the teenager complained bitterly. He had become a regular at the local pool hall and was so good at the game that he made money hustling pool. His mother decided it was time for a change of atmosphere.

After attending a multiethnic elementary school in the South Bronx, and then the High School of the Performing Arts, Snipes suddenly found himself in a predominantly black public school in Orlando, and his fast-paced style was at odds with southern sensibilities. In an interview with *Washington Post* contributor Jay Mathews, he described how he felt when he first went to Orlando: "They're just moseying along, like lemonade on the porch on a Sunday afternoon, and you're like, yo, I can't stand this. Let me outta here."

The drama department of Jones High School in Orlando soon took his mind off of what he had left behind when they started casting for *Damn Yankees*. Snipes was given a warm reception in the theater department and wasn't modest when it came to letting it be known that he had attended the High School of Performing Arts. He earned spending money in high school by joining a city-sponsored drama troupe called Struttin' Street Stuff and performed puppet shows in parks and schools for up to $70 a week. Around the same time, he also won an award for his one-man show playing Puck, a character from William Shakespeare's comedy *A Midsummer Night's Dream*, and had a successful run playing Felix Ungar in *The Odd Couple*.

Snipes told Stephen Holden of the *New York Times:* "Moving to Florida was the best thing that could have happened to me. A lot of the cats I grew up with in the South Bronx found themselves in sticky situations. Karen Rugerio, Snipes's drama teacher at Jones High, told the *Washington Post:* "He was always very focused. If you criticize the work of someone at that age, they often get upset, but Wes would always listen very carefully, wanting to learn how he could do it better."

Shaped by experiences in college

When it came time for college, Snipes auditioned for the State University of New York (SUNY) at Purchase's esteemed theater arts program and was readily accepted, receiving a Victor Borge scholarship. As Snipes explained to Larry Rohter of the *New York Times,* he fell into acting through the urging of others who saw that he was a natural. "I really wanted to be a singer and dancer, he said, and I still have a latent passion for that. When I see Alvin Ailey or Chuck Davis or Forces of Nature, I'm sitting there saying I could have been up there."

Snipes was one of only four black students in the theater arts department at SUNY Purchase, and he told *Ebony* magazine that it was a disconcerting experience: "I felt like mold on white bread.... What saved me was being exposed to Malcolm X." The emphasis on black pride found in the writings of Malcolm X helped Snipes weather a confusing period in his life: a black man coming of age while surrounded by whites. He became a Muslim for a short time, starting in the second semester of his freshman year, then abandoned the faith three years after he graduated. He revealed to Randolph: "A brother of mine used to say 'When you're drowning, grab onto a log to keep afloat. But don't hold on to the log when the boat comes by. Get on the boat and bring your butt on back home.' So Islam for me was the log to make me more conscious of what African people have accomplished, of my self-worth, to give me some self-dignity."

While in college, Snipes auditioned for Harry Belafonte's movie about break dancers called *Beat Street* and realized that in addition to applying standard acting techniques, he also had to draw from his own life experience on the street. He didn't land a part in the movie, but it was a learning experience for him. Although Snipes was never given the role of leading male in any of the university productions—in spite of his obvious talents and experience—after he left college to pursue professional work, he quickly became a leading man who was very much in demand. David Garfield, an acting teacher at SUNY Purchase, told the *Los Angeles Times* that Snipes was "obviously gifted. He was extremely funny, he could do straight drama, he could sing and he would stop shows with the dance numbers he had choreographed. He also exhibited a strong black consciousness even then."

Steady climb to fame

Snipes met his wife while a senior in college, and they married a year after he graduated in 1984. He took a job installing telephones in New York, and that same year a casting director who had spotted him at a university drama convention contacted him about Goldie Hawn's football parody *Wildcats* after the first-choice actor didn't work out. Then, along with Matt Dillon and Andrew McCarthy, Snipes procured a leading role in John Pielmeier's off-Broadway play *The Boys Of Winter,* about the ravaging effects of the Vietnam War on U.S. soldiers, and followed with a role in the Lincoln Center production of Wole Soyinka's *Death and the King's Horsemen.* After this, true to his flexible nature, he put on spike heels to portray drag queen Sister Boom-Boom in Emily Mann's Broadway play *Execution of Justice.* Mann told the *Los Angeles Times:* "I remember when he auditioned. I had never seen a man put on high heels and walk that way and all of us said 'That guy is going to be a star.'" (Snipes would don heels again for a 1995 film role, in *To Wong Foo, Thanks for Everything, Julie Newmar.*)

Because Snipes pursued an interest in martial arts, and because he has the natural grace and balance of a dancer, he was well cast as an athlete. In 1986, Snipes portrayed a boxer in the film *Streets of Gold.* Then he experienced a short lull in his career, so he turned to other pursuits for his livelihood. Therapeutic massage and parking cars were two of the things he tried in 1987 before landing a role in HBO's *Vietnam Story.* He eventually won the cable industry's ACE Award for best actor for his work in *Vietnam Story.*

In 1987 Snipes also appeared in Michael Jackson's *Bad* video, directed by Martin Scorsese, and this cameo role changed the course of his fate. Snipes portrayed a gang leader who shoved Jackson up against a wall, and in doing so, caught the attention of director Spike Lee and *New Jack City* co-screenwriter Barry Michael Cooper. Lee commented to *Premiere* magazine's Ralph Rugoff that Snipes "was so real, Michael Jackson must've been scared to death."

Vietnam Story was followed by a part in the 1989 comedy *Major League*—he turned down a smaller part in Lee's *Do the Right Thing* for this role—and later a minor role in the drug warfare film *King of New York.*

Around the same time, Snipes and his wife had a son named Jelani. They were divorced in 1990.

That same year Snipes portrayed a jazz saxophonist named Shadow Henderson in Lee's *Mo' Better Blues,* holding his own opposite heartthrob and Academy Award winner Denzel Washington. Snipes told Randolph: "I just wanted to go in, do a good job, and not let Denzel blow me off the screen." As preparation for his role as a saxophonist, Snipes watched tapes of John Coltrane and other jazz legends and visited a variety of the jazz clubs in New York City. A proficient mimic, Snipes memorized scales and fingering for all of the music played in the film.

An established leading man

The role of Harlem drug baron Nino Brown in *New Jack City* was written with Snipes in mind after his appearance in the video *Bad.* Directed by Mario Van Peebles, *New Jack City* opened March 8, 1991, and drew $22.3 million at the box office within its first three weeks—a tribute to the powerful screen presence of Snipes.

New Jack City was designed to be an antidrug and antiviolence gangster film, but a spate of shootings and violence erupted briefly at some theaters across the country after it opened. Some of the eruptions were due to the fact that few theaters were showing the film at first, and those that were sold out quickly, leaving dozens of frustrated people—usually teenagers—outside of the theater without tickets. Rohter noted: "Indeed, Mr. Snipes now finds himself in the peculiar position of fending off arguments that his portrayal (of drug lord Nino Brown) may have been too effective."

Commenting in the *Los Angeles Times* about the theaters where outbreaks occurred, Snipes asserted: "They oversold the showings by 1,500 tickets and the theater owners didn't give their money back. The same thing would happen with a Menudo concert, or the Rolling Stones."

Role in Lee's Jungle Fever

Because of Snipes's outstanding performance as Shadow in *Mo' Better Blues,* Lee decided to cast him as Flipper Purify in *Jungle Fever,* a controversial film about interracial romance, and wrote the part with Snipes in mind. Snipes told the *New York Times* that Lee had said to him on the last day of shooting *Mo' Better Blues:* "Be ready for the next one, because I got something great for you."

In *Jungle Fever,* released in June 1991, Snipes portrayed a married architect having an affair with his white secretary—an affair that ended due to economic and cultural differences between the lovers and their conflicted families. The film was a vehicle for Lee's views on interracial relationships, and Snipes told Hilary De Vries of the *Los Angeles Times:* "I don't know if the film is an argument for racial purity. I think it's about how color-conscious this society really is."

Snipes didn't have any personal experience with interracial relationships to draw from when making *Jungle Fever,* and he told Randolph in the *Ebony* interview: "It's more important to me to try and develop a good ... relationship between a black man and a black woman. That's the agenda ... and that's totally where my head is—to redefine the image of black male/female relationships and how important they are. We have to work on that ... then we can venture out. Until then, we ain't ready for it."

Snipes followed *Jungle Fever* with a leading role in Ron Shelton's 1992 release *White Men Can't Jump,* a wise-guy buddy movie about street basketball featuring Snipes and *Cheers* actor Woody Harrelson as urban hoop hustlers. The on-screen chemistry between the two stars helped make *White Men Can't Jump* one of the season's top moneymakers, and through his performance, Snipes solidified his place in American film. As he pointed out in *Entertainment Weekly,* "Rarely have you seen a young black male in this type of powerful position, who can basically make or break a project."

Following *White Men Can't Jump,* Snipes began work on Neil Jamenez's *The Waterdance,* which won several awards at the 1992 Sundance Film Festival. In the film, he portrays one of a group of hospitalized paraplegics and quadriplegics. To research his role, he spoke with patients at rehabilitation centers to understand their physical limitations and to glean emotional insight as well. This part was particularly challenging for Snipes because he relies heavily on physical expression and is physically very graceful.

In 1992 Snipes starred in a box-office success titled *Passenger 57.* His character, John Cutter, is a martial arts expert who foils a terrorist highjacking attempt. Stephen Holden of the *New York Times* wrote: "As an action hero, Mr. Snipes belongs to the school that plays it cool and tongue-in-cheek. Consistently underplaying his part, he strolls through the role with a glint in his eye that seems to acknowledge that the movie is really a live-action cartoon." Snipes also played an action hero in *Rising Sun,* a film in which he costarred with Sean Connery. Their two characters work together, trying to solve the murder of a high-priced prostitute in a Japanese-owned office building in Los Angeles. The movie met with mixed

So that he doesn't forget his roots, Snipes keeps a clothespin attached to his motorcycle. This reminds him of when he used to hang his clothes out the window to dry when he lived in the Bronx.

reviews, but Snipes was generally praised for his performance. Terrence Rafferty wrote in the *New Yorker:* "Snipes, as the bewildered-innocent half of the detective team ..., has the trickier role and brings it off flawlessly: his confusion is necessarily comic, but he never seems a buffoon."

Snipes followed *Rising Sun* with *Sugar Hill,* the jarring story of how two innocent brothers come to be brutal drug pushers and build a crime empire in Harlem's Sugar Hill section. When Snipes's character falls for an aspiring actress, he is moved to reconsider his life of crime. In *Drop Zone,* an action thriller featuring exciting sky-diving sequences released in late 1994, Snipes is again on the right side of the law, playing a government spy.

Snipes resides in the Fort Green section of Brooklyn, not far from Lee's 40 Acres and a Mule studio, and hasn't let fame change him at all. He is unusually practical, and in spite of being included in People magazine's feature "The 50 Most Beautiful People in the World, 1991," he hasn't lost sight of what is important to him. "I am never going to stop doing action-oriented projects that make me seem like I'm just one of the guys from the 'hood," Snipes told Rohter. "Audiences want to see that energy, that physicality, that toughness. But I want to do everything, and I'm blessed to be in the right place at the right time." As he told *Premiere* magazine, "I'm just thankful that I realized [acting] is what I'm supposed to be doing."

Sources

Ebony, September 1991.

Entertainment Weekly, September 27, 1991; April 10, 1992.

Los Angeles Times, April 13, 1991; May 19, 1991; June 29, 1991.

Newsweek, April 22, 1991; June 10, 1991.

New Yorker, July 26, 1993.

New York Times, August 24, 1990; March 8, 1991; March 27, 1991; June 7, 1991; November 6, 1992.

Premiere, July 1991.

Washington Post, June 7, 1991.

Sylvester Stallone

Born July 6, 1946
New York, New York

"I feel as though I haven't accomplished anything. I don't feel satisfied at all. My mind is constantly questioning: What next? Where to? Why now?"

ACTOR

S ylvester Stallone has achieved widespread recognition and fame by essentially playing two characters: Rocky and Rambo. The former endeared himself to viewers worldwide as a boxer who always overcomes insurmountable odds in order to win. And the latter, usually with the aid of incredible special effects, is able to single-handedly fight the world's oppressors. Stallone's ability to clearly delineate between good and evil, combined with the way in which good emerges truimphant in his films, has won over legions of loyal fans.

Complications during birth

Stallone is the eldest of two sons born to Frank, a hair stylist, and Jacqueline, a chorus girl. There were complications during Stallone's birth and the doctor had to use forceps (a medical instrument shaped like tongs) to help ease the baby down the birth canal. Unfortunately, the forceps cut a facial nerve, resulting in the drooping of Stallone's left eyelid and a speech impediment. The impediment caused teasing by classmates during Stallone's youth, and even his father made fun of the way he spoke.

Stallone's relationship with his father was strained because of the verbal and physical blows Frank delivered to his son. Stallone told *Sports Illustrated*: "I wouldn't say I was abused, but I was never praised." Stallone spent much of his childhood feeling lonely and isolated. He turned to comic books for escape and comfort—often envisioning himself in the role of superhero. Stallone took up weight lifting at any early age, hoping that by developing muscular strength he could become as strong as his fictional idols. Stallone was only 11 when his parents divorced. He lived with his father until the age of 15, when he went to live with his mother and her new husband in Philadelphia, Pennsylvania. Stallone was a poor student who was kicked out of 12 schools before attending Devereux Manor, which was a private high school for troubled youths. There, his years of bodybuilding paid off when he began to perform well in sports.

Decides to become actor

Because Stallone had been a less-than-model student, he had a difficult time getting into college. He tried beauty school, but found that he had no talent for cutting hair. In 1965 he won a scholarship to the American College of Switzerland, and while there he studied drama. His decision to pursue a career in acting came after he won a standing ovation for his performance as Biff, in Tennessee Williams's play *Death of a Salesman*. He remembered that moment in *Vanity Fair*: "This is it! Finally I've done something right. From here on in, I'm going for it." Just a few credits shy of graduation, Stallone dropped out of school and headed to New York City in order to pursue a career in the theater.

Writes screenplays

Stallone initially spent much of his energy writing screenplays—most of which were melodramatic and none of which sold. He also appeared in a number of off-Broadway roles, as well as some movies: *Bananas* (1971), *No Place to Hide*, (1973), *The Lords of Flatbush* (1974), *The Prisoner of Second Avenue* (1975), and *Death Race 2000* (1975). When he wasn't acting he worked in a variety of jobs to make ends meet, including selling fish, driving a truck, cooking at a diner and ushering for a movie theater.

It was while ushering that Stallone met his first wife, Sasha Czak. The two were married in December of 1974. The pair moved to Hollywood,

California, so that Stallone could try and sell some movie scripts. Sasha worked as a waitress and Stallone tried to improve his speech impediment by taping himself reading such authors as Edgar Allan Poe and William Shakespeare.

Stallone's big break came when he wrote the script that would later become *Rocky*. It was 1974 and he had recently seen a fight between world heavyweight champion Muhammad Ali and Chuck Wepner, a virtually unknown boxer. Stallone was so impressed with the dignity and pride Wepner demonstrated in the boxing ring, that he decided to include a boxer in a film script that he'd been asked to write. He named the character Rocky Balboa—"Rocky" for the great fighter Rocky Marciano, and "Balboa" for the famous Spanish explorer, Vasco Nunez de Balboa. The potential producers liked the script and asked that Stallone shift the focus of the story to the boxer. Stallone complied, and the producers agreed to back the film. There was one catch—they wanted Ryan O'Neal to play the lead. Stallone declined, telling them that he wanted the role for himself. They finally agreed and the resulting film, *Rocky* (1976), became one of the biggest box-office hits of all time.

The success of Rocky

Rocky tells the story of a down-on-his-luck boxer who is suddenly given the chance for national exposure when the reigning heavyweight champion, Apollo Creed, wants to fight Rocky as a publicity stunt. Rocky's goal is to make it through all the rounds of the fight. He thinks that by "going the distance," he can prove to himself and the shy pet-shop worker he loves, that he is "somebody." Stallone told *Sports Illustrated,* that *Rocky* was about "pride, reputation, and not being another bum from the neighborhood." Critics and viewers flocked to the film, and *Rocky* won ten Oscar nominations, receiving Academy awards for best picture, best editing and best directing. It also won a Golden Globe Award for best picture.

Stallone proceeded to make two mostly forgettable films, *F.I.S.T.* (1978) and *Paradise Alley* (1978), before returning to the character of Rocky Balboa. In all, Stallone made four sequels to the original Rocky: *Rocky II* (1980), in which the boxer has married his sweetheart, but squandered his fortune, only to be redeemed by movie's end by winning a rematch with Apollo Creed; *Rocky III* (1982), in which Rocky, now older, richer and a father, is challenged to fight the dangerous Clubber Lang; *Rocky IV,* in which Rocky fights an evil and sneaky boxer from the Soviet Union; and *Rocky V,* in which the boxer is again destitute, and finally dies in his wife's arms. Overall, the series did quite well, the simplistic plots and calculated

Stallone with Burgess Meredith in a scene from *Rocky,* 1976.

interplay between good and evil providing a cliched formula that appealed to a wide audience.

Success as "Rambo"

Stallone is equally well known for his series of *Rambo* films. Whereas the critics generally praised his *Rocky* series, they were less than kind about the gratuitous blood and violence that dominated the *Rambo* movies. Stallone portrays John Rambo, a veteran of the Vietnam War, in the series of three films: in *First Blood* (1982), Rambo is wrongly jailed by a sheriff in the Pacific Northwest and subsequently escapes and is chased through the wilderness by the police and the National Guard; in *Rambo: First Blood, Part II* (1985), Rambo returns to Vietnam to settle his own score with the Vietnamese; and in *Rambo III,* Rambo almost single-handedly attempts to drive Soviet forces out of Afghanistan. Before the film was released, the former Soviet Union had already begun to withdraw its forces from Afghanistan, thereby taking away some of the film's impact.

While audiences seem to love the Rambo/Rocky character—that of a physically strong individual who represents good while fighting seemingly insurmountable obstacles—critics have often lambasted Stallone for fighting one-dimensional enemies, often Soviets. This criticism was partly because as his movies were being released, the former Soviet Union was beginning to make friendly overtures to the democratic nations of the Western World. Stallone couldn't understand the harshness of some of the criticism aimed at him because in his mind he was simply looking for a "bad guy" to fight. Stallone told *Cosmopolitan:* "My intention was just to have an evil opponent to play against. I don't understand why people can't take it that way—as an escape fantasy-adventure."

In an attempt to break away from his "tough guy" image, Stallone tried his hand at a variety of non-action roles throughout the 1980s, all of which met with little success: *Nighthawks* (1981) was a movie about international terrorism; *Victory* (1981) concerned a young American soccer player who attempts to break out of a prisoner-of-war camp during World War II; *Rhinestone* (1984) teamed him with Dolly Parton and featured him as a New York cab driver who is taught (by Parton) to sing like the famous country-western star Johnny Cash; *Cobra* (1986) was about a policeman who has to break the rules in order to protect a model from a group of deranged killers; *Over the Top* (1987) cast Stallone as a truck driver who enters an arm-wrestling contest; *Lock Up* (1989) was about a prison inmate who is tortured by an unethical warden; and *Tango and Cash* (1989), in which he starred with actor Kurt Russel a buddy/action cop film.

Stallone continued to have bad luck into the 1990s as he tried his hand at comedy. He made *Oscar* (1991), in which he played a gangster who attempts to turn over a new leaf and bid good-bye to a life of crime. In

Stallone works out with weights for two hours a day in order to maintain his well-muscled physique.

Stop! Or My Mom Will Shoot (1992), Stallone played a policeman with a domineering mother. Both films were disastrous, and it appeared to many that Stallone had hit the bottom of his career.

He engineered a "comeback" by returning to the action-film genre. He released two thrillers in 1993: *Cliffhanger* and *Demolition Man.* In the former Stallone played a rescue ranger in Colorado's Rocky Mountains, who foils a band of international thieves as they attempt to regain the cash-filled suitcases they lost during a plane crash. In the latter, Stallone played a cop who was falsely accused of a crime and frozen in a state of suspended animation in 1996. He is then "unfrozen" when the police force of 2032 needs him to hunt down a crazed killer. Both films were huge hits and Stallone emerged once again as king of the box office. Stallone followed with a third thriller, *The Specialist,* in October 1994. This film about a demolitions expert received only lukewarm reviews.

Stormy personal life

Stallone' personal life has often been fodder for the tabloids. After ten years and several affairs, including a ten-month relationship with actress-singer Susan Anton, his troubled marriage to Sasha Czak came to an end in 1985. He then married Danish model Brigitte Niielsen, and that marriage ended after only a year and a half. After what many thought was a very stable and positive relationship with the model Jennifer Flavin, Stallone once again made media headlines when he mailed Flavin a breakup letter via Federal Express in May 1994. It turns out that Stallone had been having an affair, unbeknownst to Flavin, with model-photographer Janice Dickinson. Dickinson had given birth to a girl in February 1994, and the child is reportedly Stallone's daughter. Stallone has a son, Sage, from his first marriage.

Sources

Cosmopolitan, January 1990.

Esquire, February 1989.

People, May 2, 1994.

Sports Illustrated, November 12, 1990.

Vanity Fair, September 1990; November 1993.

Vogue, December 1991.

Patrick Stewart

Born July 13, 1940
Mirfield, Yorkshire, England

ACTOR

Patrick Stewart is best known for his portrayal of Captain Jean-Luc Picard, of the starship Enterprise, in the hit television series *Star Trek: The Next Generation*. The series, which was a sequel to the much-beloved *Star Trek* series of the 1960s, surprised many who thought that no cast of characters could ever attract the kind of loyal following that the original actors drew. Perhaps most surprising was that a Shakespearean-trained British actor playing a restrained, diplomatic leader could compete with the memory of the fiery and impetuous Captain James T. Kirk of the first *Star Trek* series. Yet, Stewart made his own indelible mark in the role of captain, and the series was at the height of its popularity when the show ended in 1994, after seven years on the air.

Playing Captain Picard has "made me a little more thoughtful. A little less impulsive. I hope, more patient. I was very short on patience and tolerance once."

Violent childhood

Stewart has described his childhood as being scary. He was born in 1940 in the small town of Mirfield, Yorkshire, England. His mother was a weaver and his father, a professional solider, was prone to fits of violence. "I wasn't beaten, but there was violence in my house," Stewart told *TV Guide*. "My father would get very angry. He would lose control." But there were also some happy times. Recently, Stewart continued, "I came across a photograph. I'm sitting on a beach, in a deck chair, and my father is tickling me. And I am squirming with laughter.... If anyone would have asked me, 'Did your father ever make you laugh?' I'd have said, absolutely not. He made me feel a lot of things, but he never made me laugh. And yet there it was. And I looked at the photograph and I could remember it. I knew what his fingers felt like on my ribs. I'd forgotten that my father made me laugh. And that's as important a memory to record as that he occasionally lost control of himself."

While still a teenager Stewart set his heart on acting as a career. He enrolled at the Bristol Old Vic Theatre School, one of the best acting academies in England. Making his stage debut in 1959 in Robert Louis Stevenson's *Treasure Island*, Stewart then toured Australia, New Zealand, and South America in Shakespeare's *Twelfth Night* and Alexandre Dumas's *Lady of the Camelias*. In 1966 he joined the prestigious Royal Shakespeare Company (RSC). For the next three decades he would enjoy great success in such RSC productions as Shakespeare's *King John, Henry IV, Hamlet, As You Like It*, and *The Taming of the Shrew*, as well as in works by contemporary playwrights, including Eugene O'Neill's *The Iceman Cometh* and Maksim Gorky's *Enemies*.

In the mid-1970s, in addition to his work in the theater, Stewart had begun accepting parts in television and film. His most notable roles of this time were of Sejanus in *I, Claudius* (1976) and of Karla in *Tinker, Tailor, Soldier, Spy* (1979). Both of these hit BBC miniseries were broadcast in the United States to critical applause. Stewart followed these productions with a number of small roles in films, including *Excalibur* (1981), *Dune* (1984), and *Lifeforce* (1985).

But it wasn't his work in the theater or in film that caught the attention of *Star Trek: The Next Generation* producer Robert Justman. Justman and his wife happened to be attending a literary reading and, after hearing Stewart perform, Justman turned to his wife and said, "We found our captain." "My closest friends were delighted and astonished, perhaps a little envious," Stewart explained to *TV Guide* his fellow actors' reactions to someone from their company making the leap from the Shakespearean stage to science-fiction television. Stewart was, himself, a little surprised when he won the role of Picard. In fact, he read for the role three times before realizing he was auditioning for the part of the captain.

Stewart and Star Trek: The Next Generation are hits

Even after he was cast in the show it took a while for Stewart to believe that he and the series would become successful. "When it first started, I didn't think I would survive beyond the pilot," he told *TV Guide*. "I did not unpack—I didn't see the point. I thought the producers would come to their senses and realize they'd made a grave error in casting me. I was certain that I'd be on my way back to London." Stewart stayed, however, and the show went on to become a great success—rivaling the popularity of the original.

Star Trek: The Next Generation takes places in the twenty-fourth century. Picard leads a starship peopled by representatives of different worlds: a Klingon who is very warrior-like, a Betazoid who intuits others' emotions, a very human-like android, and many others, including humans from Earth. They have a mission from "The United Federation of Planets" to explore the unknown in space, and to bring a message of friendship and peace with them. Along the way they suffer conflicts with alien cultures and destructive beings, yet they also learn strange and wonderful new things. Many credit the show's creator, Gene Roddenberry, with imparting a positive, life-affirming outlook to the series. According to Stewart in *TV Guide*, "Even though [*Star Trek* is] full of fun, high adventure, dazzling technology, and all kinds of bizarre creatures, it's a very serious show, and that's the way serious things should be presented."

Many people were surprised when Paramount Television announced the end of *Star Trek: The Next Generation*. As the highest-rated hour-long drama on syndicated television with more than 20 million viewers tuned in every week, *The Next Generation* seemed to be cancelled for purely financial reasons. Some speculate that Paramount realized that after seven seasons the show had just the right number of episodes (182) to ensure big profits from selling rerun rights to local stations. Any more episodes and a station might have trouble finding room to store them. Also, usually after seven years, contracts are renegotiated, and that can add hundreds of thousands of dollars in production costs to each episode. Paramount contended that they wanted to allow the actors time to appear in feature *Star Trek* films—a more profitable business.

Star Trek: Generations

When they realized that their seventh season would be the last, the cast and crew expressed mixed emotions. "My feelings when I knew this was

> Stewart wakes up at 4:30 or 5:00 every morning, reads a book and drinks hot tea before leaving for work. "To an Englishman, the day does not begin without a proper cup of tea," Stewart told *TV Guide*.

The actors who work together on *Star Trek* also enjoy spending time together socially. They visit each other's homes, and Stewart even directed four of them in a play. Stewart told *TV Guide*, "I've laughed more in the last six years than I have in my entire life."

to be the last season were a mixture of intense relief, and sadness, and an inevitable sense of loss and regret," Stewart told *TV Guide*. The cast didn't have long to miss working with each other, however, because after filming the series' last episode, they began work on a new *Star Trek* feature film. *Star Trek: Generations* was released in November 1994. The seventh feature *Star Trek* film (the previous six having focused on the cast of the original series), in *Generations* there is a symbolic changing of the guard as Captain Jean-Luc Picard meets Captain James T. Kirk by virtue of a time anomaly. The plot turns on an evil scientist, Soran, whose scheming may lead to the end of the universe. Picard enlists Kirk's help in finding Soran and putting an end to his scheme. When the *New York Times* asked Stewart how it felt to be working with members of the original cast, he replied: "There is an enormous sense of history about this. I'm acutely aware of it."

Although Stewart enjoyed playing Picard, he looks forward to returning to the stage, especially to classical theater. "Lear and Macbeth," he told James Brady in a *Parade* magazine interview. "I'm the right age now to play the heavies." In 1991 Stewart created his own Broadway show, a one-person production of Charles Dickens's *A Christmas Carol,* in which Stewart narrated portions of the tale and played 35 characters. He won rave reviews, and a Drama Desk Award for best solo performance of the 1991-92 theater season. "This was unexpectedly beautiful and thrilling," wrote theater critic Mel Gussow in his *New York Times* review of the production.

Stewart lives in the Hollywood Hills section of Los Angeles. He has a son and a daughter from his marriage to choreographer Sheila Falconer. The couple divorced in 1990, after 25 years of marriage.

Sources

Contemporary Theatre, Film, and Television Criticism, Volume 7, Gale 1989.

Current Biography, H.W. Wilson, August 1994.

Entertainment Weekly, March 6, 1992; August 26, 1994.

New York Post, December 20, 1991.

New York Times, December 15, 1991; July 24, 1994.

Parade, April 5, 1992.

TV Guide, August 31, 1991; July 31, 1993; January 15, 1994.

Variety, December 20, 1993.

SWV

"We are part of a pioneering group of women who like to speak their minds."
—*Coko Gamble*

S WV burst onto the music scene in 1992 with the release of their debut album, *It's About Time,* which sold more than 2.5 million copies. Three friends from the boroughs of New York City, Cheryl (Coko) Gamble, Leanne (Leelee) Lyons, and Tamara (Taj) Johnson began singing and harmonizing together when they were only in their teens. They'd practice anywhere—high school halls or in churches. Now they're barely over twenty and the group has completed a worldwide tour, been nominated for a Grammy Award, and filmed seven music videos. Critics and fans rave about their unapologetic lyrics and fresh, smooth sound.

All three singers originally hail from Brooklyn, New York. Before they were even teenagers, Coko and Taj sang at a local Brooklyn talent show. They soon hooked up with Leelee and formed The Female Edition, which they named after the group New Edition. By high school the fledgling trio had broken up. Coko had moved to the Bronx (another borough of Manhattan) and started a new, gospel-inspired group with some other girls. That group was also short-lived.

Renamed SWV

Their big break came when Leelee's cousin introduced her to the mother of a record producer. After meeting with the producer, Leelee called up Coko and Taj and reassembled the group. Together they made some demonstration tapes, found an agent (Maureen Singleton), and signed an eight-record deal with RCA records. It was the agent who renamed the group and gave each of the singers a stage name. Coko was named for her coffee-like complexion, Taj stands for *Tamara Antrice Johnson*, and Leelee is short for Leanne Lyons.

In October 1992 *It's About Time* was released. The album was an instant success, with the single "Weak" going platinum (selling one million copies), and two songs, "I'm So Into You" and "Right Here/Human Nature Remix," going gold (500,000 copies sold). Many of the album's songs candidly explore love and sex, and the group feels that women need to be able to speak as freely as men. "Many times women are afraid to speak about the things they want," Taj told *Ebony*. "But we decided to take a stand on songs like 'Black Pudd'n' and 'Downtown.' Sex is a natural part of life. But a lot of women don't talk about it." Critics praised the group's strong vocals and range of songs—from gospel-like ballads to hip street-sounds.

Adjusting to success

Success has affected each of the singers differently. While Coko moved to a posh New Jersey suburb and Leelee moved to Manhattan, Taj stayed in her native Brooklyn. "I've lived here for the past four years. But now I get teddy bears and fan mail on my doorstep," she explained to *Ebony*. In order to fight the stress and pressures of their hectic schedule and the music industry, Taj works out with weights regularly and plays with her shar-pei puppy.

The most difficult part of success for Coko is how men treat her differently. "Trying to talk to men in the music field is difficult because they feel like they can talk to any girl. And regular, normal men sometimes get intimidated," Coko revealed to *Ebony*. "I knew that if I got into the [music] business it would be like this, but I hate that part." Coko spends her free time with her mother, who is a gospel singer and Coko's "best friend." Coko also spends quite a bit of time with her manicurist. Well known for her four-inch-long *real* fingernails, Coko's appointments often take four hours. "I can drive with them," she told *Ebony*, "But I can't put on jewelry by myself."

For Leelee, the seemingly endless hours of work tend to drag her down. "I had no idea [being a recording artist] meant all of this. I thought it was all about the money, the fame, the fortune, but its much more than that," she explained to *Ebony*. She continued, "We don't usually have a lot of times for ourselves." When she does have time she likes to go to California and see her boyfriend, Omar, an actor and musician.

The future

The trio expects to release their second album in December 1994. This album will contain much more of the group's own writing. "We didn't really know anything before. But now we're definitely going to write and help in the production of this album," Leelee told *Ebony*. SWV's music has appeared on the soundtracks of the movies *Free Willy* and *Above the Rim*. The three also expect to appear on episodes of *The Fresh Prince of Bel-Air* and *Blossom* during the 1994-95 television season.

Sources

Ebony, June 1994.

Entertainment Weekly, December 18, 1992; July 8, 1994.

People, September 6, 1993.

Rolling Stone, May 13, 1993.

Time, July, 19 1993.

Maria Tallchief

January 25, 1925
Fairfax, Oklahoma

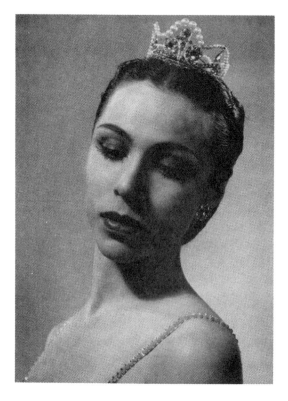

"Undoubtedly Tallchief has been Balanchine's inspiration."—Walter Terry

BALLET DANCER

Maria Tallchief is a world-renowned ballerina and one of the premiere American ballerinas of all time. She was the first American to dance at the Paris Opera and has danced with the Paris Opera Ballet, the Ballet Russe, and the Balanchine Ballet Society (New York City Ballet).

Began dancing at four

Tallchief was born on an Indian reservation; her father was a member of the Osage tribe, and her mother was of Scottish and Irish descent. Her family was wealthy. Her grandfather had helped negotiate the Osage treaty, which created the Osage Reservation in Oklahoma and later yielded a bonanza in oil revenues for some Osage people. Tallchief began dance and music lessons at age four. By age eight, she and her sister had exhausted the training resources in Oklahoma, and the family moved to Beverly Hills, California. By age twelve, Tallchief was studying under Madame Nijinska and David Lichine, a student of the renowned Russian ballerina Anna Pavlova.

Together, these teachers gave Tallchief the strong technical foundation that would later help her become one of America's most well known ballerinas.

At age fifteen at the Hollywood Bowl, Tallchief danced her first solo performance in a number choreographed by Nijinska. Following high school, it was apparent that ballet would be Tallchief's life. Instead of college, she joined the Ballet Russe de Monte Carlo, a highly acclaimed Russian ballet troupe. Tallchief was initially treated with skepticism—the Russian troupe was unwilling to recognize the Native American's greatness. When choreographer George Balanchine took control of the company, however, he recognized Tallchief's talent and selected her for the understudy role in *The Song of Norway*. Under Balanchine, Tallchief's reputation grew, and she was eventually given soloist status. In 1946 Tallchief married Balanchine, and when he moved to Paris, she went with him. The marriage was annulled in 1951, but for many years she was still his inspiration.

Becomes soloist

As with the Ballet Russe, Tallchief was initially treated with condescension in Paris. Her debut at the Paris Opera was the first ever for any American ballerina, and Tallchief's talent quickly won French audiences over. She later became the first American to dance with the Paris Opera Ballet at the Bolshoi Theatre in Moscow. She quickly became the ranking soloist and, soon after, joined the Balanchine Ballet Society, now the New York City Ballet. It was a very special era in the life of the company, and Balanchine was in full glory choreographically. The young New York City Ballet was small, and a principal dancer was in great demand, performing up to eight ballets a week. Such conditions not only developed the ballerina's impressive versatility, but also contributed to Tallchief's rise as a popular figure in dance. Tallchief was a model of dedication to her form; her life revolved around her classes and performances. At the New York City Ballet, Tallchief became recognized as one of the greatest dancers in the world. When she became the prima ballerina, she was the first American dancer to achieve this title.

In 1949, Tallchief danced what was perhaps her greatest role in the Balanchine-choreographed version of the *Firebird*. Balanchine had choreographed the role for Tallchief, and her dazzling blend of physical control and mysticism enchanted audiences. Her stamina, attack and musicality made her ideal for the tremendously demanding role that Balanchine created for her. It was a significant development for the choreographer and

Tallchief dances with Jacques d'Amboise the pas de deux from *Sylvia* on the South Lawn of the White House, June 11, 1964.

his ballerina, and had the additional bonus of enjoying popular appeal. Critical acclaim was equally enthusiastic. Walter Terry put it simply, saying, "Tallchief gave a performance of historical proportions." The ballet was obviously a powerful artistic collaboration between choreographer and ballerina. *Firebird* was followed five years later by another New York City Ballet classic, *The Nutcracker,* in which Tallchief, as a poised and commanding Sugar Plum Fairy, contributed as much to the financial as to the artistic success of Balanchine's version of this classic Christmas ballet. It became one of the most reliable box-office successes of the fledgling New York City Ballet.

Tallchief has received numerous awards, including an Achievement Award from the Women's National Press Club in 1953; a *Dance Magazine* Award in 1960; a Capezio Award in 1965; and a Distinguished Service Award from the University of Oklahoma in 1972.

In the late 1950s Balanchine began to turn his attention to the ballerina Tanquil Le Clerq. For Tallchief, experiencing Balanchine's shift in artistic infatuation was undoubtedly painful. She had dedicated herself completely to working with him and performing the pieces that had become her signature pieces. She had shown absolute, unquestioning faith in his decisions. He had reshaped her style and execution, crafting the magnificent technique associated with her performance of the Balanchine repertoire, and she perfectly represented the Balanchine style. Part of Balanchine's genius was in allowing each ballerina to do what she did best, thus developing a personal style and range of roles. He knew how to capitalize on the individuality of his ballerinas, and how to make them look wonderful. The choreographer's shift in attention to Le Clerq meant the end of a steady stream of ballets for Tallchief, although she continued to create various Balanchine roles until 1960.

Remarries and has child

In 1955 and 1956, she was a guest artist with the Ballet Russe de Monte Carlo, reportedly receiving the highest salary in ballet history. In 1956 she remarried, taking a maternity leave in 1958—her only leave from the rigors of a professional ballet career. Two years later, Tallchief joined the American Ballet Theatre. While with that company she danced *Miss Julie, Jardin aux Lilas,* and others, joining them for both a tour of the USSR and the United States.

Tallchief had no desire to dance beyond her prime, so she retired her performing career in 1966. She went to Chicago, and out of her association with the Lyric Opera Ballet attempted to craft an enterprise in the image of the New York City Ballet. Perhaps the most unfortunate decision of her career was the creation of the ill-fated Chicago City Ballet. While strong as a teacher and coach, she lacked the temperament and skills required of an artistic director. Eventually Paul Meija became resident choreographer, but in spite of tremendous support from the critics in the early years, the company collapsed in 1987. Tallchief has since renewed her alliance with the Lyric Opera Ballet School.

Sources

Chicago, February 1989.

Dance Magazine, September 1945; February 1956; December 1984; February 1991.

Interview, March 1987.

Meyers, E., *Maria Tallchief,* New York, 1966.

Theatre Arts, September 1961.

Tracy, Robert, *Balanchine's Ballerinas,* New York, 1983.

Variety, October 18, 1989.

10,000 Maniacs

ROCK GROUP

*"A lot of [our] songs are about really
frightening subjects. But we hide them in
nice little pop melodies, and it kind of lures
people in."*

10,000 Maniacs was "one of the most forceful and innovative young
bands in America," according to John Leland in *Vogue.* Composed of
lead singer and lyricist Natalie Merchant, bass player Steve Gustafson,
drummer Jerry Augustyniak, keyboard player Dennis Drew, and lead guitarist Robert Buck, the Maniacs began recording in the early 1980s but only
began enjoying substantial success with the release of their 1987 album, *In
My Tribe.* That disc, and the subsequent *Blind Man's Zoo,* made popular
10,000 Maniacs' particularly tuneful manner of social protest—their songs
take on issues such as child abuse, environmental problems, and unwanted
pregnancy. As Ira Robbins of *Rolling Stone* summed, the band's "plain-spo-
ken music is an elegant rock descendant of American and British folk traditions."

The core of the group that became 10,000 Maniacs formed around
Gustafson, Drew, and Buck in Jamestown, New York, in 1981. Soon afterwards, the band, which had played under such monikers as Still Life and
the Burn Victims, decided to change its name. The new name evolved
from a mistake about the title of a B-grade horror film, *2,000 Maniacs.* Merchant, though younger than the other group members, knew Gustafson
and Drew because they ran the student radio station at Jamestown Community College, where she attended classes. She began showing up where

the Maniacs performed, at small clubs and parties, and one night they invited her up to the microphone to sing. They liked her looks, her dancing, and her ability to improvise songs, and she quickly became an official Maniac.

Soon Merchant and the other Maniacs gained a local following in western New York. They also put out two recordings on their own label—an extended-play disc in 1982 entitled *Human Conflict Number Five,* and an album in 1983, *Secrets of the I Ching.* Both came about partially as projects of the sound-engineering program at the State University of New York at Fredonia, and the latter included protest songs like "My Mother the War" and "Grey Victory"—about the World War II atomic bombing of Hiroshima, Japan. The records received airplay on alternative and college radio stations, and drew praise and comparisons to the British folk group Fairport Convention from critics, but were commercial failures.

Sign contract with Elektra Records

The band's luck began to change in 1983, when it came under the management of Peter Leak, an Englishman who got them their first British tour, and, in 1985, a contract with Elektra Records. Elektra tried to give the band a more new wave look—"wanted to make us look like the [slick] Human League," guitarist Buck told DeCurtis. The image consultant that was called in wore leather and had "a samurai haircut," but gave up when he took his first look at 10,000 Maniacs. "He was really nice about it," recalled Buck. "He's going, 'I'm sorry. There's obviously nothing I can do for you. You people are hicks. The best thing you can do is accentuate the fact that you're hicks.'"

The Maniacs' first album for Elektra, *The Wishing Chair,* enjoyed little more commercial success than their previous efforts. Like the earlier recordings, however, it received some highly favorable reviews—for instance, Ira Robbins in *Rolling Stone* hailed it as "a thought-provoking, toe-tapping joy." Hoping to make the band's next album more salable, Elektra suggested Peter Asher as producer. Asher had produced records for many popular performers, most notably Linda Ronstadt, and during the 1960s had been half of the popular British duo Peter and Gordon. The combination proved to be winning. The resulting disc, *In My Tribe,* spawned the group's first popular hit, "Like the Weather." But as *Rolling Stone* critic J. D. Considine pointed out in his review of the album, "This [was] no slick sellout." He added that "Asher should be applauded for the fact that he has allowed 10,000 Maniacs to remain themselves." Other songs, like the controversial cut about child abuse "What's the Matter

Here," and a remake of Cat Stevens's "Peace Train," received airplay also. The band gained even more exposure when they opened a series of concerts for rock group R.E.M. Merchant explained 10,000 Maniacs' formula for success to *People*'s Steve Dougherty: "A lot of the songs are about really frightening subjects. But we hide them in nice little pop melodies, and it kind of lures people in."

That formula succeeded again with 1989's *Blind Man's Zoo*. Again using Asher as producer, the Maniacs released an album labeled both "vitriolic" (biting) and "charming" by Leland. He and David Browne of *Rolling Stone* agreed that it is probably 10,000 Maniacs' best work to date. *Blind Man's Zoo* brought the group two more hit singles—"Trouble Me," which Merchant wrote for her father while he was hospitalized, and "Eat for Two," which, in the words of *People* reviewer Andrew Abrahams, concerns "the darker side of deciding to bear a child." Other noteworthy songs from the disc include "Jubilee," a strike at religious fanatics, "The Big Parade," about a veteran of the Vietnam War, and "Hateful Hate," about the colonization of Africa. After that 10,000 Maniacs continued to win new fans with their albums *Hope Chest, Our Time in Eden* (which spawned the hit "These Are Days"), *African Violet Society,* and the hugely popular *Unplugged.*

At the height of the band's popularity, following the release of *Our Time in Eden,* Merchant announced that she would be leaving the Maniacs. Having reached the decision long before, the band decided to delay the news until after the release of the record. Citing her long tenure with the band—she had been a Maniac virtually all of her adult life—she said that she simply wanted to pursue other projects, perhaps even finish college.

Sources

People, May 23, 1988; July 3, 1989.

Rolling Stone, March 27, 1986; October 22, 1987; June 16, 1988; June 15, 1989; August 10, 1989; August 20, 1992; March 18, 1993.

Seventeen, February 1993.

Vogue, July 1989.

Robert Townsend

Born February 6, 1957
Chicago, Illinois

"People need inspiration, especially black people. If you go to the movies, you have nothing that validates that you are good, you are special, you are creative, you are talented, that you can do whatever you want to do. So I've got to fight."

ACTOR, WRITER, DIRECTOR, AND PRODUCER

Filmmaker Robert Townsend knows fully the responsibility he has taken on in pursuing his chosen profession: "I understand the effect films and movies leave on people's lives," he explained to Allison Samuels in the *Los Angeles Times.* "They affect the way we dress, comb our hair, even the way we decorate our living rooms. That's powerful stuff, and you have to treat it accordingly." Whereas fellow black filmmakers Spike Lee and John Singleton have used the medium to address social injustice and the pervasive anxiety felt by the black community—often by depicting harsh and disturbing scenes of violence and racism—Townsend has sought to rid blacks of a constraining "slave mentality" by exposing and exploding black stereotypes perpetuated by the white-dominated film industry.

In place of those cardboard images, Townsend provides his audience with characters who are neither "black" nor "white," but individuals whose actions and aspirations are not necessarily determined by racial imperatives. He also seeks to offer his audience positive values, self-esteem, heroes, a mythology—a chance to dream.

Townsend was not always a fighter, however. Born in 1957, he grew up on the west side of Chicago where, as he told Marilyn Marshall in *Ebony,* "I ran from a lot of gangs." Safe inside his home, Townsend watched hours of television, his imagination stimulated by entertainers as varied as comedian Red Skelton and actor Sidney Poitier. His creative ability and sense of self-worth were also spurred by his divorced mother, who raised her four children to believe they could accomplish anything. "Because of that," Townsend explained to Clifford Terry in the *Chicago Tribune,* "I never believed in limitations."

Townsend dreamed of becoming a basketball player; but growing up in a neighborhood that produced National Basketball Association stars Isiah Thomas and Mark Aguirre, he fared only well enough to make the team and then sit on the bench. To pass the time, he did impersonations, making his teammates laugh—much to the chagrin of his coaches. Heeding his fellow players' observation—"Townsend, you can't play—but you're funny," as he recalled in an interview with Donna Brit for the *Washington Post*—Townsend decided to sharpen his comedic skills and pursue acting instead of athletics.

Honed acting skills

At the age of 16 he joined Chicago's Experimental Black Actors Guild, becoming its youngest member. Through this group Townsend learned the skills of acting and directing and gained his first screen role, a small part in the 1975 production *Cooley High.* "My most memorable line was 'Somebody should kick his [butt]," he told the *Chicago Tribune*'s Terry. "What a way to come onto the silver screen! I remember my mother going to the movie, saying, 'He's up there cursin.'" During this period Townsend also studied improvisation with the renowned comedy troupe Second City, but after graduating from high school he deferred to his mother's wishes and attended college at Illinois State University, where he studied radio-TV communications. He subsequently transferred to William Patterson College in New Jersey, commuting to New York City to work with the Negro Ensemble Company and study acting with famed dramatic coach Stella Adler. Townsend finally ended his academic career at Hunter College in New York, dividing his time between studying, acting in Off-Broadway productions, and performing stand-up routines in comedy clubs.

In 1982 Townsend headed west to California with his friend Keenan Ivory Wayans, who later went on to create Fox TV's hit comedy series *In Living Color.* For the first time in his life, Townsend was confronted with limitations. Although after a few years he was able to secure small roles in mainstream productions such as *Streets of Fire, A Soldier's Story,* and *American Flyers,* for the most part Townsend was offered the typical fare available to aspiring black actors: pimps, slaves, and servants.

What Townsend had discovered was the separate and unequal sphere into which blacks were put in Hollywood; they were never just actors and directors who made films for audiences, but black actors and black directors who made black films for black audiences. Townsend wanted to change this perception, as he explained in *Dollars & Sense:* "Whites sit down after dinner and say, 'Hey honey, let's go see a black film tonight.' The problem is that the films made by black filmmakers cross the spectrum, just like all other films do. We need to be looked at in that way. Until then, the money will be spread thin to the various films. We will all lose." This sense of loss can be appreciated, Townsend and others believe, if we imagine what would have happened if the film industry and audiences perceived a film like *The Godfather* strictly as an Italian-American film, or *Dances with Wolves* as primarily a Native American film. The relevance of these films clearly extends far beyond their immediate setting; to pigeonhole them according to a specific culture would be to obscure their universal themes and access.

Film parodied Hollywood's "black" view

"There ain't nothin' to it but to do it," a character says in Townsend's first film as a director, *Hollywood Shuffle* (1987), which he co-wrote with Wayans. That line perhaps became a mantra for the filmmaker during his discouraging apprenticeship in Hollywood. A satirical and pointed look at Hollywood's treatment and view of blacks, *Hollywood Shuffle,* which was filmed intermittently over two and a half years, cost $100,000 to make—paltry by Hollywood standards. The initial $60,000 came from money Townsend had saved from acting jobs; the remaining $40,000 he charged on every MasterCard and Visa he could obtain. He paid his actors minimum film wages; when he couldn't pay them, he filled their cars with gas on his charge accounts. He finished the film during a whirlwind 14-day span, shooting scenes in one take, then moving on to avoid being caught without location permits. When the film was completed, he booked a screening room—on credit—invited every film distribution company in Hollywood, and then signed a deal with Goldwyn studios, which promptly settled his debts and his actors' remaining wages. Townsend's gamble paid off big time: in the first month after its release, *Hollywood Shuffle* grossed $850,000. It eventually earned more than $10 million.

The hero of the film is Bobby Taylor, played by Townsend. Bobby, kind and respectful, lives at home in Los Angeles with his grandmother, mother, and younger brother and works at a hot dog stand, Winky Dinky Dog, the manager of which dreams of Bobby taking over the business. But Bobby has a different idea; to the exasperation of his fellow workers and his manager, he continuously misses work to attend film auditions in hopes of becoming an actor. But Bobby lands only one role—a jive-talking pimp in a "blaxploitation" picture, a genre made popular in the 1970s in which blacks are roundly stereotyped. Mirroring Townsend's own experiences, Bobby is frustrated by the gap between his acting abilities and his acting opportunities.

Throughout the film are comical vignettes, reveries, and nightmares that Bobby experiences as he seeks his dream; he imagines himself starring as a hero in films like *Rambro: First Young Blood, King Lear,* and *The Death of a Breakdancer,* a black-and-white film in which he plays a private detective named Sam Ace. But Bobby is also frightened when he imagines being a graduate of the "Black Actors School," where white instructors—through courses such as Jive Talk and Shuffling—teach classically trained black actors how to play pimps and hustlers. In perhaps the funniest vignette, "Sneakin' in the Movies," Bobby imagines that he and a friend are Speed and Tyrone, two streetwise young film critics who slip into movie theaters to view films and then determine whether one should pay to see them. Both gave thumbs down to movies such as *Dirty Larry* and *Amadeus and Salieri* but heartily endorsed *Attack of the Street Pimps,* declaring: "The director captured the essence of street life in a whore-type situation.... It was live."

With *Hollywood Shuffle,* Townsend parodied the white Hollywood establishment that makes black actors perform "black" according to a white vision. "The movie's comic range derives from the strength of such bitterness—Townsend's disbelief over the grotesque choices open to black actors," David Denby observed in *New York.* Michael Konik, writing in *Reason,* believed the film, in its parody and spoof, was an evolutionary step in the black film genre, elevating "blacks from supporting players, stereotypical caricatures, and fast-talking liars to people, people who are interesting and challenging enough to earn the attention, sympathy, and enthusiasm" of all viewers, regardless of color. Echoing the acclaim of many reviewers of the film, *Time*'s Richard Corliss praised Townsend's human insight: "[He] knows Bobby fully lives where we all live, in dreams of glory, agony, love—of life's infinite possibilities. In real life, most of those dreams are dashed or deferred. So who wouldn't be pleased enough to pay the price of a movie ticket to see Townsend's come true?"

The success of *Hollywood Shuffle* thrust Townsend into the limelight. Comedian and film star Eddie Murphy asked Townsend to direct his 1987 concert film, *Raw*. The filmmaker also directed the HBO comedy special *Partners in Crime*, which showcased new comedic talent from around the country. After *Shuffle* Townsend was also featured in the 1989 mystery film *The Mighty Quinn*, playing a free-spirited Caribbean hustler who is a suspect in a murder investigation led by his friend, the local police chief, portrayed by actor Denzel Washington.

Difficulties remain for black filmmakers

Despite the success of his first film, his growing stature in Hollywood, and the emergence of strong films by other black writers and directors, Townsend had difficulty receiving financial backing for his second feature, *The Five Heartbeats*. It took four years to make the film; *The Five Heartbeats* made the rounds of the studios, including Warner Bros., with which Townsend had signed a deal after the success of *Hollywood Shuffle*. Finally, Twentieth Century-Fox agreed to back the film, releasing it in 1991.

The Five Heartbeats is about a fictitious legendary R&B male singing group. The film begins by flashing back to 1965 and then moves forward, following the group through the 1980s. The themes explored as the group and its individual members are depicted include racism, exploitation, drug abuse, and the testing of friendship by the pressures of success. Townsend wanted to make a film that was "pure comedy, but it took another shape," he told the *Los Angeles Times*'s Samuels. "I traveled on the road for a few months with an actual group from the '60s, the Dells, and heard their stories of being ripped off and taken advantage of by people in the business. After spending time with that group I felt sad. I kept telling myself, it isn't about jokes, Robert, it isn't about jokes."

What the film is primarily about, according to Townsend, is friendship. "The story is a positive look at five young black men with an attempt to break away from any of the negative stereotypes that are tagged to us through the media," he explained to Samuels. "Each character is totally different from the other. One might be what most people expect from the black male, while the others take you in completely different directions. I want to show people something they haven't seen before."

Few critics felt Townsend completely accomplished this ideal, but most found his attempt noteworthy. "Its characterizations are often sketchy, its story awkwardly paced, and its dialogue much too familiar," Janet Maslin wrote in the *New York Times*. "Even the musical sequences, the very source of the Heartbeats' appeal, are not entirely convincing. But *The Five Heartbeats* also conveys an obvious love of its material and a fundamental sweetness and sincerity." Dave Kehr, reviewing the film for the *Chicago Tribune*, agreed: "None of the characters is far from cliché, but Townsend's affectionate direction somehow makes their familiarity seem a warming virtue."

Townsend's continued desire to provide audiences, especially black audiences, with positive universal values and role models was evident in his next production, *The Meteor Man*, which was released in 1993. The film, in which Townsend plays an inner-city high school teacher who is actually an alien with superhuman powers, was a Hollywood first: no black had ever before played a comic-book-type superhero. Townsend thought the time was overdue. "We haven't seen even one movie where the hero is black and he's talking to everybody," he pointed out in *Interview*. "I just want one to cheer for. Like I cheer for Terminator, I cheer for Rambo, I cheer for James Bond. I just want one.... He doesn't have to be super, just a hero."

Sources

American Film, December 1987.

American Visions, February/March 1993.

Chicago Tribune, March 10, 1991; March 29, 1991; March 31, 1991.

Dollars & Sense, January 1992.

Ebony, July 1987; September 1987.

Interview, February 1991.

Jet, August 9, 1993.

Los Angeles Times, September 9, 1990.

New Statesman, April 8, 1988.

Newsweek, April 6, 1987; July 13, 1992.

New York, April 6, 1987.

New York Times, March 4, 1990; March 29, 1991; October 18, 1992.

Reason, November 1987.

Time, April 27, 1987.

Washington Post, March 31, 1991.

Denzel Washington

Born in December 1954
Mt. Vernon, New York

ACTOR

"I'm going to continue to take chances—fall on my face sometimes—but hopefully learn from the experiences. I've grown and learned so much from acting about black history. That's the thing I'm most happy about."

Academy Award winner Denzel Washington has ridden a series of cinematic successes to superstardom in Hollywood. He is a performer who is equally at home in light comedy and serious drama, and his romantic good looks have earned him fans all over the world. Film director Ed Zwick told the *Philadelphia Daily News* of Washington: "Whatever that mysterious electrochemical process is that makes the camera love someone, he has more of it than any one person should."

An actor blessed with good looks and a wide range of talent, Washington has chosen his roles with care. *Washington Post* contributor Donna Britt noted: "It's ironic that this man whose race almost certainly has diminished his opportunities as an actor has used his career to explore his blackness." Washington admits that he has felt stifled by the "role model" and "torch bearer" tags by which critics identify him, but at the same time he is a dedicated artist seeking to make an impression. "All I can do is play the part," he told the *Washington Post.* "I can't do [a] part for 40 million black people or orange or green. On the other hand I'm not going to do anything to embarrass my people."

Denzel Washington was born late in 1954, the son of a Pentecostal minister and a gospel singer. He grew up right on the edge of the Bronx, in the middle-class neighborhood of Mt. Vernon, New York. "My father was down on the movies, and his idea of something worthwhile would be *The King of Kings, The Ten Commandments* and *101 Dalmatians,*" the actor told the *Chicago Tribune.* "And I knew no actors. It's a wonder I ever went into acting." Washington was a good student as a youth, and he drew his friends from the melting pot of races that formed the Bronx. He described his childhood as "a good background for somebody in my business. My friends were West Indians, blacks, Irish, Italians, so I learned a lot of different cultures."

When Washington was 14, his parents divorced. The subject is still sensitive for him, although he remains on cordial terms with both his mother and his father. "I guess it made me angry," he told the *Washington Post.* "I went through a phase where I got into a lot of fights. Working it out, you know." A guidance counselor at his high school suggested that Washington apply to a private boarding school ("very rich and very white") in upstate New York. He did, and to his astonishment was accepted with a full scholarship. After graduating from that academy, he attended Fordham University in the Bronx, where he declared a pre-med major. In retrospect, Washington attributes his strong showing as a youngster to his mother's influence. "She was very, very tough, a tough disciplinarian," he told the *Washington Post.* "Even when I was 15 or 16, I had to be home by the time the street lights went on. She saw to it I was exposed to a lot of things. She couldn't afford it, but she was very intelligent. She is basically responsible for my success."

Decided on acting career

A long-standing membership in the YMCA also contributed to Washington's career choice. In college he drifted through several majors, including biology and journalism, and took an acting workshop "but underwent no great revelation." During the summer recess, however, he served as a counselor at a YMCA-sponsored camp. "I had grown up in the organization and had worked as a leader," he told the *Chicago Tribune.* "I organized a talent show, and someone told me, 'You seem real natural on the stage; did you ever think of becoming an actor?' Bing! That's all it took." When he returned to Fordham in the fall, he auditioned for the university's production of Eugene O'Neill's *The Emperor Jones,* and won the lead over a number of theater majors. He went on to star in several more dramas at Fordham, including Shakespeare's *Othello.*

Robinson Stone, a retired actor, was Washington's drama instructor at Fordham. Remembering his gifted student, Stone told the *Chicago Tribune:* "Oh, God, he was thrilling even then. Denzel was from the Bronx campus, not even a theater major—and he got the lead in the school production of *Othello.* He was easily the best Othello I had ever seen, and I had seen Paul Robeson play it. I remember Jose Ferrer came to look at it. He and I agreed that Denzel had a brilliant career ahead of him. He played Othello with so much majesty and beauty but also rage and hate that I dragged agents to come and see it."

Cast in television's St. Elsewhere *series*

The agents too were impressed. Even before Washington graduated from Fordham he was offered a small role in a television drama, *Wilma,* based on the life of Olympic runner Wilma Rudolph. After he earned his degree, Washington embarked on a hectic round of professional activities, including theater work, television, and films. Early in his career he appeared opposite George Segal in *Carbon Copy,* a comic movie, and he also took a role in the television miniseries *Flesh and Blood.* These parts introduced Washington to the Hollywood production companies, and he was cast as doctor Phillip Chandler in the television drama *St. Elsewhere.* Although he was not nearly as demanding of himself in his *St. Elsewhere* role as he has since become, Washington was nevertheless able to infuse the role with non-stereotyped humanity. *Washington Post* writer Megan Rosenfeld concluded that the actor's five-year association with *St. Elsewhere* gained him "the kind of popular recognition that is both the boon and the curse of serious actors. Chandler is an intelligent and ambitious young man, portrayed not as a black paragon, but as a human being with all the flaws and problems of anyone else."

It was a stage role that assured Washington's success, however. Early in the 1980s he was cast in the pivotal role of Private Peterson in the drama *A Soldier's Play.* The part won Washington an Obie Award for his off-Broadway performance, and he was invited to work as Peterson in the film version of the play. Washington took a break from *St. Elsewhere* to undertake the film role, and he was quite pleased when the renamed *A Soldier's Story* earned the respect of film critics worldwide. In *A Soldier's Story,* Washington turned in a memorable performance as the young private goaded to murder by an abusive drill sergeant. After viewing *A Sol-*

dier's Story, Chicago Tribune correspondent Bob Thomas called Washington "one of the most versatile of the new acting generation."

The Hollywood establishment recognized that Washington possessed a near phenomenal potential. He was at once handsome, articulate, and dignified, and he appeared to be at ease in both comic and dramatic situations. Inevitably (and unfortunately), his race still restricted the number and size of roles he was offered. Even after he appeared in the Oscar-nominated role of activist Steven Biko in *Cry Freedom,* he was still not considered a high-visibility star. As late as 1989 the actor told the *Washington Post* that he often found himself "waiting for an opportunity to come [my] way but realizing there's no group of people like [me] who are successful, who can give you the faith to say, 'Well, if I wait, it will come.' So you end up taking [roles] ... that are not necessarily the best, that aren't optimum."

Insisted that the script for Glory *be revised*

One of the roles Washington did not consider "optimum" was that of the runaway slave Trip in the film *Glory.* The original script for *Glory* concentrated on Civil War general Robert Gould Shaw, who led the first black regiment into battle and died with them in an unsuccessful assault. At Washington's suggestion, the screenplay for *Glory* was significantly revised in order to explore the concerns of the black foot soldiers. Satisfied with the revisions, Washington accepted the part of Trip. He studied histories of the Civil War and of slavery in the South, learning enough to assure that both he and his character would be in a fit of controlled rage. "When we were making *Glory,*" he told the *Chicago Tribune,* "people kept asking me, 'Why are you so angry?' I haven't been through anything like [slavery and soldiering], but I've read about it. I've studied the history, and that's enough to make you angry. How can I be 35 and never been taught about black soldiers being a part of the Civil War. That's something to ask: How can that happen?"

Washington's performance in *Glory* earned him an Academy Award for best supporting actor in 1990. It was his second nomination, but more importantly, it was only the fifth Oscar ever won by a black actor. The award finally brought him the visibility and clout he needed to secure work that met his standards. After starring as a jazz trumpeter in Spike Lee's *Mo' Better Blues* in 1990, he appeared in *Mississippi Masala,* a drama about an interracial love affair, and then took the lead in *Malcolm X.*

The three-and-a-half-hour *Malcolm X* was released in November 1992 to overwhelming critical praise. *Philadelphia Inquirer* movie critic Desmond

Washington with Jihmi Kennedy and Morgan Freeman in a scene from *Glory, 1989.*

Ryan wrote: "Denzel Washington's often-mesmerizing portrait of Malcolm will surely be the performance to beat when the Oscars are handed out.... When Washington draws us into Malcolm X's inner turmoil and torment, we can almost feel the fire that forged his iron will." *New York Times Magazine* reporter Lena Williams likewise maintained that Washington "has caught the Muslim leader's vocal cadences exactly, the quiet intensity of his rapid-fire delivery, the underlying humor of his logic. For those moments the cameras are rolling, it is 1963—and Malcolm speaks."

In 1993 Washington starred with Julia Roberts in the film adaptation of John Grisham's best-selling novel *The Pelican Brief*. Washington portrays an investigative reporter who teams up with a law student to unravel a political murder plot. This same year Washington also starred in the highly acclaimed film *Philadelphia* as a personal injury lawyer named Joe Miller. Miller, who hates homosexuals, represents Andrew Beckett, who was fired from his law firm because he had AIDS.

Washington is not particularly forthcoming about his private life, but his family is very important to him. In his rare moments of leisure he stays home, avoiding the celebrated Hollywood party circuit. In the *Washington Post*, the actor called his wife and two children "the base that keeps me solid." He added: "Acting is just a way of making a living. Family is life. When you experience a child, you know that's life." The actor is careful to keep a humble perspective on the praise he has received, and he completely refuses to consider himself "sexy" despite persistent claims in the press. Acting, he said, is a way for him to explore the spiritual self, irrespective of race or creed. "I enjoy acting," he told the *Washington Post*. "This is when I feel most natural. This is really my world. I was obviously destined to get into this, and I guess I have the equipment to do it."

Sources

Boston Globe, February 1, 1990.

Chicago Tribune, March 15, 1986; December 30, 1987; August 5, 1990.

Detroit Free Press, July 29, 1990.

Interview, December 1993.

Jet, December 20, 1993; January 31, 1994.

New York Times Magazine, October 25, 1992

Philadelphia Daily News, October 24, 1992; November 12, 1992; November 17, 1992, November 18, 1992.

Philadelphia Inquirer, November 18, 1992.

Time, February 15, 1993.

Washington Post, September 18, 1985; August 25, 1989.

Sigourney Weaver

Born October 8, 1949
New York, New York

"I like doing off-beat, extreme stuff; traditional roles bore me. I became an actress because I'm so curious about everything. Every time I start a new picture, I can explore a new world."

ACTRESS

Sigourney Weaver has pursued her acting career with a sense of adventure and amusement, pushing herself to find unusual, sometimes even bizarre, comic and dramatic film and stage roles. "A seamless fusion of beauty and intelligence," as *Newsweek* observed, Weaver combines professionalism with a spirit of playfulness and risk-taking. Primarily a movie actress who started in off-Broadway productions and continues to act in them, Weaver courts the humorous and the horrific, along with a sense of seriousness, in the parts she carefully selects.

Weaver has explored "new worlds" with the oddest list of credits for an actress of her reputation and stature. She has not shied away from movies as different from each other as *Alien, Ghostbusters,* and *Half Moon Street.* And each time she has forged an original and memorable screen character. "By training, temperament, and spectacular good looks, Sigourney Weaver seems a natural for stardom in this era; she's scaled to be a modern heroine," judged the *New Yorker*'s Pauline Kael.

In *Alien* (1979), her first movie, *Newsweek*'s Jack Kroll recognized her unusual talent when he concluded his review by writing: "And newcomer Sigourney Weaver, a strong young actress with a touch of Jane Fonda, takes the classic B-movie woman's role—all the heavings and hysterics of noble women like Fay Wray, Faith Domergue and Julie Adams—and raises it to a kind of abstract energy and ambushed grace that's like watching a ballet of pure terror." Weaver inspires such praise, even in movies where a high-level performance is not always easy to accomplish and critical opinion is divided or even negative. Ivan Reitman, director of *Ghostbusters,* simply called Weaver "the perfect contemporary heroine."

Born into a wealthy family, Weaver described her childhood to *Time*'s Richard Corliss: "I was a privileged, pampered, sheltered child.... It was as though every day had a happy ending." Her father is Sylvester "Pat" Weaver, a television pioneer and innovator who served as president of NBC during the 1950s and created the "Today" and "Tonight Shows," which are still the anchors of the network's programming, as well as cable programming. Her mother is British stage actress Elizabeth Inglis. Weaver's grandfather was a prosperous businessman in Los Angeles and her grandmother composed opera.

She and her brother Trajan, who was named after the Roman emperor, spent their childhoods moving frequently. The Weavers had an estate at Sands Point, Long Island, and Weaver recalls regular visits from the television stars of the 1950s—Milton Berle, Steve Allen, Jessica Tandy, and even the chimpanzee from the *Today Show,* J. Fred Muggs, "a vicious little beast. He once tried to rip my dress!" When he was home, her father watched multiple televisions to keep abreast of the competition.

At 14 Weaver changed her name from Susan to Sigourney, the aunt of Jordan Baker in F. Scott Fitzgerald's novel *The Great Gatsby.* "To my ear Sigourney was a stage name—long and curvy, with a musical ring," Weaver has often explained. She was also called "Junior Birdman" in school, "a real honor—it meant I was the funniest in the class." She sampled summer stock in Connecticut. "By then I was close to six feet tall and exceedingly clumsy. Directors told me I was uncastable. But my mother saved the day. She kept telling me it was wonderful to be so 'stately,' a kind way of putting it to this giant. If she hadn't said that, I might have gotten even more self-conscious about my height."

Weaver attended Stanford University, from which she graduated with a degree in English. Weaver described her 1960s undergraduate days for

Time: "Every day was a happening.... I wore an elf costume—red pantaloons, vest and hat, all festooned with blue pompons—and lived with my boyfriend in a tree house, dining on vegetables we stole from the experimental garden. One day, for a linguistics presentation, we threw pies at each other, then tossed tiny parachutes at the other class members. The professor gave us both A's."

Attends Yale graduate school

Weaver's experience at the Yale Drama School, where she enrolled in the fall of 1971, was a shock. "Yale was a joyless experience. It almost destroyed my career. I had so much confidence when I got there, and so little when I left," she said. She did become friends, however, with student playwrights John Guare (*House of Blue Lights*), Wendy Wasserstein (*Uncommon Women and Others*), and Christopher Durang (*Sister Mary Ignatius Explains It All for You*). Weaver acted in their student productions, but the Yale Drama School had seriously damaged her interest in theater.

"I had no intention of going into show business. There was so much tension and competition at Yale, I thought I wanted a nice, safe job—like working in a bank," Weaver admitted. Durang, however, offered her a part in the off-Broadway production of *The Nature and Purpose of the Universe*. Other acting jobs followed, including a role in Somerset Maugham's *The Constant Wife* with film star Ingrid Bergman. She also appeared in fellow Yale colleague Guare's *Marco Polo Sings a Solo*.

Big break with Alien

Weaver's big break in movies came when she was cast as Ripley in the science fiction film *Alien* in 1979. Directed by Ridley Scott, whose previous credit at the time was *The Duellists*, *Alien* was a box-office hit but received mixed reviews, though critics agreed that on a sheer horror level it was extremely terrifying. Jack Kroll described *Alien* in *Newsweek* as a movie that "just boils everything down to the pure, ravishingly vulgar essence of fright." David Denby in *New York Magazine*, however, objected to Scott's manipulation of the audience and called the movie "terrifying, but not in a way that is remotely enjoyable" and "the killings are so gratuitously horrible that we jump every time."

Drawing inspiration from the popularity of the other science fiction and space fantasy movies of the 1970s, *Alien* has more in common with haunted-house horror movie techniques than the playful intentions of the *Star Wars* and *Star Trek* movies. The crew of the space craft Nostromo (the name is taken from a Joseph Conrad novel) are returning home when a signal is picked up from a crashed space ship on an unknown planet. The crew investigates and discovers an alien life form, an octopus-like creature "unclouded by conscience or delusions of morality."

The alien changes form at will as it induces terror and shock. It tracks down one crew member after another, with Ripley and her pet cat being the lone survivors. "Sigourney Weaver," wrote Vincent Canby in the *New York Times*, "is impressive and funny ... a young woman who manages to act tough, efficient and sexy all at the same time."

Weaver next appeared in the 1981 production *Eyewitness.* Originally titled *The Janitor, Eyewitness* has a plot in which William Hurt plays Daryll Deever, a Vietnam veteran and janitor whose passions in life are his motorcycle and television news reporter Tony Sokolow, played by Weaver. When Sokolow is assigned to cover a murder that took place in the building where Hurt works, he pretends to know more than he does to gain her interest, which also attracts the attention of the real killers.

Weaver's portrayal of Jillian Bryant in Peter Weir's 1983 romantic melodrama *The Year of Living Dangerously* cast her opposite actor Mel Gibson who, as Guy Hamilton, plays an Australian journalist on assignment in Djakarta, Indonesia, right before the fall of President Sukarno in 1965. Weir set the film's love story in the context of international intrigue on the brink of the Sukarno overthrow and the anticommunist purge of Indonesia. Although *The Year of Living Dangerously* (the title is from a Sukarno speech) loosely interprets actual historical facts and conditions, the movie has a convincing surface reality—it was filmed in the Philippines and Australia—with many fine performances.

Weaver set loose her wacky comedic sensibility in Ivan Reitman's *Ghostbusters,* an instant box-office hit also starring Bill Murray, Dan Aykroyd, and Harold Ramis. Weaver appears as Dana Barrett, a symphony cellist who turns to the services of the *Ghostbusters*—"no job is too big, no fee is too big"—when her apartment becomes possessed by spirits. She herself is eventually possessed by the demon Zuul in this rich lampoon of spirit-world myths. Of Weaver's performance in the film, *Newsweek*'s Ansen noted that director Friedkin "gets to show what a fine and sexy comedienne she can be." *Ghostbusters* is possibly the leading example of contemporary comedy in its deadpan treatment of an essentially silly situation—New York City being overrun by ghosts rising from the dead on the eve of the apocalypse and then being trapped by three scientists with their own high-tech ghostbusting equipment.

On cover of Time *for* Aliens

Weaver received a flood of media attention for her reprise of Ripley in *Aliens,* the sequel to *Alien,* including a *Time* cover story. As the lone human survivor of *Alien,* Ripley, in hyper-sleep, returns to earth 57 years later to learn that the forbidden planet has been colonized, and no communication has been received from the inhabitants. Ripley's story of horror is not believed, but she is recruited to accompany a Marine troop to investigate.

Director James Cameron (*The Terminator*) changes direction from the original film's emphasis on terror to combat, with plenty of horrible alien monsters to kill. The queen of the creatures is pitted against Ripley for the survival of the one remaining colonist, a small child named Newt, in this space battle on the theme of motherhood. "At its core," explained *Newsweek*'s Ansen, "is the ferociously urgent performance of Sigourney Weaver, who hurls herself into her warrior role, with muscular grace and a sense of conviction that matches Cameron's step for step. Next to her wonderfully human macho, most recent male action heroes look like very thin cardboard."

In a complete departure from Ripley, as Dr. Lauren Slaughter in British director Bob Swaim's film *Half Moon Street,* Weaver played an American academic living in London who works at an Arab-Anglo Institute specializing in Middle Eastern studies. Ambitious and bored, she becomes a call girl whose clientele includes a number of her associates from her day job. One of these is Lord Dulbeck (Michael Caine), a liberal politician who falls in love with her. She is, however, badly used in an international power game that she does not understand and that reveals the difference between sexual and political power.

Weaver's next film was *One Woman or Two,* a 1987 release in which she played Jessica Fitzgerald, an American advertising executive who tries to convince a paleontologist (Gerard Depardieu) who has discovered a two-million-year-old woman to permit her to use his discovery as the promotional symbol of a new perfume. In a casting quirk, Dr. Ruth Westheimer plays an American philanthropist who rapturously covets the clay dummy the scientist reconstructs from his paleontological discovery. In a further oddity, the clay model and Dr. Ruth bear an uncanny resemblance.

All of Weaver's subsequent films have portrayed strong and independent women. In 1988's *Gorillas in the Mist,* Weaver portrayed Dian

Fossey, who gained fame for her work with gorillas in Africa. Fossey's efforts to stave off poachers, however, ended up getting her killed. In *Working Girl,* released in 1991, Weaver plays a tough business executive who attempts to sabotage a sweet secretary played by Melanie Griffith. She revisited the character of Ripley in *Alien 3,* which was the third and final story in the *Alien* series and was released in 1992. Most recently Weaver played the first lady to Kevin Kline's president in the 1993 comedy *Dave.* A box-office success, this movie revolves around a mild mannered temp-agency owner who is an exact double for the president. When the president unexpectedly dies, his double is called in to pretend he is the president and his innocence ultimately helps to clean up the corruption in the White House.

Primarily a screen actress, Weaver has pursued a parallel off-Broadway stage career. Her most important role was in the 1984 production of David Rabe's play *Hurlyburly,* directed by Mike Nichols. A three-hour-plus black comedy about a group of disaffected males and the women in their lives set in the Hollywood Hills, *Hurlyburly* combines philosophical speculation with raw sexual conflict. The play received critical praise for its superb acting and high production values. Weaver played Darlene, the love interest of both Eddie, played by William Hurt, and then Mickey, played by Christopher Walken, in a cast that also included Harvey Keitel, Jerry Stiller, Cynthia Nixon, and Judith Ivey.

Works with actor-husband

In 1986 Weaver appeared in the Classic Stage Company's production of Shakespeare's *The Merchant of Venice* as Portia. Her husband, James Simpson, also a Yale Drama School alumnus, who has established a reputation as an interpreter of contemporary drama for the Williamstown Theater Festival, the Public Theater, and the Ensemble Studio Theater, directed. "Together, the director and star seem disoriented by Shakespeare," wrote Mel Gussow in the *New York Times.* "Except for her height and her beauty, Ms. Weaver is an average Portia."

Simpson, a child actor who grew up in Hawaii and had the start of a lucrative career on the television series *Hawaii Five-O* by the time he was 17, now concentrates on his directing career. He and Weaver met at the Williamstown Theater Festival, and Weaver admits to asking him out originally. About their relationship, Weaver told Leslie Bennetts of the *New York Times,* "Movies are usually the product of a lot of conventional thinking, and just being around Jim has brought me back to a world I might have been stepping out of."

Sources

American Film, October 1983; July-August 1986; September-October 1986.

Boxoffice, September 1986; December 1986; May 1987.

Chicago Tribune, July 13, 1986.

Detroit Free Press, July 18, 1986.

Detroit News, July 16, 1986; November 7, 1986; February 12, 1987.

Film Commentary, September-October 1979; May 1984; July-August 1984; March-April 1985; August 1986; November-December 1986; August 1992.

Glamour, September 1986; June 1992.

Los Angeles Times Calendar, July 13, 1986.

Maclean's, July 28, 1986.

Ms., April 1983.

Nation, February 19, 1983; September 20, 1983.

New Republic, June 16, 1979; March 7, 1981; February 7, 1983.

New Statesman, June 17, 1983.

Newsweek, May 28, 1979; March 2, 1981; January 24, 1983; June 11, 1984; July 2, 1984; July 21, 1986.

New York, June 4, 1979; March 2, 1981; January 24, 1983; June 11, 1984; July 16, 1984; July 28, 1986; November 24, 1986; March 2, 1987.

New Yorker, June 11, 1979; March 23, 1981; February 23, 1983; July 2, 1984; April 11, 1986, August 11, 1986.

New York Times, February 18, 1979; May 25, 1979; May 27, 1979; February 27, 1981; April 3, 1981; April 5, 1981; October 15, 1981; November 4, 1981; January 16, 1983; January 21, 1983; January 23, 1983; June 8, 1984; June 22, 1984; July 1, 1984; July 2, 1984; July 18, 1984; July 18, 1986; August 3, 1986; August 22, 1986; November 7, 1986; December 21, 1986; December 22, 1986.

Parade, March 1, 1987.

People, July 28, 1986; September 8, 1986; October 13, 1986; November 10, 1986; February 16, 1987; May 17, 1993.

Rolling Stone, August 28, 1986.

Time, June 4, 1979; March 2, 1981; January 17, 1983; June 11, 1984; July 28, 1986; May 10, 1993.

USA Weekend, July 4-6, 1986.

Washington Post, August 17, 1986.

Robin Williams

Born July 21, 1952
Chicago, Illinois

ACTOR AND COMEDIAN

"I feel Robin was put on Earth to make us laugh."—Laurie Williams

Comedian Robin Williams has achieved international superstardom for his work on both stage and screen. Having catapulted to fame in the television situation comedy *Mork & Mindy,* Williams has since appeared as the lead in such films as *Good Morning, Vietnam* and *Mrs. Doubtfire* and in comic specials for Home Box Office (HBO). Spontaneous, irreverent, and often entirely off-the-cuff as a comic, Williams ranges from topic to topic, often skewering conventional wisdom and always inciting gut-wrenching laughter. Writer Brad Darrach observed in *People* magazine that Williams "barks like a demented seal ... running at the mouth like a power hose at a race riot." This comic style, which draws heavily from such improvisational comedians as Jonathan Winters, Sid Caesar, and Lenny Bruce, has generated for Williams a strong and devoted following and has been brilliantly utilized in several of his films. However, in an effort to avoid being pigeonholed, the actor-comedian has accepted a wide range of serious parts as well.

Williams had an active imagination as a child. Born in Chicago on July 21, 1952, the son of a well-to-do, frequently transferred automobile executive, Williams grew up in Chicago and Detroit and attended eight different schools in an eight-year period. Williams was often without friends his own age and remembers that he would stage mock battles with an army of toy soldiers or study the television routines of his comic idol, Jonathan Winters. Short and overweight—for which he was constantly teased by his classmates—Williams discovered refuge in comedy. He attended high school at Detroit Country Day School—an exclusive private academy with high scholastic standards—and as a senior moved with his family to affluent Tiburon, California, a suburb of San Francisco. There Williams enrolled in Redwood High School, a public facility noted for its counter culture-influenced curriculum. "I think the turning point for Robin came when he left Detroit Country Day School, which was a bunch of boys wearing very proper white shirts, and we moved to [California]," Laurie Williams, his mother, told the *Chicago Tribune*. "He went to Redwood High School and began bringing home some pretty wild and wooly friends. I don't think they would have been drawn to him if he hadn't been pretty wild himself." California and its lifestyle were indeed liberating for Williams. He lost weight and grew interested in sports, including wrestling, an activity he would one day dramatize in *The World According to Garp*. His classmates voted him "Most Humorous" and "Least Likely to Succeed."

Williams attended Claremont Men's College briefly and intended to study political science. However, he discovered theater, and soon thereafter his other interests paled in comparison to acting. With the hesitant support of his parents, he transferred to Marin College in Kentfield, California, and majored in classical drama. He worked weekends with a San Francisco improvisational group, the Committee. Laurie Williams recalled in the *Chicago Tribune* that his "exposure to improvisation with 'The Committee' was very exciting for him. People would call out a single line, and he was very good at improvising from just that." Williams won a full scholarship to the prestigious Juilliard School in 1973. There he studied speech and drama, but his irrepressible humor began to reveal itself in classes. His teachers—including actor John Houseman—urged him to be serious, but audiences lined up to see his whiteface mime performances in front of the Metropolitan Museum of Art. Williams returned to San Francisco in 1976 and joined a comedy workshop. He tended bar on the side, and it was at the tavern where he worked that he met Valerie Velardi, a graduate student who was supporting herself as a waitress. Velardi proved to have the ambitious spirit that Williams lacked. She helped him hone his routines and persuaded him to leave San Francisco for Los Angeles.

Gains huge following with Mork & Mindy

Williams debuted in Los Angeles on "open mike" night at the Comedy Store. He told *TV Guide* that the club was a "terrorizing combination of Roman arena and the Gong Show." His routine was a hit, and he became a regular at the club. Television offers followed, including stints in three unsuccessful shows: a revived *Laugh-In, The Richard Pryor Show,* and *America 2-Night,* which starred comedian/actor Martin Mull. Williams auditioned in 1977 for the producers of *Happy Days* and won a guest appearance as the space alien Mork from the plant Ork. Mork drew a strong positive response from the *Happy Days* viewers, and producer Garry Marshall devised a situation comedy, *Mork & Mindy.* Starring Williams and Pam Dawber, *Mork & Mindy* eclipsed even *Happy Days* in popularity; it topped the Nielsen ratings in 1978 and 1979 and averaged 60 million viewers per episode. Critics delighted in the inspired pastiches of mime and clowning Williams created in the show. He was given free reign to ad-lib during taping—very unusual in television—often bringing his fellow performers to tears in their efforts to suppress their laughter.

Williams was clearly a huge success, but he indulged himself in a way he now calls "degrading" and "humiliating." His June 1978 marriage to Velardi notwithstanding, Williams engaged in extramarital affairs and abused both alcohol and drugs. Williams continued to perform at a high level, however. He continued his club work, cut an album called *Reality ... What a Concept* that went platinum (selling one million copies), and became a frequent visitor to *Saturday Night Live.*

He also began to accept film work, but success in that medium proved somewhat more difficult. The 1980 film *Popeye*—in which he portrayed the famous cartoon sailor—was a disappointment that never lived up to its advanced billing; only the advent of home video spared it from financial failure. Two more serious efforts—*The World According to Garp* in 1982 and *Moscow on the Hudson* in 1984—were only modest successes by Hollywood standards. In *The World According to Garp,* Williams played the title character, a sensitive young man who matures from teen to adult amidst the most unusual circumstances. In *Moscow on the Hudson,* he portrayed a Russian musician who defects in New York and eventually becomes an American citizen. *Chicago Tribune* critic Gene Siskel has suggested that as a film actor Williams has suffered from the fact that his roles do not give his fans what they either expect or want. This was especially true of *The*

Williams has won a number of awards, including a Grammy for best comedy album for *Reality ... What a Concept* in 1979; a Golden Apple Award, a Golden Globe Award, and a People's Choice Award for *Mork & Mindy*; a Golden Globe Award and an Academy Award nomination, both for best actor, both for *Good Morning, Vietnam* in 1988; an Academy Award nomination and a Golden Globe Award nomination, both for best actor, both for *Dead Poets Society* in 1989; a Golden Globe Award for best actor in a musical or comedy and an Academy Award nomination for best actor for *The Fisher King* in 1992.

Best of Times and *Club Paradise*, two 1985 films that—to quote Darrach—"thoroughly trashed his reputation."

Quits using drugs and alcohol

Williams claims he reached the crossroads in his life in early 1983. Two dramatic events forced him to reassess his drug-dominated lifestyle: his wife, Valerie, became pregnant, and friend John Belushi died of a drug overdose only a few hours after sharing some cocaine with Williams at the Chateau Marmont Hotel. "The Belushi tragedy was frightening," Williams told *People*. "He was the strongest. A bull with incredible energy. His death scared a whole group of show business people. It caused a big exodus from drugs. And for me there was the baby coming. I knew I couldn't be a father and live that sort of life."

Williams quit alcohol and drugs cold turkey, explaining in an interview with *New York*: "Zach was about to be born, and I didn't want to miss it because I was coked up or drinking." With sobriety, however, Williams realized that his marriage was empty. In 1986 he and Velardi separated and in 1988 Velardi filed for divorce. While his parents were experiencing marital difficulties, Zachary began having some behavioral problems. When he was one, Marsha Garces came into his life as a nanny and in a year his tantrums disappeared. She then became Williams's personal assistant on his national tour. Although initially both he and Garces were seeing other people, within the year the two had become romantically involved. In 1989 the couple was married in Lake Tahoe.

With his personal life now on track, Williams appeared in a succession of impressive films. In 1988 he achieved critical and commercial success with the film *Good Morning, Vietnam,* the story of a Saigon disc jockey who spins records for American combat troops. Siskel contended that in *Good Morning, Vietnam,* Williams's "trademark spontaneity is expressed within both a story and a setting that are as compelling as his humor." Other critics were equally enthusiastic. Williams, who received an Academy Award nomination for his performance, told the *Seattle Post Intelligencer* that a successful film "moves you up the food chain. It's like life in the Precambrian sea. There is a food chain of scripts, and success can give you access to better scripts." Barry Levinson, the director of *Good Morning, Vietnam,* allowed Williams to improvise more than 20 minutes of disc jockey patter for the film; Darrach characterized it as a "wild and hectic stream of consciousness with a hell-in-a-handbasket abandon."

Williams received another Academy Award nomination for his work in *Dead Poets Society,* released in 1989. In it Williams plays a dedicated English teacher who tries to instill a love for literature and an open mind in his students at a boys prep school. Another serious role followed in *Awakenings,* a film based on the real-life experience of Dr. Oliver Sachs, a physician whose work brought virtually comatose patients briefly back to a conscious state. In 1991 *The Fisher King* centered on an academic who has hallucinations after his wife's sudden death. He again earned an Academy Award nomination. The same year Williams appeared in *Hook,* playing an adult Peter Pan who attempts to regain his childhood by returning to Never Never Land. Despite an all-star cast and the direction of Steven Spielberg, the film was a box-office disappointment.

Most recently Williams found phenomenal success as the voice of Genie in the Disney animated adventure *Aladdin.* Wanting to leave a memorable performance for his kids, Williams exceeded Disney's expectations by improvising about 30 hours of tape. He also scored big at the box office in 1993 with *Mrs. Doubtfire,* a film that focuses on an unemployed actor who is denied joint custody of his three children when his wife sues for divorce. Desperate to maintain contact with his children, Williams's character dresses up as an older British lady and lands the job of nanny for his own family.

Williams is a subdued person when not in the limelight. He told the *Chicago Tribune* that he is reading studies on creativity and trying to determine how "a person standing alone on the stage ... can enter into a state in which he is liberated to say things and make connections he might otherwise hold back. Trying to maximize the brain without assaulting it anymore—that's my goal." Williams described his monologues to the *Boston Globe* as arising from "reflexes, instinct. It's Zen-like. I don't know where the stuff comes from. Something kicks in. You're not in control. That's what's scary.... When it's happening, you sometimes feel like a voyeur. When it works, it's like jazz, maybe like scat singing. When it doesn't work, it's painful, worse than constipation." But moments of failure are rare indeed for Williams.

Sources

Boston Globe, January 15, 1988.

Chicago Tribune, January 10, 1988; April 1, 1988.

Newsweek, May 7, 1979; July 7, 1986; January 4, 1988.

New York, October 13, 1986; November 22, 1993.

New Yorker, August 11, 1986; January 11, 1988; September 20, 1993.

New York Times, December 28, 1978.

People, October 30, 1978; October 29, 1979; September 13, 1982; February 22, 1988; November 29, 1993.

Rolling Stone, November 2, 1978; February 25, 1988.

Seattle Post Intelligencer, February 1, 1988.

Time, October 2, 1978; February 24, 1986; December 28, 1987; November 29, 1993.

TV Guide, October 28, 1978.

Vanessa Williams

Born March 18, 1963
New York, New York

SINGER, SONGWRITER, AND ACTRESS

M any performers must overcome stagger-ing odds to achieve fame. In Vanessa Williams's case, those odds were compounded by scandal and deep embarrassment. A recording artist and stage star with two gold records to her credit, Williams was the first black woman to be elected Miss America and the first to relinquish her crown after a maga-zine published nude photographs of her. The road back to respectability has been a long one for Williams, but her talents as a singer and dancer—precisely those that won her the 1983 Miss America title—have enabled her to estab-lish a thriving career.

"I recall my mother telling me that just because you are Black, you are going to have to work 100 percent more than everyone else just to be considered equal. That is unfair, but it is the reality of the situation."

Ebony correspondent Lynn Norment wrote of Vanessa Williams: "The entertainer has not let obstacles defer her dreams so far, and it is doubtful that they will encumber her in the future." Indeed, the biggest obstacles are probably behind Williams. The singer and actress observed in Ebony that being crowned Miss America—considered the honor of a lifetime by much of

Middle America—was for her a stumbling block that almost ruined her chances for work in show business. "I think being Miss America was a major detour to what I wanted to do professionally," she said. "If [producers] think you are Miss America, they think you are an airhead ... a bimbo."

In Williams's case, nothing could be further from the truth. Even before the scandal that ended her Miss America reign, she was known as one of the most hard working and outspoken Miss Americas. She refused to be pegged as a symbol because she was black. She freely voiced her opinions on abortion, government policies, and race relations and presented herself as an articulate woman with well-defined goals for a career as an entertainer. "My parents really taught me that there are no limitations, that you can do anything you want," Williams told an *Ebony* correspondent.

Vanessa Williams was born on March 18, 1963, in the Bronx, New York. Both of her parents had college educations and considerable musical talent. When Williams was just one year old, the family moved to Millwood, New York, an upscale community some 30 miles north of Manhattan. There both parents worked as public school music teachers. According to Elizabeth Kaye in *Rolling Stone,* Williams "was the only black child in her school until she was seven. When she was six, another child called her a 'nigger.' She didn't know what it was. Her mother began to teach her about her heritage, using black-history flashcards that detailed the achievements of [Underground Railroad conductor] Harriet Tubman and [former slave and abolitionist] Frederick Douglass. Soon she had black-pride posters in her bedroom. She decided that she wanted to be the first black Rockette."

Laid foundations for a musical career

By the time Williams turned ten she had immersed herself in music and dance. She took French horn, piano, and violin lessons, studied classical and jazz dance, and appeared in numerous school plays. Kaye noted that when Williams performed, "her father was invariably the first to start applauding and the last to stop. Her mother was more circumspect. 'Nice job, 'Ness,' she would say." Williams entered high school as a highly popular, if somewhat rebellious, student. Her interests continued to be theater and music, and she graduated from high school with a prestigious Presidential Scholarship for Drama. Although she was one of only 12 students accepted into the Carnegie Mellon University theater arts program in Pittsburgh that year, she decided to stay closer to home and attend Syracuse University.

During the summer after her freshman year at Syracuse, Williams returned to Millwood. She took a job as a receptionist and makeup artist for local photographer Tom Chiapel. Chiapel did nude photography of young women, and Williams—who was 19 at the time—became curious about the process. "I had worked there for a month and a half when Tom Chiapel mentioned several times that he'd like to shoot me in the nude," Williams recalled in *People*. "He assured me that none of the photographs would ever leave the studio. *He assured me*." Williams did one nude session by herself and another in silhouette lighting with a second female model. Later that summer, on a visit to New York City, she did a third session with a Manhattan photographer. She was so distressed by the nature of that session—which involved leather gear and highly provocative shots—that she asked for the negatives and thought they had been destroyed.

At summer's end Williams returned to Syracuse, where she continued to excel in theater and music. She was appearing in a college musical when she was approached by the director of the Miss Greater Syracuse pageant, one of the steps toward the Miss America contest. Williams was not enthusiastic about entering a beauty pageant, but her parents convinced her to do it. She won Miss Greater Syracuse handily and went on to be crowned Miss New York in 1983.

No black woman had ever been crowned Miss America before. If the pageant favored a certain type, it was usually the blue-eyed, blonde southern woman. Williams pointed out in *GQ* that the *New York Daily News* ran a story saying no black woman would ever win the Miss America title. "I knew I had the talent and brains," she said. "I just didn't feel comfortable in front of all those people in a swimsuit. I never thought I'd win. I mean, I was pro-choice and pro-ERA, not 'Little Miss Seawall' at the age of 5. The southern girls said I'd never win because I didn't fit the profile. They said it was all in the breeding."

A new breed of Miss America

On September 14, 1983, just six months after entering her first beauty pageant, Vanessa Williams was chosen Miss America. Her closest competitor, Suzette Charles, was also black. Williams won the pageant by singing a torchy rendition of "Happy Days Are Here Again" and impressed the judges with her honest and witty answers to their questions. Her parents and her entire hometown rejoiced as she won a $25,000 scholarship and the potential of earning many times that much for personal appearances and product endorsements.

Williams embarked on a hectic tour in keeping with her duties as Miss America. Because she was black, she came under unusual scrutiny from the press and public. As a *People* correspondent put it, "Vanessa Williams was perceived not simply as Miss America but as an emblem of social change—not Miss America at all, in that sense, but Miss New America, embodiment of a kind of collective national redemption." Not surprisingly, Williams rebelled against such symbolism, pointing out that she had never felt discriminated against while growing up and that she did not feel race was an issue in her selection. "People are reading too much into it," she remarked in *People*.

The outspoken but poised Miss America was nearing the end of her reign in July 1984 when the scandal broke. The provocative photographs Chiapel had taken of her with another woman—the ones she insists she never signed for release—found their way into the pages of *Penthouse* magazine. After glimpsing the pictures, the shocked Miss America pageant board of directors asked Williams to resign.

Hit rock bottom

A weeping Williams consulted with her family, her attorney, and a public relations man—Ramon Hervey II—who was called in to help allay the damage. Within 72 hours of the revelation that the photographs would be published, Williams called a press conference and stepped down with dignity and dry eyes. Her losses were immense. Although pageant officials said she could keep the scholarship money, she was dropped from several major product endorsements worth an estimated $2 million. She was also barred from appearing at the 1984 Miss America pageant and was dropped from a Bob Hope television special. Williams confided in *People:* "I feel as if I were just a sacrificial lamb. The past just came up and kicked me. I felt betrayed and violated like I had been raped.... I think this would have to be the worst thing that has happened in my life. But I can't go anyplace but up. I've hit rock bottom."

Williams had to deny in print that she was a lesbian. She was hounded by obscene telephone calls at home and taunted on the streets. Movie scripts came pouring in for her, but all of them featured excessive nudity and near-pornography. On the other hand, as *Penthouse* publisher Bob Guccione himself observed, the photographs gained Williams media exposure that eluded many former Miss Americas.

Williams may have earned a spot in the public eye, but she was hardly the toast of Hollywood. *Ebony*'s Norment wrote: "The following years were exceptionally trying for the young woman. After the furor over her giving up the Miss America crown subsided, Vanessa continued to pursue her dream of a show business career. She knocked on doors that wouldn't open. She auditioned for parts but never got called back. She met with record company executives, but nobody took her seriously."

Nobody, that is, except Ramon Hervey II, who became Williams's manager in 1985 and her husband in 1987. Hervey helped Williams to choose film roles that would not further tarnish her image, such as the 1987 movie *The Pick Up Artist*. He also paved the way for a recording contract with PolyGram's Wing Records division, a rhythm and blues subsidiary. "There's no way [Vanessa] would have been taken seriously as an actress in Hollywood," Hervey conceded in *GQ*. "We decided it would be better to concentrate on her musical talents, which we could control. We made a conscious effort to build a base in the black community with a rhythm-and-blues album. If Vanessa didn't succeed in black music first, then she'd never succeed. We had to convince the black media to give Vanessa a chance to become a whole person again."

Williams's first album, *The Right Stuff*, was released in 1988. The album went gold in sales (selling one million copies), and placed three singles in the Top Ten on the rhythm and blues music charts. Williams helped to make the work a hit by appearing in high-energy music videos and by touring the United States and Europe for live shows. Her efforts won her the best new female recording artist award from the National Association for the Advancement of Colored People (NAACP) in 1988. She was also nominated for three Grammy awards in the rhythm and blues category. *GQ* contributor Pat Jordan declared: "For the first time in years, the name 'Vanessa Williams' became synonymous not with scandal but with success and a kind of relentless courage. Her life was no longer defined solely by a single aberration from her past."

"Success is the best revenge"

Williams followed her hit debut album in 1991 with another well-received work, *The Comfort Zone*. The LP yielded her first Number One single, "Save the Best for Last," a song co-written by Williams. "Save the Best for Last" stayed at Number One on the pop, rhythm and blues, and adult contemporary charts for five weeks, even as Michael Jackson's "Remember the Time" failed to make a showing. Superstar recording artist Luther Vandross told an *Entertainment Weekly* correspondent: "I couldn't be more thrilled about what's happening for [Vanessa] right now. The way she looks, the way she sings, that inexplicable something called charisma all work in her favor."

Williams was honored with the Image Award for best new artist—female from the National Association for the Advancement of Colored People (NAACP) in 1988; Grammy Award nominations for best new artist and best R&B vocal performance—female for "The Right Stuff" in 1988 and for "Dreamin'" in 1989; Grammy Award nominations for record of the year, female vocal solo—pop, and female vocal solo—R&B for "Save the Best for Last" in 1992; and she has earned two gold records.

Williams also appeared in feature films and television movies, among them *Another You, Harley Davidson and the Marlboro Man, Stompin' at the Savoy, Candyman,* and *New Jack City.* During the 1992-93 season, Williams costarred in the television series *Melrose Place.* She also established what looked to be a significant stage career as the title character of Broadway's *Kiss of the Spider Woman,* all the more impressive in that she assumed the role from the much-lauded originator of the part, veteran performer Chita Rivera. In between recording sessions, tours, and film and stage work, Williams and Hervey managed to have two daughters, Melanie and Jillian, and a son, Devin Christian.

Williams told a *People* correspondent that she knows some Americans will always remember the *Penthouse* pictures, and she knows she will have to explain them to her children someday. "The incident was a part of my life that was pretty devastating," she confessed. "But in the context of my whole life, I got over it." The versatile performer added in *Ebony,* "I'm not dwelling on [the past] now. I'm just moving on, for there is nothing I can do to change that, so I just have to deal with it and move on.... If situations arose where I could get revenge, I absolutely would. But at this point, success is the best revenge."

Sources

Ebony, April 1987; December 1988; April 1990.

Entertainment Weekly, April 24, 1992.

Essence, January 1993.

GQ, June 1990.

Jet, September 16, 1991; February 3, 1992; May 3, 1993; July 26, 1993.

Newsweek, August 6, 1984.

New York Times, July 31, 1994.

Oakland Press (Oakland County, Ml), June 14, 1992.

People, October 3, 1983; December 26, 1983-January 2, 1984; August 6, 1984; September 10, 1984; December 24-31, 1984; January 30, 1989.

Rolling Stone, January 31, 1985; April 16, 1992; April 30, 1992; May 14, 1992.

Time, August 6, 1984.

Oprah Winfrey

Born January 29, 1954
Kosciusko, Mississippi

TALK SHOW HOST, ACTRESS, AND
PRODUCER

Nearly everyone knows Oprah Winfrey—
one of the richest women in the entertainment business—from her television talk
show or from her films. What is less familiar is
the story of her rise from poverty to stardom.
Oprah Gail Winfrey was born on January 29,
1954, in the small town of Kosciusko, Mississippi. Her parents, Vernita Lee and Vernon
Winfrey, were never married. Vernon Winfrey,
20 years old and in the service at the time, was
home on furlough from Fort Rucker in Alaba-
ma when Oprah was conceived. When his
leave was over, Vernon returned to duty and
had no knowledge of his fatherhood until Vernita Lee mailed a card to him announcing the
baby's arrival and requesting clothing. Vernita
had intended to name the baby Orpah after a character in the biblical
Book of Ruth, but someone, perhaps the midwife who attended the delivery, the clerk at the courthouse, or even Vernita Lee herself, misspelled
the name by transposing the "p" and the "r."

> "Oprah is a wonderful, wonderful person.
> Who she is on-camera is exactly what she
> is off-camera.... She's a totally
> approachable, real, warm person."
> —Sherry Burns

There was little work for a young, unskilled black woman in Kosciusko. But Lee had heard that jobs were more plentiful and higher paying in Milwaukee, Wisconsin, and so, shortly after Oprah's birth, she moved there, leaving the baby in the care of Vernon Winfrey's mother. Grandmother Winfrey was a churchgoing woman of strong character. Accordingly, much of Oprah's early life was spent at church, which furnished her with several early opportunities to display her talents. It soon became apparent that this child was exceptional. Her ability to read, speak, and memorize was phenomenal. She made her first speaking appearance during an Easter program. Later, at Christmastime, she was on the program again. She was just three years old.

At home, however, Oprah found that she was not to be heard so readily. She spent a great deal of time with adults but was expected to be quiet when in their presence. This kind of restraint proved very difficult for an articulate child who longed for the company and attention of the people around her.

When she recalls her childhood, Winfrey indicates that she began to wish that she were white when she was about six years old. She relates that she slept with a clothespin on her nose, and prayed for corkscrew curls. She felt, she says, that being white would have rescued her from all of the physical discipline to which she was subjected in the form of frequent spankings. Though she viewed her life as unsatisfactory, her spirit was not broken. She would not be subdued, and her grandmother would not compromise. Her grandmother soon appealed to Vernita Lee for relief and Oprah was sent to live with her mother in Milwaukee.

Vernita, having been so young and inexperienced when her child was born, did not fully realize her duties as a mother. And the combination of welfare money and her wages as a maid was still insufficient to afford the two even the minimal comforts of a home. As she became more and more aware of city life, Winfrey became increasingly rebellious and resentful of her poverty. As she had proven to be too difficult for her grandmother, so too she exhausted her mother.

It was Vernon Winfrey's turn now. He had moved to Nashville, Tennessee, upon completing his military commitment and was now married. He and his wife welcomed Oprah during the summer of 1962, just after she had finished first grade. The young girl soon found that she would not be able to wear her new parents down as she had her mother and grandmother. Vernon, an active Baptist, brought his daughter with him not only for Sunday church services, but for youth activities, holiday programs, and other church-sponsored community activities. Oprah, again, became known as a bright student and a dependable performer in the various pageants and presentations of the church and community. But within a year Vernita Lee wanted to see her daughter. The Vernon Winfreys hesitated and then relented because they knew that it was important to support the natural mother-daughter relationship.

During their time together, Vernita persuaded Oprah that life "at home" could now be much more pleasant than it had been earlier. She was soon to marry a Milwaukee man with whom she had maintained a relationship for several years. The new family would include the man's two children, a son and a daughter. It was quite a blow for the Winfreys, but they felt a certain respect for Lee's wishes, and so the agreement was made. Unfortunately, the return to Milwaukee led to disastrous consequences.

Winfrey suffers in silence

Again Winfrey developed a painful concern relating to skin color and standards of physical attractiveness. She became convinced that she was neglected in favor of her lighter-skinned stepsister. She felt cast off, and her pain was all the more intense because it seemed to her that her mother was as guilty of her mistreatment as anyone else. Not surprisingly, she more and more often sought refuge in books. Her bookish bent only increased her isolation from the family, who placed little value on superior intelligence and intellectual or scholastic achievement. Having been moved back and forth between her parents according to their preference, she began to fear that neither of them really wanted her as a part of their lives. The seeds of rebellion were soon firmly sowed in her mind, and her conduct began to deteriorate.

It was also during this period, beginning as early as her tenth year, that Winfrey became the victim of frequent sexual abuse. She suffered these attacks in silence because she did not know what else to do. In every instance the abusive episodes involved male family members or trusted acquaintances.

In spite of her miserable home life, Winfrey remained a good student. Gene Abrams, one of her teachers at the inner-city Lincoln Middle School, recognized her exceptional abilities and took an active interest in her. He helped her to get a scholarship to a prestigious suburban school in the affluent Fox Point area. Winfrey encountered few scholastic problems there, but her emotional problems were multiplying and her behavior was reflecting the chaos she was experiencing. Out of her fertile mind,

Winfrey was hatching and staging one absurd scheme after another. On several occasions she destroyed family belongings, and she pretended that their apartment had been burglarized in order to get herself a more fashionable pair of glasses. Twice she ran away from home. Winfrey's mother was constantly bewildered by her increasingly frequent escapades and was brought again to the acknowledgement of her inability to deal with her rebellious daughter. During the summer of 1968 Oprah, now 14 years old, went back to Nashville to live with her father and his wife.

Life takes a new course

It was a vastly different Oprah who returned to Nashville after the five years spent in Milwaukee. Adjustment between father and daughter was not easy, but Vernon Winfrey was able to prevail. He set high standards of conduct and achievement for his daughter and stuck with her to see that she met them. She enrolled in Nashville's East High School and she was soon involved in numerous school activities, especially those having to do with public speaking and dramatics.

By the time Oprah entered her senior year of 1970-71, she had focused her interests and knew that her future lay in the performing arts. She was chosen to attend the 1970 White House Conference on Youth in Washington. She went to Los Angeles to speak at a church and toured Hollywood while she was there. And she won various titles, including "Miss Fire Prevention" and "Miss Black Tennessee."

The local radio station, WVOL, managed and operated by blacks, hired Winfrey to read the news. She was soon ready to enter college and hoped to attend an institution far removed from Nashville, perhaps in New England. But once again, Vernon Winfrey made a decision that countered his daughter's preferences. She would attend Tennessee State University in Nashville. An academic scholarship won in an oratorical contest sponsored by the local Elks Lodge helped to finance her college studies, which were to feature a major in the English language arts.

Media opportunities open

Winfrey continued her work as a news announcer at WVOL and was soon hired away by WLAC, a major radio station. It was not long before she moved to WLAC-TV (later WTVF) as a reporter-anchor. Although she was earning a five-figure salary while she was in college, her father had not softened his strict requirements of her in terms of conduct or scholarship, and with each succeeding year she was finding his restraints on her social life harder and harder to accept. She began to look beyond Nashville and found a new position at WJZ-TV in Baltimore, Maryland, in 1976. She was only a few months short of her college graduation, but she left Nashville and Tennessee State University without having earned her bachelor's degree.

Winfrey became the object of an intensive makeover effort on the part of WJZ. The management sought to develop for her an entirely new persona. The attempt was not completely successful. She had little formal training in journalism or mass communications, and her reporting often failed to achieve the desired degree of objectivity. Indeed, she resisted the necessity to be objective, preferring to approach a story from the inside and react to it in a subjective manner.

Winfrey finds her niche

Winfrey was well-protected by the contract she had with the station, however; management was forced to find a better use of her talents. She was assigned to cohost a local morning show called *People Are Talking*. Neither she nor her employers recognized the fact right off, but Winfrey had found her niche. Her engaging personality and her amazing ability to communicate with a diverse audience were indisputable assets in her new assignment.

As the popularity of her show began to grow, as well as her satisfaction and enjoyment of it, Winfrey began sending tapes of her broadcasts to other markets around the country. She sensed that she was ready for big-time broadcasting. The woman who had been coproducer of *People Are Talking* left Baltimore in 1984 for a new position on *A.M. Chicago,* a morning talk show broadcast by the ABC-TV Chicago affiliate, WLS-TV. The station manager had observed Winfrey on some of the tapes his new producer had screened for him and quickly decided to hire her for *A.M. Chicago,* which would compete with the *Phil Donahue Show,* the well-established favorite in the local and national market. With Winfrey's arrival, *A.M. Chicago* took off and quickly outdistanced *Donahue* in the ratings. In early 1985 Phil Donahue moved his show to New York and left Chicago to Winfrey.

Winfrey exercises acting talent

In high school and college Winfrey had pursued an interest in dramatics and had attracted favorable attention as an actress, so she found the idea of portraying Sofia in the Quincy Jones/Steven Spielberg 1985 film pro-

Oprah Winfrey lives in a luxury condominium decorated in white overlooking Chicago's Lake Michigan. She also has a farm in Indiana.

duction of Alice Walker's novel *The Color Purple* very appealing. She took leave from her show and went south to create her role. The film opened to mixed reviews and much discussion, but most professional critics praised Winfrey's performance, and it earned her an Academy Award nomination. Close on the heels of *The Color Purple,* she appeared in 1986 in a motion picture based on Richard Wright's novel *Native Son.* Hers was not a major role. The film was neither a critical success nor a popular one and was not widely distributed. Still, Winfrey's performance was noticed.

Winfrey's *A.M. Chicago* show having become such a sensation, WLS-TV decided to allot it a full hour instead of its former 30 minutes and changed its title to *The Oprah Winfrey Show.* By late 1986 the show was in syndication. It was reported that the syndication deal grossed $125 million and that its star would receive more than $30 million in 1987-88 and become the highest-paid performer in show business.

Winfrey forms own company

Winfrey had become one of the best-known figures of the 1980s. She could finally devote much of her prodigious energy to the pursuit of the numerous dreams that she had cherished throughout the years of her swift ascent to the pinnacle of her profession. Since the achievement of her full-blown success, Winfrey has formed her own company, Harpo (Oprah spelled backwards) Productions, and purchased a gigantic studio to house its operations. Harpo has taken over the ownership and production of *The Oprah Winfrey Show,* over which she maintains full control and responsibility, thus demonstrating her astuteness as a businesswoman. The company plans to bring to the screen productions that convey important social and spiritual messages that might not be deemed by others to be commercially promising.

Winfrey speaks to numerous youth groups and urges her audiences on to higher achievement. She presses them to strive for higher standards and to seek to be all that they can be. She seeks to raise the level of confidence and self-esteem of her female listeners of all ages. She speaks of a goal of helping women to win self-empowerment.

In 1988 Winfrey was invited to deliver the main address at commencement exercises at Tennessee State University. At that ceremony the university awarded her a diploma in recognition of her accomplishments, although she had left the institution without having completed degree

Winfrey and audience at Southwestern High School in Baltimore, Maryland, during a taping of *Oprah*, 1988.

requirements. For her part, Winfrey established a scholarship fund at her alma mater that will furnish payment of expenses for ten students enrolled in the university each year. Characteristically, she reserves the right to choose the students who receive these annual awards. She maintains a personal relationship with each recipient and requires that each student keep a "B" average. She writes letters to them and reassures them: "I understand that the first year is really difficult, and there are a lot of adjustments to be made. I believe in you. We all made an agreement that it would be a three-point average, not a 2.483, and I know you want to uphold your end of the agreement, because I intend to uphold mine."

In January 1994 President Clinton signed the "Oprah Bill," which is a new law to protect children. Winfrey drafted the legislation with the help of former Illinois governor James Thompson. Its aim is to screen all potential day care workers by establishing a registry of convicted child abusers.

The Oprah Winfrey Show is viewed by 20 million people each weekday. Winfrey's rise to stardom is an extraordinary story of personal achievement. Her appeal is unusually broad, and her name is perhaps the best-known of any woman now performing on national television.

Sources

Black Collegian, November/December 1990.

Ebony, October 1988.

Essence, October 1986.

Good Housekeeping, August 1986.

Jet, November 29, 1993; November 10, 1994.

King, Norman, *Everybody Loves Oprah!,* Morrow, 1987.

Ladies' Home Journal, December 1988.

Ms., November 1988; January/February 1989.

New York Times Magazine, June 11, 1989.

People, November 29, 1992; November 29, 1994.

Time, August 30, 1993.

Photo Credits

The photographs appearing in *Performing Artists: From Alvin Ailey to Julia Roberts* were received from the following sources:

AP/Wide World Photos: cover photographs (Robert Townsend, Julia Roberts, Andy García), pages 1, 4, 10, 15, 24, 30, 49, 67, 71, 77, 93, 106, 113, 120, 126, 138, 152, 157, 159, 166, 175, 178, 190, 208, 212, 220, 226, 249, 258, 264, 271, 275, 284, 289, 295, 299, 302, 306, 309, 314, 319, 323, 347, 350, 355, 357, 363, 371, 374, 380, 384, 400, 404, 407, 417, 425, 432, 435, 446, 458, 464, 492, 502, 512, 516, 519, 523, 533, 537, 547, 552, 556, 567, 571, 575, 585, 593, 599, 606, 610, 620, 623, 628, 656, 662, 666, 668, 675, 681, 693; UPI/Bettmann: pages 22, 53, 185, 255, 544, 596, 635, 650; The Bettmann Archive: pages 35, 38; UPI/Bettmann Newsphotos: pages 40, 55; Reuters/Bettmann: pages 61, 101, 104, 131, 182, 280, 393; Archive Photos/Fotos International: pages 81, 168, 172, 335, 641; Patrick Harbron/Sygma: page 87; Archive Photos/Saga: page 97; Courtesy of A&M Records: page 146; Archive Photos/Popperfoto: page 162; Copyright © 1985 Columbia Pictures Industries, Inc.: page 195; Archive Photos/Saga/P. Iovino: page 201; Archive Photos: pages 252, 282; Courtesy of Arista: page 330; Photograph by Harrison Funk, © 1991 Sire Records Company: page 341; Archive Photos/American Stock: page 369; Archive Photos/Express News: page 413; Courtesy of ICM Artists, Ltd.: page 442; Photograph by Chris Cuffaro, © 1991 The David Geffen Company: page 487; Courtesy of Priority Records: page 498; Photograph by Lance Mercer, © 1993, Sony Music, courtesy of Epic Records: page 527; Photograph by Ernie Panicioli, © 1991 Sony Music: page 561; Photograph by Chris Cuffaro/Visages, © 1991 Warner Bros. Records: page 580; Archive Photos/Darlene Hammond: pages 615, 624; Springer/Bettmann Film Archive: page 638.

Index

Bold denotes profiles and volume numbers.

A

Abbey Road **1**: 59
Abbruzzese, Dave **3**: 526
Abdul, Paula 1: 1-3, 199
Absolute Torch and Twang **2**: 378
The Accused **1**: 217
Ace Ventura: Pet Detective **1**: 97, 99
The Addams Family **2**: 360
The African Queen **2**: 312, 336
African Violet Society **3**: 655
Aftermath **3**: 594
The Age of Innocence **1**: 169-170, **3**: 542
Age to Age **2**: 272
Agon **2**: 447
Aida **3**: 556, 559
Aida: A Picture Book for All Ages **3**: 560
Ailey, Alvin 1: 4-9, 2: 285, 355
Aladdin **3**: 679
Alien **3**: 668-670, 672
Alien 3 **3**: 673
All About Eve **1**: 165
Allen, Debbie 1: 10-14
Allen, Tim 1: 15-21
All Hail the Queen **3**: 568
Allman, Gregg **1**: 109
All of Me **2**: 425-426, 430
All the President's Men **2**: 321, **3**: 576
All the Right Moves **1**: 142
Alonso, Alicia 1: 22-29
Alonso, Maria Conchita 1: 30-34
Alvin Ailey American Dance Theater **1**: 4-5, **2**: 408, 456

A.M. Chicago **3**: 691, 692
American Ballet Theatre **1**: 23, 28, 50-51, **3**: 651
American Me **3**: 517
Am I Not Your Girl? **3**: 505
Amos and Andrew **1**: 85
Anchors Aweigh **2**: 372
And ... A Time To Dance **2**: 401
And a Voice to Sing With **1**: 41, 44
And in This Corner **3**: 625
Angel With a Lariat **2**: 376-377
The Anniversary **1**: 165
Any Day Now **1**: 43
Any Which Way You Can **1**: 187
Apocalypse '91: The Enemy Strikes Black **3**: 563
Apocalypse Now **1**: 202
Appetite for Destruction **3**: 600, 602
Aria **1**: 209
Arnold, Tom **3**: 609
The Arsenio Hall Show **2**: 292
Astaire, Adele **1**: 36
Astaire, Fred 1: 6, 35-39, 2: 254, 369
Augustyniak, Jerry **3**: 653
Awakenings **3**: 679
The Awful Truth **2**: 277

B

Back to the Future **1**: 220, 223
Back to the Future Part II **1**: 224
Bad **3**: 631
Baez, Joan 1: 40-46

Bagdad Cafe **2:** 268

Balanchine, George **3:** 649

The Ballad of Gregorio Cortez **3:** 514

Ballet Alicia Alonso **1:** 25

Ballet Nacional de Cuba **1:** 22, 26-28

Ballet Russe de Monte Carlo **3:** 648-649, 651

The Band Wagon **1:** 36

Baptism **1:** 43

Barefoot in the Park **3:** 574

The Barkleys of Broadway **1:** 37-38

Baryshnikov, Mikhail 1: 47-52, **2:** 317

Batman **2:** 363, 364, 366

Batman Forever **1:** 100, **2:** 367

Batman Returns **2:** 367, **3:** 542

Beaches **2:** 439-440

The Beatles 1: 53-60

The Beatles **1:** 58

Beatrice di Tenda **3:** 524

Beetlejuice **2:** 363, 366

Beggar's Banquet **3:** 595

The Belle of New York **1:** 38

Ben **2:** 352

Benny and Joon **1:** 176

Bergen, Candice 1: 61-66

Bergen, Edgar **1:** 61, 63

The Best Little Whorehouse in Texas **3:** 521

The Best of Times **3:** 678

Beyond the Forest **1:** 165

Big **2:** 302

Big Business **2:** 439

The Big Chill **1:** 133

The Bill Cosby Show **1:** 128

Billy Bathgate **2:** 322

Bird **1:** 187

Birdy **1:** 83

Bittersweet White Light **1:** 109

Black and Blue **3:** 596

Blackboard Jungle **3:** 547

Black Rain **2:** 251

Blade Runner **3:** 514

Blades, Rubén 1: 67-70

Bleach **3:** 488-489

Blessed Are ... **1:** 43, 44

Blind Man's Zoo **3:** 653, 655

Blood Sugar Sex Magik **3:** 583-584

Bluesbreakers **1:** 115

"Blue Suede Shoes" **3:** 553

Bobby **1:** 80

Bobby McFerrin **2:** 433

Bodies, Rest and Motion **1:** 211

Body Count **2:** 345

The Bodyguard **1:** 136, **2:** 333

Body of Evidence **2:** 410

Bono, Sonny **1:** 106-107

Bopha **1:** 230, **2:** 294

Born on the Fourth of July **1:** 143

Bosom Buddies **2:** 300-301

The Boys From Brazil **3:** 510

Boyz N the Hood **1:** 201, 204-205

The Breakfast Club **1:** 195, 197

Breakin' **2:** 342

Bright Lights, Big City **1:** 224

Bringing Up Baby **2:** 277, 311

Brooks, Garth 1: 71-76

Brown, Bobby 1: 77-80, **2:** 333, **3:** 534

Brown, Bryon **1:** 143

Buck and the Preacher **3:** 548

Buck, Robert **3:** 653

Bugsy Malone **1:** 214

Bull Durham **1:** 131, 135

Burnin' **2:** 419

Burton, Richard **2:** 324

Butch Cassidy and the Sundance Kid **3:** 574

By the Light of the Moon **2:** 402

C

Cadence **1:** 204

Cage, Nicolas 1: 81-86, 173, 211

The Candidate **3:** 575
Candleshoe **1:** 214
Candy, John 1: 87-92, 153-154, **2:** 302
Carey, Mariah 1: 93-96
Carnal Knowledge **1:** 64, **2:** 454
Carrey, Jim 1: 97-100
Carrie **3:** 510
Carvey, Dana 1: 101-105, **2:** 468
Casualties of War **1:** 224
Catch a Fire **2:** 419
Change of Seasons **2:** 325
Charade **2:** 278
The Chase **1:** 74
Cher 1: 84, **106-112**, **3:** 539-540
Cher **1:** 109, 111
Chicago City Ballet **3:** 651
A Child Is Waiting **2:** 256
City Slickers **1:** 146, 150-151
City Slickers II: The Legend of Curly's Gold **1:** 151
Clams on the Half Shell Revue **2:** 438
Clapton, Eric 1: 113-119, **2:** 419
Clara's Heart **2:** 307
Class Action **1:** 204
Clean and Sober **2:** 364, 366
Clean Slate **1:** 105
Cliffhanger **3:** 640
Clinton, George **3:** 581-582
Club Paradise **3:** 678
Cobain, Kurt **3:** 487-491, 528
Cobra **3:** 639
Cocktail **1:** 143
The Color of Money **1:** 142
The Color Purple **2:** 258, 260-261, 266, **3:** 692
Colors **1:** 31, **2:** 343
Come Back to the Five and Dime, Jimmy Dean, Jimmy Dean **1:** 110
The Comfort Zone **3:** 685
Comic Relief **1:** 88, 90, **2:** 267
Comin' Uptown **2:** 316
Coming to America **2:** 291-292

Commando **3:** 612
Conan, The Barbarian **3:** 610, 612
Conan, The Destroyer **3:** 612
Conga **1:** 192
Connery, Sean 1: 120-125, **2:** 322, **3:** 542, 633
Control **2:** 347-349
Coogan's Bluff **1:** 186
Cool Runnings **1:** 91
"Cop Killer" **2:** 345
Coppola, Francis Ford **1:** 82
Cosby, Bill 1: 126-130, 149 **2:** 433, 454, **3:** 622
The Cosby Show **1:** 10, 126, 129, **2:** 286, 434, **3:** 622
Costner, Kevin 1: 131-137, **2:** 282, 333
Cotton Club **2:** 316
Cover Girl **2:** 372-373
Crimes and Misdemeanors **2:** 339
Crooklyn **2:** 391
Crossover Dreams **1:** 69
The Crow **2:** 382-383
Cruise, Tom 1: 138-145
Cry Baby **1:** 174
Cry Freedom **3:** 665
Crystal, Billy 1: 146-151, **2:** 267, 317
Culkin, Macaulay 1: 152-155
Cuts Both Ways **1:** 193

D

d'Amboise, Jacques 1: 156-161
The Dance of Death **3:** 510
Dance Theater of Harlem **2:** 446, 449
Dances With Wolves **1:** 136, **2:** 280-283
Dangerous **1:** 164
Dangerous Liaisons **3:** 542
Dave **3:** 673
David's Album **1:** 43

Davis, Bette **1**: 162-167, **2**: 435
Day-Lewis, Daniel **1**: 168-171, **3**: 543
Days of Thunder **1**: 143
The Dead **2**: 338
Dead Poets Society **3**: 679
The Dead Pool **1**: 98, 186
Death of a Salesman **2**: 322
Deep Cover **1**: 201, 206
Demolition Man **3**: 640
Depp, Johnny **1**: 172-177
Desperately Seeking Susan **2**: 409
Destiny **2**: 352
Diamonds Are Forever **1**: 123-124
Dick Tracy **2**: 322
A Different World **1**: 13-14, **2**: 284, 286, **3**: 622, 627
Diff'rent Strokes **2**: 347
Dirty Harry **1**: 186
Dirty Rotten Scoundrels **2**: 430
Dirty Work **3**: 597
Doc Hollywood **1**: 224
Dogg, Snoop Doggy **1**: 178-181
Doggystyle **1**: 178-180
Dollywood **3**: 521
"Don't Be Cruel" **3**: 553
Don't Be Cruel **1**: 78, 80
"Don't Worry, Be Happy" **2**: 433
Doogie Howser, M.D. **2**: 306
Do the Right Thing **2**: 384, 388, **3**: 535, 564
Down and Out in Beverly Hills **2**: 439
Downhill Racer **3**: 574
Drew, Dennis **3**: 653
Driving Miss Daisy **1**: 226, 229-230
Dr. No **1**: 122-123
The Duck Factory **1**: 98
Duet **2**: 434
Dumb and Dumber **1**: 100
Dying Young **3**: 589
Dylan, Bob **1**: 40, 43

E

Earth Girls Are Easy **1**: 98
Easter Parade **1**: 38, **2**: 254
Eastwood, Clint **1**: 182-189, 230
The Ed Sullivan Show **1**: 56
Edward Scissorhands **1**: 176
Efil4zaggin **3**: 500
8 Million Ways to Die **2**: 250
The Electric Company **2**: 454
Electric Company Album **2**: 451
The Electric Horseman **3**: 576
Emotions **1**: 95
Enemies: A Love Story **2**: 339
The Enforcer **1**: 186
The Entertainer **3**: 510
Epstein, Brian **1**: 54, 57
Equus **2**: 325
Eric Clapton **1**: 116
Erotica **2**: 410
Esmond, Jill **3**: 510
Estefan, Gloria **1**: 190-194
Estevez, Emilio **1**: 3, 195-200
Eubie! **2**: 316
Eve of Destruction **2**: 317
Every Which Way but Loose **1**: 186
Exile on Main Street **3**: 595
Exodus **2**: 420
Experience the Divine **2**: 440
Eyen, Tom **2**: 437
Eyes of Innocence **1**: 192
Eyewitness **3**: 671

F

The Fabulous Baker Boys **3**: 542
Fame **1**: 12-13, **2**: 285, 348
Family Business **2**: 322
Family Ties **1**: 220, 222-223, 225
Far and Away **1**: 143
Fatal Beauty **1**: 69

Fat Albert and the Cosby Kids **1**: 126, 128

Father of the Bride **2**: 425, 430

Fearless **3**: 535

Feel My Power **2**: 297

A Few Good Men **1**: 144

Field of Dreams **1**: 136

Figaro **3**: 494

"Fight the Power" **3**: 564

A Fine Mess **1**: 34

Firebird **3**: 649, 651

Firefox **1**: 186

The Firm **1**: 144

First Blood **3**: 639

Fishburne, Laurence 1: 201-207

The Fisher King **3**: 679

A Fistful of Dollars **1**: 184-185

Five Corners **1**: 218

The Five Heartbeats **3**: 660

Flatliners **3**: 589

Folksingers 'Round Harvard Square **1**: 42

Fonda, Bridget 1: 208-211

For a Few Dollars More **1**: 185

Forever Your Girl **1**: 1-3

For Love or Money **1**: 224

For Me and My Gal **2**: 370, 372

Forrest Gump **2**: 303

For the Boys **2**: 440

Foster, Jodie 1: 212-219, **2**: 327, **3**: 535

The Four Seasons **2**: 455

461 Ocean Blvd **1**: 117

Foxes and Carny **1**: 217

Fox, Michael J. 1: 210, **220-225**

Foxy Lady **1**: 109

Frankie and Johnny **3**: 542

Freaky Friday **1**: 214

Freaky Styley **3**: 582

Freeman, Morgan 1: 226-231, **2**: 294

The Fresh Prince of Bel-Air **3**: 624, 626

From Russia With Love **1**: 123

The Funky Headhunter **2**: 298

G

Gamble, Cheryl (Coko) **3**: 645

García, Andy 2: 249-251

Gardens of Stone **2**: 338

Garland, Judy 2: 252-257, 370, 372

Garth Brooks **1**: 73

The Gauntlet **1**: 186

Getting Even With Dad **1**: 155

Ghost **2**: 268

Ghostbusters **3**: 668, 671

Ghostbusters II **1**: 79

Gillespie, Ben **2**: 436

Giselle **1**: 22, 23, 25, 27, 28

Glory **1**: 226, 230, **3**: 665

Glover, Danny 2: 258-263

Goat's Head Soup **3**: 595

The Godfather Part III **2**: 251

Goldberg, Whoopi 2: 264-270, 307, **3**: 626

Goldfinger **1**: 123

Good Morning, Vietnam **3**: 675, 678

The Good Son **1**: 155

The Good, the Bad, and the Ugly **1**: 185

Good Times **2**: 347

Gorillas in the Mist **3**: 672

Gossard, Stone **3**: 526

Got To Be There **2**: 351

The Graduate **2**: 319-321

Grand Canyon **2**: 262, 430

Grant, Amy 2: 271-274

Grant, Cary 2: 275-279, 311

Grease 2 **3**: 538

Greene, Graham 2: 280-283

The Grifters **2**: 339

Grohl, Dave **3**: 488-489

The Group **1**: 63

Guarding Tess **1**: 85

Guess Who's Coming to Dinner **2**: 312, **3**: 548

Gung Ho **2**: 363

Guns N' Roses **3**: 599

Gustafson, Steve **3**: 653
Guy, Jasmine 2: 284-288
Gypsy **2**: 440

H

Half Moon Street **3**: 668, 672
Hall, Arsenio 2: 289-294
Hamlet **3**: 510
Hammer 2: 295-298
Hang 'em High **1**: 186
Hanks, Tom 1: 90, **2: 299-305**
Happy Birthday, Gemini **2**: 455
Happy Days **2**: 460
A Hard Day's Night **1**: 56
Harlem Nights **2**: 287
Harris, Neil Patrick 2: 306-308
Harrison, George **1**: 53-54
The Harvey Girls **2**: 254
Havana **3**: 577
Hazme Sentir **1**: 32
"Heartbreak Hotel" **3**: 553
Heart in Motion **2**: 273-274
Heart of Stone **1**: 111
Help **1**: 56
Henry V **3**: 510
Hepburn, Katharine 2: 277, **309-313**, **3**: 548
"Here You Come Again" **3**: 521
Hero **2**: 251
He's the DJ, I'm the Rapper **3**: 625
High Plains Drifter **1**: 186
Hindman, Earl **1**: 19
Hines, Gregory 1: 150, **2: 314-318**
His Girl Friday **2**: 277
History of the World, Part I **2**: 316
Hitchcock, Alfred **2**: 278
Hocus Pocus **2**: 440
Hoffman, Dustin 1: 143, **2: 319-322**
Holiday **2**: 277, 311
Hollywood Shuffle **3**: 658660
Home Alone **1**: 152-155

Home Alone 2: Lost in New York **1**: 154
Home Improvement **1**: 15, 18, 20
Home Invasion **2**: 345
Honkytonk Man **1**: 186-187
Hook **2**: 322, **3**: 589, 679
Hope Chest **3**: 655
Hopkins, Anthony 1: 105, **2: 323-329**, **3**: 507
Horton, Lester **1**: 6, 8
Hotel New Hampshire **1**: 217
"Hound Dog" **3**: 553
Houston, Whitney 1: 80, **2: 330-334**
How Will the Wolf Survive? **2**: 402
Humanitas International **1**: 44
The Hunt for Red October **1**: 124
Huston, Anjelica 2: 335-340

I

Ice Pirates **2**: 338
Ice-T 2: 341-346
The Iceberg/Freedom of Speech ... Just Watch What You Say **2**: 343
Idomeneo **3**: 525
I Do Not Want What I Haven't Got **3**: 504
"I Got You, Babe" **1**: 107, 111
I Love Trouble **3**: 590
I'm Breathless **2**: 410
I'm Your Baby Tonight **2**: 333
Indecent Proposal **3**: 578
Indiana Jones and the Temple of Doom **1**: 124
Ingenue **2**: 374, 378
In Living Color **1**: 97, 99, **2**: 332, **3**: 534
In My Tribe **3**: 653, 655
In Pieces **1**: 74
Internal Affairs **2**: 251
Interview With the Vampire **1**: 144
In the Line of Fire **1**: 187

In the Name of the Father **1:** 170
Into the Light **1:** 194
Into the Night **3:** 539
In Utero **3:** 490
Invitation to the Dance **2:** 372
"I Shot the Sheriff" **1:** 117, **2:** 419
"Islands in the Stream" **3:** 521
I Spy **1:** 126-128
It Could Happen to You **1:** 85, 211, **3:** 535
It's About Time **3:** 645-646
It's Always Fair Weather **2:** 372
It's Only Rock and Roll **3:** 595
It Takes a Nation of Millions to Hold Us Back **3:** 563
"I Will Always Love You" **2:** 333

J

Jackson 5 **2:** 351-352
Jackson, Janet **1:** 2, **2:** 332, **347-349**
Jackson, Michael **2:** 347, 350-354, **3:** 631
The Jacksons Live **2:** 352
Jagger, Mick **3:** 592-598
Jamison, Judith **1:** 9
Janet Jackson's Rhythm Nation 1814 **2:** 347, 349
Jasmine Guy **2:** 287
Jelly's Last Jam **2:** 317
Jennifer Eight **2:** 251
Jeremiah Johnson **3:** 575
The Jerk **2:** 425, 428
Jezebel **1:** 164
JFK **1:** 136
Joan Baez **1:** 42, 45
Joan Baez in Concert Part Two **1:** 43
Joffrey Ballet **2:** 355-356
Joffrey, Robert **2:** 355-359
John Henry **2:** 448
Johnny Dangerously **2:** 365
Johnson, Tamara (Taj) **3:** 645

Jo Jo Dancer, Your Life Is Calling **1:** 13
Judgment at Nuremberg **2:** 256
Julia, Raul **2:** 360-362
Jungle Fever **2:** 389, **3:** 632-633
Just Another Band From East L.A: A Collection **2:** 400, 403

K

The Karate Kid **2:** 458-461
The Karate Kid, Part II **2:** 462
The Karate Kid III **2:** 462
Keaton, Michael **2:** 363-368
Kelley, David **3:** 543
Kelly, Gene **1:** 6, **2:** 254, **369-373**
Kelly's Heroes **1:** 186
Kidman, Nicole **1:** 143
Kiko and the Lavender Moon **2:** 403
The King and I **2:** 453
King of New York **1:** 204
"King Tut" **2:** 428
Kirov Ballet **1:** 50
Kiss of the Spider Woman **2:** 362
Knock Wood **1:** 62
Kramer vs. Kramer **2:** 319, 321-322

L

La Bamba **2:** 403
Ladyhawke **3:** 538
La Fille du regiment **3:** 524
lang, k. d. **2:** 374-378
La Pistola y El Corazon **2:** 403
Laser Mission **2:** 381
The Last Action Hero **3:** 613
The Last of the Mohicans **1:** 168-170
L.A. Story **2:** 430
Late Night with David Letterman **2:** 394
"Layla" **1:** 117
Lead Me On **2:** 273

A League of Their Own **2:** 303, 410

Lean on Me **1:** 226

Leap of Faith **2:** 430

Lee, Brandon 2: 380-383

Lee, Spike 1: 203, **2:** 384-392, **3:** 535, 631

Legacy of Rage **2:** 381

Legal Eagles **3:** 577

Leigh, Vivian **3:** 510

Lennon, John **1:** 53

Lenny **2:** 321

Lethal Weapon **2:** 258, 261

Lethal Weapon 2 **2:** 258, 261

Let It Be **1:** 58-59

Let It Bleed **3:** 595

Let It Loose **1:** 192-193

Let's Get It Started **2:** 297

The Letter **1:** 164

Letterman, David 2: 293, **393-398**

Life With Mikey **1:** 224

The Light of Day **1:** 224

Like a Prayer **2:** 410

Like a Virgin **2:** 409-410

Lilies of the Field **3:** 545, 548

The Lion and the Cobra **3:** 503

Little Big Man **2:** 322

The Little Foxes **1:** 164

The Little Girl Who Lives Down the Lane **1:** 216

Little Man Tate **1:** 219

Little Nikita **3:** 549

Little Women **2:** 311

Lock Up **3:** 639

Lollapalooza **2:** 345

The Long Walk Home **2:** 268

Losin' It **1:** 140

Los Lobos 2: 399-403

Love, Courtney **3:** 491

Love Hurts **1:** 111

"Love Me Tender" **3:** 553

Lovett, Lyle **3:** 590

Lyons, Leanne (Leelee) **3:** 645

M

Made in America **2:** 269, **3:** 624, 626

Madonna 2: 407-412

Madonna **2:** 409

Magic **2:** 325

Magical Mystery Tour **1:** 57

Magnum Force **1:** 186

"Mainline Florida" **1:** 117

Malcolm X **2:** 384, 389-391, **3:** 665

Malle, Louis **1:** 65

Manhattan Murder Mystery **2:** 339

Manilow, Barry **2:** 437

The Man Who Came to Dinner **1:** 165

Marathon Man **2:** 321

Maria Conchita **1:** 30, 32

Mariah Carey **1:** 94

Mark, Marky 2: 413-416

Marky Mark **2:** 414

Marley, Bob 2: 417-424, **3:** 505

Marlowe, Pop! **2:** 454

Married to the Mob **3:** 541

Martin, Steve 2: 425-431

Mask **1:** 110

The Mask **1:** 97, 99

"*Master Harold*" ... *and the Boys* **2:** 258-259

Ma, Yo-Yo 2: 404-406

McCartney, Paul **1:** 53-54

McCready, Mike **3:** 526

McFerrin, Bobby 2: 432-434

Me and My Gal **2:** 254

Medicine Man **1:** 125

Meet Me in St. Louis **2:** 254

Memories of Me **1:** 150

Menace on the Mountains **1:** 214

Menendez: A Murder in Beverly Hills **3:** 517

Merchant, Natalie **3:** 653

Mermaids **1:** 111

The Meteor Man **3:** 661

Miami Vice **3:** 512, 515

Midler, Bette 2: 435-441

Midnight Cowboy **2:** 319-322

Midori 2: 442-446

The Mighty Quinn **3:** 660

The Milagro Beanfield War **1:** 69, **3:** 571

Mississippi Masala **3:** 665

Mitchell, Arthur 2: 446-450

Mo' Better Blues **2:** 388-389, **3:** 632, 665

Moonstruck **1:** 83-84, 106, 111

Moreno, Rita 2: 451-457

Morita, Noriyuki "Pat" 2: 458-463

Mork & Mindy **3:** 675, 677

Morris, Mark **1:** 51, **2:** 355

Moscow on the Hudson **1:** 31, **3:** 677-678

Mother's Milk **3:** 580, 582-583

Mr. Mom **2:** 363, 365

Mr. Saturday Night **1:** 150

Mrs. Doubtfire **3:** 675, 679

Mr. T. and Tina **2:** 460

The Muppet Show **2:** 451, 455

Murphy Brown **1:** 65

Music Box **1:** 95

Music for the People **2:** 414

My Beautiful Laundrette **1:** 168-169

Myers, Mike 1: 103, **2: 464-469**

My Girl **1:** 154

My Left Foot **1:** 169-170

My Life **2:** 367

My Lives **3:** 609

Mystic Pizza **3:** 587-588

N

The Name of the Rose **1:** 124

Napoleon and Samantha **1:** 214

National Dance Institute **1:** 156, 160

Native Son **3:** 692

Natty Dread **2:** 419

The Natural **3:** 577

Nevermind **3:** 488, 490

Never Say Never Again **1:** 124

New Edition **1:** 78-79

New Jack City **2:** 344, **3:** 631-632

New Kids on the Block **2:** 413

New York City Ballet **1:** 156, 158, **2:** 447, **3:** 648-651

Nicholson, Jack **2:** 335, 337, 454, **3:** 539, 543

Nighthawks **3:** 639

Nightmare on Elm Street **1:** 173

The Night of the Following Day **2:** 454

Night on Earth **3:** 535

Night Shift **2:** 363, 365

"The Night They Drove Old Dixie Down" **1:** 44

"Nine to Five" **3:** 521

Nine to Five **2:** 455, 521

Nirvana 3: 487-491, 526

No Fences **1:** 73-74

None But the Lonely Heart **2:** 277

Norma **3:** 525

Norman, Jessye 3: 492-497

North by Northwest **2:** 278

Northern Exposure **2:** 280, 283

Nothing but the Truth **1:** 69

"Nothing Compares 2 U" **3:** 504

Nothing in Common **2:** 302

Notorious **2:** 278

Novoselic, Krist **3:** 488

No Way Out **1:** 131, 134-135

Now Voyager **1:** 165

The Nutcracker **3:** 651

N.W.A. 2: 297, 341, **3: 498-501**

O

O'Connor, Sinead 3: 502-506

O Ella o Yo **1:** 32

Off the Wall **2:** 352

O.G.—Original Gangster **2:** 344

Old Acquaintance **1:** 165

Olivier, Laurence 2: 323, **3: 507-511**

Olmos, Edward James 3: 512-518
One Good Cop 2: 367
One Little Indian 1: 214
One of the Boys 1: 32
One Woman or Two 3: 672
On Golden Pond 2: 313
Only Angels Have Wings 2: 277
Ono, Yoko 1: 58
On the Town 2: 372-373
Opportunity Knocks 1: 103
The Oprah Winfrey Show 3: 692-693
Ordinary People 3: 576
Oscar 3: 639
Othello 3: 510
Our Time in Eden 3: 655
The Outlaw Josey Wales 1: 186
Out of Africa 3: 577
Outrageous Fortune 2: 439
The Outsiders 1: 140-141, 196
Over the Top 3: 639

P

Pacific Heights 2: 367
Pale Rider 1: 186
Pal Joey 2: 370
The Paper 2: 367
Papillon 2: 321
Parenthood 2: 425, 430
"Parents Just Don't Understand" 3: 625
Paris Opera Ballet 3: 648-649
Parton, Dolly 3: 519-522, 587, 639
Passenger 57 3: 633
Pavarotti, Luciano 3: 523-525
Pearl Jam 3: 526-532
Peggy Sue Got Married 1: 83-84, 98
The Pelican Brief 3: 590, 667
Penn, Sean 2: 410
Penny Serenade 2: 277
Perez, Rosie 3: 533-536
A Perfect World 1: 136

Pfieffer, Michelle 1: 170, 2: 367, 3: 537-543
Philadelphia 2: 303, 3: 667
The Philadelphia Story 2: 312
Picasso at the Lapin Agile 2: 430
The Pick Up Artist 3: 685
The Pirate 2: 372
Places in the Heart 2: 258, 260
Planes, Trains, and Automobiles 1: 91, 2: 426, 430
The Player 2: 269
Play Me Backwards 1: 45
Play Misty for Me 1: 186-187
Please Hammer Don't Hurt 'Em 2: 297
Plowright, Joan 3: 511
Point of No Return 1: 208, 211
Poitier, Sidney 3: 544-551, 626
Popeye 3: 677
Power 2: 343
The Power of One 1: 230
Predator II 1: 69
Presley, Elvis 3: 552-555
Presumed Innocent 2: 362
Pretty Woman 3: 585-586, 588
Price, Leontyne 3: 556-560
Pride and Prejudice 3: 509
Primitive Love 1: 192
The Prince and the Showgirl 3: 510
The Private Lives of Elizabeth and Essex 1: 164
Prizzi's Honor 2: 338
Public Enemy 3: 561-566
Pumping Iron 3: 610, 612
Punchline 2: 302
Pushkin, Alexander 1: 50

Q

Quayle, Dan 1: 66
Queen Latifah 3: 567-570

R

Rabbit Test **1:** 148
A Rage in Harlem **2:** 317
Ragtime **1:** 13
Rain Man **1:** 143, **2:** 319, 322
Raising Arizona **1:** 83
A Raisin in the Sun **3:** 545, 547
Rambo **3:** 639
Rambo: First Blood, Part II **3:** 639
Rambo III **3:** 639
Rapid Fire **2:** 382
Rashad, Phylicia **1:** 10, 129
Rastaman Vibration **2:** 419
Raw **3:** 660
Raw Deal **3:** 612
Rawhide **1:** 184-185
Rebecca **3:** 509
Redford, Robert 3: 571-579
The Red Hot Chili Peppers 3: 527, 530, **580-584**
The Red Hot Chili Peppers **3:** 581
Red Rock West **1:** 85
The Remains of the Day **2:** 327
Renacer **1:** 191
Repo Man **1:** 195-197
Resource Center for Nonviolence **1:** 43
Revelations **1:** 5, 8, 10
Revolver **1:** 56
Rhinestone **3:** 521, 639
Rhyme Pays **2:** 342
Rhythm Nation 1814 **2:** 347, 349
Rich and Famous **1:** 65
Richardson, Patricia **1:** 19
Richard III **3:** 510
Ricochet **2:** 344
The Right Stuff **3:** 685
Ringo **1:** 59
Rising Sun **1:** 125, **3:** 633
Risky Business **1:** 141-142
The Ritz **2:** 451, 455

A River Runs Through It **3:** 571, 577-578
The Road to Wellville **1:** 105, **2:** 328
Roberts, Julia 3: 585-591, 667
Robin Hood: Prince of Thieves **1:** 136, 230
The Rockford Files **2:** 451, 455
Rock the House **3:** 625
Rocky **3:** 637, 639
Rocky II **3:** 637
Rocky III **3:** 637
Rocky IV **3:** 637
Rocky V **3:** 637
Roddenberry, Gene **3:** 643
Rogers, Ginger **1:** 37
Rogers, Mimi **1:** 143
The Rolling Stones 3: 592-598
Romero **2:** 362
A Room With a View **1:** 168-169
Ropin' the Wind **1:** 71, 74
The Rose **2:** 438
Roseanne 3: 606-609
Roseanne **1:** 18, **3:** 606-607
Roseanne: My Life as a Woman **3:** 609
Rose, Axl 3: 599-605
Rose, Leonard **2:** 405
"Round Midnight" **2:** 433
Roxanne **2:** 425-426, 430
Royal Wedding **1:** 38
Rubber Soul **1:** 56
Running Man **1:** 31
Running Scared **1:** 150, **2:** 317
Russia House **3:** 542
Ruthless People **2:** 439

S

Sarafina: The Movie **2:** 269
Saturday Night Live **1:** 89-90, 101-102, 104-105, 146, 149-150, **2:** 428, 464, 466468, **3:** 504-505, 677
Scandal **1:** 208-209

Scarface **3:** 538

Scenes From a Mall **2:** 440

School Daze **1:** 203, **2:** 286, 387-388

Schwarzenegger, Arnold **1:** 31, 105, **3: 610-614**

SCTV **1:** 89-90

Searching for Bobby Fisher **1:** 206

Second City Comedy Troupe **1:** 87, 89

The Secret of My Success **1:** 224

Secrets of the I Ching **3:** 654

Seinfeld **3:** 616-617

Seinfeld, Jerry **3: 615-619**

Seinlanguage **3:** 618

Sesame Street **2:** 454

The Seven-Per-Cent Solution **3:** 510

Sex **2:** 410

Sgt. Pepper's Lonely Hearts Club Band **1:** 57

Shadowlands **2:** 328, 374, 377

She's Gotta Have It **2:** 386-387

Shoot to Kill **3:** 550

Showdown in Little Tokyo **2:** 381

Shriver, Maria **3:** 610, 614

Siembra **1:** 68

Siesta **1:** 218

The Sign in Sidney Brustein's Window **2:** 453

The Silence of the Lambs **1:** 219, **2:** 324, 327

Silkwood **1:** 110

Silverado **1:** 133, **2:** 260

Simple Pleasures **2:** 433

Sinbad **3: 620-623**

The Sinbad Show **3:** 622

Singles **1:** 210, **3:** 529

Single White Female **1:** 208, 210

Sister Act **2:** 269

Sister Act 2 **2:** 269

Six Degrees of Separation **3:** 624, 626

Sleeping With the Enemy **3:** 589

Sleepless in Seattle **2:** 300, 303

Slowhand **1:** 117

"Smells Like Teen Spirit" **3:** 490

Smith, Will **3: 624-627**

Sneakers **3:** 550, 578

Snipes, Wesley **1:** 204, **3: 628-634**

Soap **1:** 146, 148

So I Married an Axe Murderer **2:** 469

A Soldier's Play **3:** 664

A Soldier's Story **3:** 664

Some Girls **3:** 597

Something of Value **3:** 545

Songs of Freedom **2:** 422

The Sonny and Cher Comedy Hour **1:** 108-109

Sophisticated Ladies **2:** 316

The Spaghetti Incident? **3:** 600, 604

Speaking of Dreams **1:** 45

Special Look **1:** 14

Spellbound **1:** 3

Splash **1:** 88-91, **2:** 300, 302

Spontaneous Inventions **2:** 433

The Spook Show **2:** 265

Stage Door **2:** 311

Stallone, Sylvester **3: 635-640**

Stand and Deliver **3:** 516-517

A Star Is Born **2:** 255

Star Trek **3:** 641

Star Trek: Generations **3:** 643

Star Trek: The Next Generation **2:** 268, **3:** 641-643

Starr, Ringo **1:** 53-54

Stars and Bars **1:** 169

Starting Over **1:** 65

Stealing Home **1:** 219

Steel Magnolias **3:** 521, 587-588

Steel Wheels **3:** 597

St. Elmo's Fire **1:** 195, 197

St. Elsewhere **3:** 664

Stewart, Patrick **3: 641-644**

Sticky Fingers **3:** 595

The Sting **3:** 574-575

Stir Crazy **3:** 549

A Stolen Life **1:** 165

Stop! Or My Mom Will Shoot **3:** 640

Straight Outta Compton **3**: 499-500
Straight Time **2**: 321
Strait, George **1**: 72
Straw Dogs **2**: 321
A Streetcar Named Desire **2**: 448
Street Smart **1**: 229-230
Sudden Impact **1**: 186
Summer Stock **2**: 373
Sundance Institute **3**: 571
Suspect **1**: 111
Suspicion **2**: 278
Sutherland, Kiefer **3**: 590
Sweet Charity **1**: 13
Sweet Liberty **3**: 539
SWV 3: 645-647

T

Talent for the Game **3**: 513
Tallchief, Maria 3: 648-652
Tango and Cash **3**: 639
Tap **2**: 317
Taps **1**: 140
Taxi Driver **1**: 213, 216
"Tears in Heaven" **1**: 118
Teen Wolf **1**: 224
Tell Them Willie Boy Is Here **3**: 574
Ten **3**: 526-529
10,000 Maniacs 3: 653-655
Tequila Sunrise **3**: 542
The Terminator **3**: 612
Terminator 2: Judgment Day **3**: 613
Tex **1**: 196, 198
Tharp, Twyla **1**: 51, **2**: 355
That Hamilton Woman **3**: 509
That Was Then ... This Is Now **1**: 197-198
Their Satanic Majesties Request **3**: 594
This Is Cher **1**: 109
This Life **3**: 544
This n' That **1**: 165
Three Days of the Condor **3**: 575

The Three Sisters **3**: 510
Thriller **2**: 352
Throw Momma From the Train **1**: 150
Thunderball **1**: 123
"Tiburon" **1**: 68
Tightrope **1**: 186
To Catch a Thief **2**: 278
Too Legit to Quit **2**: 298
Tootsie **2**: 319, 322
Top Gun **1**: 142
To Sleep with Anger **2**: 261
Total Recall **3**: 613
Townsend, Robert 3: 656-661
Tracy, Spencer **2**: 312
Triumph **2**: 352
True Blue **2**: 410
True Lies **3**: 613
A Truly Western Experience **2**: 376
Truth or Dare **2**: 410
21 Jump Street **1**: 172, 174, 176
Twins **3**: 612-613
Two Mules for Sister Sara **1**: 186
Two Trains Running **1**: 205

U

"U Can't Touch This" **2**: 297
The Unbearable Lightness of Being **1**: 169, 171
Uncle Buck **1**: 91, 153-154
Unforgiven **1**: 187, 230
Unguarded **2**: 271, 273
Unplugged **1**: 95, 118, **3**: 655
Untamed Heart **3**: 535
The Untouchables **1**: 124, 131, 134, **2**: 250
The Uplift Mofo Party Plan **3**: 582
Use Your Illusion I and II **3**: 600, 603

V

Valley Girl **1**: 83

Vedder, Eddie **3:** 526-532
Victory **3:** 639
A View from a Broad **2:** 437
"Vision of Love" **1:** 93-94
The Voice **2:** 433
Volunteers **1:** 88, **2:** 300
Voodoo Lounge **3:** 597-598
Vs. **3:** 530-531

W

Wagon's East **1:** 91
A Walk With Love and Death **2:** 337
Washington, Denzel 3: 660, 632, **662-667**
The Waterdance **3:** 633
Wayans, Damon **1:** 99
Wayans, Keenan Ivory **1:** 99, **3:** 658
Wayne's World **1:** 101, 103, **2:** 464-465, 468, 469
Wayne's World 2 **1:** 101, 105, **2:** 464, 468
The Way We Were **3:** 575
Weaver, Sigourney 3: 668-674
West Side Story **1:** 12, **2:** 451, 453, 455
The Whales of August **1:** 166
Whatever Happened to Baby Jane? **1:** 165
What's Eating Gilbert Grape? **1:** 176
What's Love Got to Do With It? **1:** 206
When a Man Loves a Woman **2:** 251
When Harry Met Sally **1:** 146, 150
Where Are You Now, My Son? **1:** 44
Where in the World Is Carmen Santiago? **2:** 456
The White Album **1:** 58
White Men Can't Jump **3:** 535, 633
White Nights **2:** 317
White Oak Dance Project **1:** 47, 51

Whitney **2:** 332
Whitney Houston **2:** 331
Whoopi Goldberg **2:** 267
Wild at Heart **1:** 84
Williams, Robin 2: 267, 322, 367, **3:** **675-680**
Williams, Vanessa 3: 681-686
Winfrey, Oprah 3: 687-694
Wisdom **1:** 198
The Wishing Chair **3:** 654
The Witches of Eastwick **1:** 111, **3:** 539-541
With a Song in My Heart **3:** 496
Witness **2:** 258, 260
The Wizard of Oz **2:** 252, 254
Wolf **3:** 542-543
Wolfen **2:** 316, **3:** 514
Woman of the Year **2:** 312
"Wonderful Tonight" **1:** 117
Woodstock **1:** 40, 43
Working Girl **3:** 673
The World According to Garp **3:** 676-677
Wuthering Heights **3:** 509
Wyatt Earp **1:** 136

Y

The Year of Living Dangerously **3:** 671
Yellow Submarine **1:** 58
Yo! Bum Rush the Show **3:** 563
You Can't Hurry Love **1:** 209
You Gotta Believe **2:** 414
You Only Live Twice **1:** 123

Z

Zoot Suit **3:** 513, 514